Praise for *Skating on Thin Ice*

"As a female survivor of sexual abuse in sport and an expert in the space, I read this book with goosebumps and validation. I continually found myself saying 'oh, you so get it,' and this is rare. I commend the authors for their diligence and thoroughness. Regardless of my own lived experience, today I am a proud hockey mom. This book will help me raise hockey boys to be the hockey men of the future!"

Allison Forsyth, Two-Time Olympian, Safe Sport Advocate, and Partner and COO of ITP Sport & Recreation

"*Skating on Thin Ice* provides a sociological and psychological road map that describes the sanctioned rape culture of professional hockey. It argues that the depraved actions of hockey players are not the result of some group mental illness, but the logical outcome of a culture that is highly privileged and deeply misogynistic, and that defines masculinity through a prism of physical and sexual violence. A must-read, especially for sports fans."

Laura Robinson, Author of *Crossing the Line: Violence and Sexual Assault in Canada's National Sport*

"*Skating on Thin Ice* blends seasoned social science analysis and deep familiarity with the world of professional hockey to provide a compelling exploration of the toxic culture of misogyny and violence against women that pervades so much of high-level professional sports. This is a powerful, insightful, and profoundly troubling book that should be read by anyone concerned with the integrity and moral character of sport today."

Elliott P. Currie, Professor of Criminology, Law, and Society, University of California, Irvine

"This book is about opening the conversation to the culture that exists in all sports for change. We as women have sat on the bench for too long, and it is time to play. When reading this book, how will you measure the success of your child versus the damage to succeed?"

Brenda Andress, Founder and CEO of SheIS Sports Network and Former Founding Commissioner of the Canadian Women's Hockey League

"Every so often a book comes along that deepens the way we think about the depth of misogyny inherent in patriarchy. *Skating on Thin Ice* is one such book, offering a critical and nuanced analysis of hegemonic masculinity in general and ice hockey culture in particular. Especially refreshing and innovative is the way this book focuses on strategies for change and refuses to accept the status quo. Given the levels of male violence against women, we need more books like this."

Gail Dines, Professor Emerita of Sociology, Wheelock College, and Founder and President of Culture Reframed

WALTER S. DEKESEREDY
STU COWAN
MARTIN D. SCHWARTZ

SKATING
ON
THIN ICE

PROFESSIONAL HOCKEY, RAPE CULTURE,
& VIOLENCE AGAINST WOMEN

FOREWORD BY HEATHER MALLICK
AFTERWORD BY JACK TODD

ÆVO UTP

Aevo UTP
An imprint of University of Toronto Press
Toronto Buffalo London
utorontopress.com

Library and Archives Canada Cataloguing in Publication

Title: Skating on thin ice : professional hockey, rape culture, & violence against women / Walter S. DeKeseredy, Stu Cowan, and Martin D. Schwartz ; foreword by Heather Mallick ; afterword by Jack Todd.
Names: DeKeseredy, Walter S., 1959– author. | Cowan, Stu, author. | Schwartz, Martin D., author.
Description: Includes bibliographical references and index.
Identifiers: Canadiana (print) 20230459099 | Canadiana (ebook) 20230459110 | ISBN 9781487547103 (cloth) | ISBN 9781487550844 (EPUB) | ISBN 9781487548858 (PDF)
Subjects: LCSH: Women – Violence against. | LCSH: Hockey players – Sexual behavior. | LCSH: Men – Sexual behavior. | LCSH: Rape culture. | LCSH: Hockey – Social aspects.
Classification: LCC HV6250.4.W65 D45 2023 | DDC 362.88082 – dc23

ISBN 978-1-4875-4710-3 (cloth)   ISBN 978-1-4875-5084-4 (EPUB)
                                     ISBN 978-1-4875-4885-8 (PDF)

Printed in the USA

Cover design: Elke Barter
Cover image: iStock.com/shironosov

We wish to acknowledge the land on which the University of Toronto Press operates. This land is the traditional territory of the Wendat, the Anishnaabeg, the Haudenosaunee, the Métis, and the Mississaugas of the Credit First Nation.

University of Toronto Press acknowledges the financial support of the Government of Canada, the Canada Council for the Arts, and the Ontario Arts Council, an agency of the Government of Ontario, for its publishing activities.

Canada Council
for the Arts

Conseil des Arts
du Canada

ONTARIO ARTS COUNCIL
CONSEIL DES ARTS DE L'ONTARIO
an Ontario government agency
un organisme du gouvernement de l'Ontario

Funded by the   Financé par le
Government   gouvernement
of Canada   du Canada

This book is dedicated to Saul "Red" Fisher and Michael D. Smith, two major sources of inspiration and knowledge. We also dedicate this book to the female survivors of male violence and the frontline workers who tirelessly help them.

Contents

Foreword

The great sport of hockey was always something of a castle in the air, had we but known it at the time – but we didn't. We loved hockey. Hockey was us. Loving the game itself is at the core of *Skating on Thin Ice: Professional Hockey, Rape Culture, and Violence against Women*, a remarkable book about a vanishing castle.

As a teenager in Kapuskasing, Ontario, a municipal snow fortress that still serves as General Motors' cold weather testing center, I idolized the Montreal Canadiens. They won and won and won. After all, they had the imprimatur of storied coach Scotty Bowman, whose dark eyes were cold and whose brain you could see humming, their goalie Ken Dryden was rumored to be an intellectual, and I followed a number of high and low scorers, as one does. There was no women's NHL and girls had to crush on someone.

Girls in the north especially were huge fans. The great journalist Adam Gopnik, in his 2011 collection of Massey Lectures,

Winter: Five Windows on the Season, writes that hockey is "a clan sport and a craft sport – even an art sport." It's hard to play; its intricacy demands full attention.

Hockey, he writes, "is played at incredibly high speed, reveals and rewards situational and spatial intelligence at a degree of difficulty that no other sport possesses." You could tell the players were always in danger on ice – anything could happen – but we also loved the sounds of hockey, the whoosh of skates, the huge knock of the slapshot, the stick on the ice, the thunder clump into the boards. We heard that classic soundtrack at our own local rinks.

It was a visceral game in an era when girls were more likely to be raised to be polite, admiring, and avoidant of physical risk. So we admired the boys and men who played this great game on national TV, just as girls did until recently.

Those same boys and men did not admire us, as this extraordinary book makes clear.

The authors of *Skating on Thin Ice*, Walter S. DeKeseredy, Stu Cowan, and Martin D. Schwartz, are hockey fans too. The degree of disappointment they feel at uncovering the foul sexual violence of young hockey players raised to treat all females with casual contempt, the contortions of the hockey establishment to protect them, and the damage inflicted on young women pains them so.

Now they see the sport besmirched, soaked in misogyny, the sour hatred emanating from older officials and players having steeped into the boys and young men brought into the sport.

Some of the money used to pay off victims and force them to sign non-disclosure agreements came from hockey families, the loving, trusting parents of kids going into the system. This shocks. This hurts.

I said hockey was a castle in the air. Turrets and towers first began dropping off in the 1970s as pro hockey became thuggish on the ice. The sport became corporatized, coarsened.

What were pro hockey players going to be like off the ice with their female fans? With their families? They'd display sexual brutality plus intense misogyny, a mindset they were taught and never questioned.

I read *Skating on Thin Ice* often in tears, some pages too painful to dwell on. The authors make their case beautifully, offering context for the sport and the industry, revealing the history of violence and the roots of misogyny, telling agonizing stories of female humiliation and horror, and showing how the castle was really a structure for turning young boys into hateful men.

Toxic masculinity soaks our lives, more so since a huge backlash has formed against hard-won women's rights in recent decades. We have to talk about it. Talking opens windows, opens minds. Boys and girls aren't born enemies.

Skating on Thin Ice is an important book, always hopeful that junior hockey and pro hockey need not be hellish but joyous, the greatest winter sport of all.

Thank you, Walter, Stu, and Martin. How heartening to find such intelligence, compassion, and journalistic skill put in the service of the defense of women. Although you uncovered a grim history, you offer hope for the sport – that hockey players and the establishment that rules them can change and become a force for sanity and goodwill.

Heather Mallick
Staff Columnist, *Toronto Star*, and Author of
Cake or Death: The Excruciating Choices of Everyday Life

Preface

This book was conceived in the early morning of July 24, 2021. Walter DeKeseredy began that day like any other. He poured himself a strong cup of coffee and then turned his undivided attention to the hockey section of the *Montreal Gazette*. As his good friends know all too well, he always wants the latest news on the Montreal Canadiens, something he has looked for since becoming a huge Habs fan as a young boy living in Hudson, Quebec, in the mid-1960s. It was then that Walter's babysitter, Mrs. Burbridge, first introduced him to the Canadiens. Occasionally, Walter's parents would go out for dinner or to a party on a Saturday night, and Mrs. Burbridge was kind enough to look after him. However, there was one major condition – she had to watch CBC's *Hockey Night in Canada*, which is not unusual given that this is what most Canadians did (and arguably still do) on Saturday nights. There was no way she was going to miss the Habs game, and Walter has since followed in her footsteps.

Walter fondly remembers the elderly Mrs. Burbridge knitting while he played with his toys and hearing her cheer loudly when Montreal scored, particularly when Jean Béliveau got a goal against the Toronto Maple Leafs. Mrs. Burbridge's passion for the Habs rubbed off on Walter, and it never wavered until that morning of July 24 when he read Stu Cowan's column in the *Gazette* titled "Logan Mailloux Was Surprised Canadiens Decided to Draft Him."

"The day the music died" is a powerful lyric in Don McLean's haunting 1971 song "American Pie." For baby boomers who are familiar with this ballad, it may be painfully obvious, but it is worth stating anyway: this song is about the 1959 plane crash that killed rock and roll icons Buddy Holly, Ritchie Valens, and The Big Bopper. For Walter, July 24 was the day that his allegiance to the Habs temporarily died, because he learned that this storied franchise unexpectedly selected a convicted sex offender in the first round of the NHL draft on Friday, July 23. This deeply disturbing action rocked the hockey world, and it continues to be the subject of much discussion and debate today.

While playing in Sweden in 2020, Mailloux, as will be described in greater detail in chapter 1, secretly photographed an eighteen-year-old woman he had consensual sex with and then shared the picture and her identity with his SK Lejon teammates. Mailloux was charged with defamation and offensive photography and fined USD$1,650 by a Swedish court in December 2020. After reading this, Walter asked himself, "How could this happen? How could such a classy team stoop to this level?" For readers who don't know (and there probably aren't many), the Montreal Canadiens have won twenty-four Stanley Cups, and their rosters over the years have included some of the world's greatest players, including Jacques Plante, Maurice "Rocket" Richard, Guy Lafleur, Frank Mahovlich, and Ken Dryden. Walter was deeply concerned, not only because he was a fan but also because he had spent nearly forty years of his life studying various types of face-to-face and online violence against women and had been involved in progressive struggles to end these harms. He felt he had to do something right away and thus emailed Stu Cowan on July 25. What follows is a copy of Walter's message:

Dear Mr. Cowan,
First, let me introduce myself. My name is Dr. Walter DeKeseredy. I am a Canadian citizen who works at West Virginia University and who is a big Habs fan – until now.
I have devoted 36 years of my life to studying violence against women, including conducting the 1992 Canadian national survey on woman abuse in university/college dating. My work also focuses on the harms caused by the Habs' first round draft pick. What [Mailloux] did is defined by leading experts in the field as "Image-Based Sexual Abuse." Attached are two articles I published on this topic.
I would be more than happy to talk to you about this problem. Also note that I subscribe to the *Montreal Gazette* and I am an avid reader of your columns. More information about me can be found below my signature.

Stu got back to Walter the next day and interviewed him for two columns that appeared in the *Montreal Gazette* on July 27:

"Canadiens Drafting Mailloux 'Reflects Deep Insensitivity': Expert," and "Canadiens' Pick Logan Mailloux Has Lots of Work to Do Off Ice: Expert." Around the same time, Walter's close friend and colleague, Martin D. Schwartz, published an important article on patriarchal masculinities, sport, and male-on-female violence in the widely read and cited scientific journal *Violence against Women*. In this piece, titled "Masculinities, Sport, and Violence against Women," Martin pointed out that while there had been a burst of creative investigation into the relationship between sport and woman abuse in the 1980s and 1990s, unfortunately this connection had been ignored in recent years. He also declared that it was time to go back and take up this topic again. This is one of the key reasons we decided to team up and write this book.

Drawing on decades of rigorous sociological research and Stu Cowan's rich experience as a sports journalist specializing in hockey-related issues, *Skating on Thin Ice* supplies salient examples of abusive, misogynistic, racist, and homophobic behaviors in the world of professional hockey and examines the larger societal forces that perpetuate and legitimate the harms covered in each chapter. Much attention is given to the voices of survivors in chapter 2 because effective means of preventing what happened to them must be rooted in respect for their experiential knowledge.

Why is the abuse of women so common in professional hockey? Based on numerous years of careful, hands-on research done by Walter DeKeseredy and Martin Schwartz (and their colleagues), we answer this question in chapter 3 by introducing a new *male peer support theory*, which deals with the many influences, including having sexist and abusive peers, that convince men that they are entitled to the privileges of patriarchy and that on some occasions it is acceptable to use force to compel women to behave accordingly. Our theory, though, does not put all the blame on professional hockey. We show that young men like Logan Mailloux enter the world of professional hockey already trained and primed to treat women as objects and to commit violent acts against them.

It is not only male peer support that contributes to professional hockey players' violence against women and senior team officials' tolerance of their hurtful behavior. In chapter 4 we thus center on the broader social factors that uphold toxic hockey culture. These include patriarchal structures in society that affect the socialization patterns of men and the ways they learn to do masculinity. Many men learn that it is appropriate to abuse women; this often flows naturally from the objectification of women, the acceptance of rape myths, and the lessons learned from today's often violent and racist pornography.

What is to be done about this toxic hockey culture? Chapter 5 provides progressive answers to this question, but it does not simply repeat what others have already called for. Instead, we supplement previous suggestions with more contemporary initiatives. Informed by our male peer support theory, considerable attention is devoted to outlining the role that progressive men can play in preventing the pain and suffering that we have identified. Our wish is that this book helps make a difference. It is not enough to simply look at what we know about an issue or experience. We then must ask how this knowledge helps define and change individual experiences – how this knowledge reflects or changes power dynamics, institutions like professional hockey, and relationships in society.

Obviously, the three of us do not have all the possible solutions, but as critical thinkers with a passion for hockey, what we do know for sure is what Simon Winlow, Steve Hall, James Treadwell, and Daniel Briggs state in their 2015 book *Riots and Political Protest*: "Things cannot go on as they are." Hopefully, the world of professional hockey will be a better place when you finish reading this book.

1

More Than a Few Bad Men

And so, while one part of the equation that constructs masculinity has been turned upside-down by a global economy and a move toward equality for women, the other side has worked twice as hard at providing constant affirmation of male strength and aggression in the face of such challenges. This is just one of the many unspoken jobs for which the young men who play the game from October to May are responsible.

– Laura Robinson[1]

Elite hockey players are under enormous pressure, especially in large cities such as Montreal, where the legendary Montreal Canadiens are what Michael McKinley, among many others, defines as a "secular religion."[2] Montreal fans always expect their team to win the National Hockey League's (NHL) coveted Stanley Cup. This enormously high expectation often results in certain players becoming objects of fan and journalist ridicule, which, in turn, leads some of them to experience debilitating forms of mental illness.

Canadiens forward Jonathan Drouin is one such player. The spring of 2021 was an exciting but unexpected time for the Canadiens because of their weak regular season performance. They surprisingly made the playoffs and, against all odds, went to the Stanley Cup finals. Unfortunately, Drouin could not help his teammates. He missed the latter part of the season and the playoffs because he was suffering from anxiety and insomnia, ailments that have plagued him for years. In a one-on-one television interview with Chantal Machabée on Reseau des sports (RDS) on September 20, 2021, Drouin revealed that he stopped playing hockey on April 23: "That week was difficult for me ... I had fallen ill to the point where I was no longer controlling my body. That was really the moment when I realized that I need to take a break from hockey, to take a step back."

Goaltender Carey Price is also a prominent member of the Montreal Canadiens franchise. Though he helped his team reach the 2021 Stanley Cup finals with a stellar playoff performance and much praise from the media and fans, he did not start the 2021–2 season. Price voluntarily took some much-needed personal time off to enter the NHL/NHL Players Association (NHLPA) player assistance program, which helps players and their families address mental health, substance abuse, and other issues.

What happened? In a column written for the *Montreal Gazette* on October 7, 2021, Brendan Kelly suggests that Montreal's intense hockey atmosphere could be a major contributing factor:

> Are the issues that sent him to the assistance program due to the intense pressure of playing in a city where we are obsessed with our hockey team and treat it like our shared religion? Or is it something he's been carrying with him from long before? We just don't know.[3]

On November 9, 2021, the truth about Price's condition emerged shortly before the Canadiens were to play a home game against the Los Angeles Kings. He entered a residential treatment facility for substance abuse, a mental health–related problem that can be exacerbated by work-related stress. Price issued this statement on his Instagram account about his time in the player assistance program:

> Over the last few years I have let myself get to a very dark place and I didn't have the tools to cope with that struggle … Things had reached a point that I realized I needed to prioritize my health for both myself and for my family. Asking for help when you need it is what we encourage our kids to do, and it was what I needed to do.
>
> I am working through years of neglecting my own mental health which will take some time to repair; all I can do is take it day by day. With that comes some uncertainty when I will return to play.[4]

It is not only male professional hockey players who experience what Drouin and Price did because they are expected to meet exceedingly high performance standards. Consider US gymnast Simone Biles who withdrew from a July 27, 2021, Olympic team event, citing pressure and mental health problems. Earlier that same year, tennis star Naomi Osaka opted out of the French Open and Wimbledon because of anxiety and other mental health issues. The pressure to succeed as a high-level, competitive athlete knows no age, sex, gender identity, race, or class boundaries. Yet, there is a different type of pressure that primarily exists among groups of male athletes who participate in contact sports like professional hockey.

This pressure is the central focus of our book. It involves prioritizing a relentless quest for victory but also living up to the principles of *hegemonic masculinity*, which is the dominant form of masculinity in North America, Australia, the United Kingdom, and in many other parts of the world.[5] The basic components of hegemonic masculinity suggest that men must (a) avoid all things feminine; (b) engage in frequent sexual relations with women; (c) show toughness and aggression; (d) exhibit self-reliance; (e) exhibit non-relational attitudes toward sexuality; and (f) actively engage in homophobia.

Many rugby clubs exemplify these principles, and the following observation made nearly four decades ago still holds true today:

> Rugby clubs from the beginning were places for testing, expressing, and accentuating masculinity; by mocking and vilifying women in obscene songs; by ridiculing homosexuality through songs and male stripteases; by extremes of

drunkenness; by initiation ceremonies in which initiates were stripped, often forcibly, and their genitals defiled with noxious substances; by exceedingly rough and violent behavior on the field of play. These traditions have lasted wherever rugby is played, though usually in diluted form.[6]

More recent evidence is provided by the London School of Economics (LSE) rugby club. In 2014, it was banned after constantly engaging in sexist, racist, homophobic, and misogynistic behaviors. What is more, prior to this date, punitive action was taken against the club for doing the following:

- "Blacking up," dressing as Guantanamo Bay prisoners, and imitating Muslim students' prayers as they left their place of prayer;
- being involved in Nazi-themed drinking games, which resulted in a Jewish student's nose being broken;
- damaging LSE property; and
- running naked through LSE and urinating on school buildings.[7]

Elite hockey is not immune from similar types of misconduct. For instance, a class-action lawsuit filed in late June 2020 against the Canadian Hockey League (CHL), the Western Hockey League (WHL), the Ontario Hockey League (OHL), and the Quebec Major Junior Hockey League (QMJHL) alleged that players were forced to masturbate in front of teammates and their coaches, and that they were coerced to sexually assault teammates, consume the saliva, urine, and feces of other players, and to sexually abuse animals.[8] Though the suit did not move forward, it also alleged that players had heavy objects tied to their genitals, had their genitals dipped in noxious substances, and had objects like hockey sticks forced into their anuses.[9]

The sexual, physical, economic, and psychological abuse of women is another ugly feature of hegemonic masculinity. This gender-based problem is not a new epidemic in the world of professional and junior hockey. Actually, the concept of an "epidemic" is out of place here. To health officials, an epidemic is a disease that devastates a population before eventually subsiding. The abuse of women, however, is deeply entrenched in the elite hockey world as well as in other all-male contact sports. Thus, woman abuse in hockey can be more accurately seen as *endemic*, a long-term and perhaps even permanent feature to be found among certain people in certain places. The problem is much broader than a few bad men involved in this sport at many levels.

Every sport rooted in competitive masculinity produces some troublesome men, from sailing to skiing to tennis to video gaming and esports. And there is also no question that North American professional football, hockey, basketball, and baseball, like British rugby, seem to produce more than their share of violent, racist, homophobic, and misogynist men. While it is true that all sports produce violent men, studies that have compared violence against women across various sports find major differences. Most of these crimes are committed by male athletes in "revenue producing contact sports" such as professional hockey. These findings demonstrate the problem of "clumping all sport environments together under the rubric of athletic affiliation."[10] A study of male athletes versus nonathletes might not find major differences, but a study of popular money-making sports versus everyone else certainly will.

The contemporary data offered in this book and other sources confirm what Michael Messner, a leading expert on the connection between gender, sports, and violence, concluded in 2005. In his analysis of the part sports plays in the construction of white, heterosexual masculinity, Messner found that "male athletes' off-the-field violence is generated from the normal, everyday dynamics at the center of male athletic culture."[11] Some sociologists even go as far to contend that in a culture that produces high rates of violence against women supported by the presence of all-male, pro-abuse subcultures, it is male athletes who *do not* sexually harass, beat, and rape women who are the deviants.[12] The norm is to engage in this behavior.

Noxious male athletic culture, on top of producing men who abuse women, frequently generates male players, coaches, team presidents, and others who engage in offline and online racist and homophobic means of communication. Former Las Vegas Raiders coach Jon Gruden is a recent case in point. The *Wall Street Journal* reported that back in July 2011, Gruden sent a racist email to Bruce Allen, then president of the Washington Redskins (now the Washington Commanders), remarking that NFL (National Football League) Players Association executive director DeMaurice Smith (who is Black) "has the lips the size of michellin [*sic*] tires."[13] In a public response on October 10, 2021, Gruden said, "I'm really sorry ... I don't have a racial bone in my body, and I've proven that for 58 years."[14] He is right. For *USA Today* columnist Nancy Armour, "It is more like a metric ton. Along with misogyny, homophobia and every other brand of bigotry."[15]

Support for Armour's contention emerged on Monday, October 11, when the *New York Times* published excerpts of Gruden's emails that were sent between 2011 and 2018 and obtained by the NFL in its investigation of the Washington team's toxic culture and abusive behaviors that flourished under the leadership of owner Daniel Snyder. The inquiry resulted in a minimal (for billionaires) USD$10 million fine, but the NFL also made sure there was no written report and gave Snyder the power to permanently suppress any information from the investigation, such as the accusations that he personally engaged in sexual harassment.

On June 22, 2022, the US House Committee on Oversight and Reform released a twenty-nine-page memo detailing the results of its eight-month inquiry into how the Commanders and the NFL dealt with claims of unbridled sexual harassment of the team's female employees. The memo includes evidence showing Snyder's role in creating a hostile work environment and his attempts to discredit victims and witnesses by launching a shadow investigation to influence the NFL's internal investigation into workplace misconduct at the Commanders.[16] It should also be noted that Snyder and his team were twice subjects of an NFL-led investigation into sexual harassment and workplace misconduct, the second of which began in early 2022.[17]

Returning to Gruden's wrongdoings, while broadcasting for ESPN, he sent emails from his personal account to Allen's team account. The *New York Times* found that Gruden's messages included homophobic slurs directed at NFL commissioner Roger Godell and a derogatory statement about one team's decision to draft a gay player. Gruden also exchanged pictures of topless cheerleaders with Allen and other men associated with the NFL, ridiculed trans woman Caitlyn Jenner, denounced the NFL's hiring of female referees, and called for the firing of players who, in support of the Black Lives Matter movement, kneel during the US national anthem. Interestingly, Carl Nassib, the first gay NFL player to publicly come out, currently plays for the Raiders.

After these revelations, Gruden resigned as Raiders' coach on the evening of October 11, 2021, saying, "I love the Raiders and do not want to be a distraction ... I'm sorry, I never meant to hurt anyone."[18] As is typical in the NFL, we are left with Gruden's insincere apologies but no accompanying moves to provide major organizational culture shifts. This is part and parcel of the consequences of the injuries done by Gruden and others like him who are affiliated with the NFL.[19] The same can be said about the NHL, and the case of Logan Mailloux immediately comes to mind.

Prior to December 2020, Logan Mailloux looked forward to an unblemished professional hockey career. He was destined to play in the NHL for the Canadiens. But, in late summer of 2021, his future with them was unclear, and so was his opportunity to rejoin the London Knights, which is a prestigious OHL team. On September 2, 2021, the OHL suspended him indefinitely for violating the league's code of conduct.

Deemed by many hockey fans to be a forgivable mistake, Mailloux photographed a woman without her consent while performing a consensual sexual act while on loan from the

Knights to SK Lejon, a Swedish amateur team, during the COVID-19 pandemic. Mailloux then shared this image and her name with his teammates on Snapchat. He was charged with, and convicted of, defamation and offensive photography and fined USD$1,650 by a Swedish court in December 2020. This outcome surprised many because most perpetrators of image-based sexual abuse (also commonly referred to as "revenge porn") never face serious legal consequences. Rather, their female targets are the ones who suffer. Many, if not most, survivors experience one or more of these outcomes: victim-blaming; ridicule; lost employment opportunities; and alienation from family members, friends, and community members.[20]

Ponder the case of a 2012 rape in Steubenville, a small city of about 18,000 in a predominately rural county located in the Appalachian region of eastern Ohio.[21] The events in Steubenville should give us pause to contemplate the seriousness of image-based sexual abuse in real-life terms, for in this town, two high school football players were convicted of raping a local girl of high school age while she was intoxicated after attending several parties held on August 11, right before the new school year began. What brought the incident to light were the videos and photographs posted on YouTube, Instagram, and Facebook by those who were there.

This example highlights those who callously posted their exploits on social media outlets, others at the party who did nothing to stop the abuse, the pedestal on which football is placed in this economically declining area, and the tight-knit relationships between the sheriff and other community leaders and the football coach, team, and parents and players.

It is also about the trauma experienced by the rape survivor. After the two perpetrators were found guilty on March 17, 2013, she was threatened by people siding with the players, and she experienced other harrowing indicators of victim blaming that left her "wondering if she has any friends in the world."[22]

In Steubenville, the players involved were not good enough to play professional ball, but Mailloux was a star with professional potential. However, he renounced himself from the 2021 summer NHL draft because, in his words,

> this is a huge mistake I've made. A stupid, childish mistake. I was selfish. I want the victim and her family to know how sincerely sorry I am and how remorseful I am. I know now how it can affect their family. I regret doing it, but there is nothing I can do about that now. I hope they can forgive me one day.[23]

Though Mailloux publicly asked not to be drafted, a player cannot remove himself from the draft. Although other teams ignored the talented player and he slid down the draft board, the Canadiens took advantage of this rule and ignored Mailloux's request. Instead, they selected him as a first-round pick. After the move was heavily criticized, team officials provided this rationale for their highly questionable behavior:

> By drafting prospect Logan Mailloux with the 31st overall pick, the Montreal Canadiens not only selected a promising hockey player, but also a young man who recently admitted to making a serious mistake. The Canadiens are aware of the situation and by no means minimize the severity of Logan's

actions. Logan understands the impact of his actions. His recent public statement is a genuine acknowledgement of his poor behavior and the first step on his personal journey.

We are making a commitment to accompany Logan on his journey by providing him with the tools to mature and the necessary support to guide him in his development. We are also committed to raising awareness among our players about the repercussions of their actions on the lives of others.[24]

Former Canadiens general manager Marc Bergevin added to the above justification by stating, "He's 17 years old and he's willing and understanding and remorseful and he has a lot of work to do, but he's already started to put it behind him and have a hockey career."[25] Nevertheless, the woman Mailloux abused told *The Athletic* that his apologies were not sincere. She also said, "I do not think that Logan has understood the seriousness of his behavior ... All I wanted was a heartfelt apology for his behavior."[26]

Mailloux did not stay off the ice for long. On December 29, 2021, the OHL reinstated him. Nowhere in its rationale for doing so, however, was there any evidence of Mailloux making amends to the survivor of his abuse or any reference to the needs she has for rebuilding her life:

Since the time of suspension, with the support of the London Knights, Logan Mailloux has participated in therapy and counselling with Dr. Lindsay Forbes, and a personal development plan under the leadership of Wendy Glover. Ms. Glover is a London-based, experienced holistic athletic development practitioner, academic and personal development advisor, teacher and member of the Ontario School Counsellors Association.

After reviewing the program, speaking with the player and Ms. Glover, and receiving a commitment from the player to continue with his personal development program, the League is satisfied that Logan Mailloux has undertaken the necessary steps and will reinstate him, effective January 1, 2022.[27]

Put another way, blatantly missing from the OHL's actions is a *victim-centered* approach, one that prioritizes the notion of *parallel justice*. This involves seeking a path for justice for survivors of woman abuse that parallels what hockey organizations like the London Knights and OHL offer to offenders like Mailloux.[28] Certainly, his victim deserves equal assistance, and more will be said about potentially effective parallel justice efforts in chapter 5.

Mailloux's crime was not Bergevin's first experience with sexual abuse. He was the Chicago Blackhawks director of player personnel in 2010 when two players made sexual assault allegations against then video coach Brad Aldrich and the Blackhawks front office executives chose not to report these incidents to the police. When, shortly before the draft of Mailloux occurred, the media asked Bergevin to comment on the accusations, he tersely retorted that he was unaware of the alleged sexual assaults or of a team management meeting to discuss Aldrich:

It came out recently, there was a meeting that I heard was done in Chicago. I was not part of any meeting, and I was not part of any decision based on that. I was unaware of what was going on at the time. You can go on the record with that.[29]

One can only speculate about Bergevin's reaction to the independent Jenner & Block law firm's 107-page report on how the Blackhawks dealt with the sexual assault allegations against Aldrich.[30] The report was released on October 26, 2021, and it resulted in the Blackhawks being fined USD$2 million by the NHL due to "the organization's inadequate internal procedures and insufficient and untimely response" to the complaints.[31] Additionally, Stan Bowman, Chicago's general manager and president of hockey operations, resigned from his job and his position as general manager of the 2022 US Olympic men's hockey team. Al MacIsaac, vice president of hockey operations, also resigned, and NHL commissioner Gary Bettman announced his intention to meet with then Florida Panthers coach Joel Quenneville and current Winnipeg Jets general manager Kevin Cheveldayoff. These two men also attended the team management meeting, were named in the report, and were Blackhawks employees when the sexual assault allegations were first brought to light.

Kyle Beach, one of the two survivors of Aldrich's abuse, came forward with his experiences in a TSN SportsCentre interview with Rick Westhead the day after the report was released. Beach talked about how much pain he endured and made this statement, which closely resembles those recounted by thousands of female survivors of sexual assault: "Until very recently, I did not talk about it, I did not discuss it, I didn't think about it. And now that I'm beginning to heal, I begin to look back and it definitely had impacts on my life … I acted out, I snapped … I did things that I never could imagine doing. I relied on alcohol, I relied on drugs."[32]

The same day as Beach's highly emotional interview, Quenneville was behind the bench coaching the Florida Panthers as if nothing had happened. His exemption from negative consequences for his part in mishandling Beach's allegation, however, was short-lived. Two days later, on October 28, 2021, he resigned his position as coach shortly after meeting with Bettman, but the Cheveldayoff–Bettman summit that occurred the next day led to Cheveldayoff keeping his job, which might be interpreted as a statement on his (non) culpability. And what about Bergevin? His role in drafting Mailloux, along with the worst start to a season in Canadiens' history (and other factors), led to the Canadiens firing him as well as assistant general manager Trevor Timmins, and Paul Wilson, senior vice president of public affairs and communications, on November 28, 2021.[33] Will Bergevin ever be implicated in the case of Kyle Beach? Only time will tell.

Since Bettman left the door open for Quenneville to eventually return to the NHL, many skeptics question whether his resignation and his ostensibly remorseful statement that accompanied it are heartfelt or just more barefaced instances of institutional damage control. After his meeting with Quenneville, Bettman said:

We thank the Panthers' organization for working with us to ensure that a thorough process was followed. Given the result, there is no need for any further action by the NHL regarding Mr. Quenneville at this time. However, should he wish to re-enter the League in some capacity in the future,

I will require a meeting with him in advance in order to determine the appropriate conditions under which such new employment might take place.[34]

And what does one make of Blackhawks captain Jonathan Toews's response to the Jenner & Block report the day after it was released? Toews was quoted in *USA Today* as saying, "It wasn't something that was taken super seriously at the time." To be fair, he expressed *some* sympathy for Beach, but he seemed to express significantly more for Bowman and MacIsaac:

> Make any argument you want, they're not directly complicit in the activities that happened … It's not up to me to comment on whether they would like to deal with it differently or not. I just know them as people and I've had a relationship and friendship with them for a long time as being part of the Blackhawks family.
>
> How this situation went down, what the timeline was, what they knew, I can't really comment on that. It's obviously a tough day. Regardless of the mistakes that may have been made, for someone like Stan who has done so much for the Blackhawks, and Al as well, to lose everything they care about and their livelihoods as well, I don't understand how that makes it go away – just delete them from existence and that's it, we'll never hear from them. So, I have a lot of respect for them as good people. They're good people.[35]

It is often said that "everyone is entitled to their opinion," and that individuals are sometimes good to certain people but bad to others. Our view, however, is that those who are considered "good people" overall don't do what Bowman, Aldrich, and their colleagues did to Beach. Good people also wouldn't contribute to the subsequent atrocity perpetrated by Aldrich. After the Blackhawks won the 2010 Stanley Cup, Aldrich was given the option to resign, which he did, and the Jenner & Block report reveals that Quenneville gave him a letter of endorsement that enabled him to get jobs with USA Hockey, Miami University in Ohio (where two sexual assault allegations were brought against him), and the high school in Houghton, Michigan, where he was convicted of sexually assaulting a teenager in 2013. Good people, as *USA Today* reporter Nancy Armour makes clear, would not allow "lives to be ruined so they could add their names to the Stanley Cup."[36]

Were there any repercussions from the Blackhawks sexual abuse cover-up besides the Jenner & Block report and people losing their jobs? *Toronto Star* reporter Chris Johnston asserts that the NHL's "cone of silence has been punctured."[37] What is Johnston's rationale for drawing this conclusion? For him, it was a major step forward that the day after Beach relayed his experiences to Westhead, the NHL sent a memo to all team governors, presidents, general managers, and head coaches stating that all league and team personnel, including players, must instantly report inappropriate or criminal conduct to Gary Bettman or NHL deputy commissioner Bill Daly.

The reports can be made, anonymously if preferred, directly or through a hotline administered by Deloitte.[38] This hotline was set up in December 2019 following the resignation of Calgary Flames coach Bill Peters that November after it was revealed that he directed racist slurs at Nigerian-born former Flames player Akim Aliu. Reports can also be made by email, by speaking to a live operator, or by leaving a voicemail message in one of nine languages commonly used by NHL players. Based on the implementation of the NHL's new strategy, the attention given to the Kyle Beach case, and the November 10, 2021, resignation of Anaheim Ducks general manager Bill Murray due to allegations of an ongoing pattern of verbally abusing members of the Ducks organization, Johnston assumes that "a culture of secrecy in the back hallways of NHL organizations is getting peeled back and examined under new light ... More people in hockey are talking than ever before. And they're starting to be heard."[39]

While we commend Johnston's optimism, it will take much more than a recent string of events to, as Laura Robinson puts it, "change the lineup." Robinson is also spot on to specify that "we can't change a few policies and procedures in hockey and expect that [things] will change for the better ... The culture needs to change."[40] We concur, and ways of doing so are proposed in chapter 5.

The highly injurious behaviors described in this chapter and throughout this book are, again, not isolated incidents or the acts of a select few deviant men. As Rachel Doerrie, contributor to *EP Rinkside* and OHL scout, correctly noted in her July 19, 2021, column, they are a product of a broader culture that needs to change:

> Quite clearly, hockey culture is a terrible place ... It's in a place where it's fine to draft players guilty of sex crimes or racial bullying and or [sic] to hire those accused of domestic violence

to front office jobs. This is the culture that's been accepted in the game: As long as you can skate, shoot, hit and contribute on the ice, you can be a deplorable human off of it.[41]

Doerrie is not exaggerating. There are many more hockey players like Mailloux who could easily be identified here. He is certainly not among a unique minority who abuse women and who, as Gianluca Agostinelli puts it in his contribution to *The Conversation*, "treat social media as virtual locker rooms, where they brag of their sexual achievements and share their sordid stories of their 'conquests' of women."[42] For example, in October 2021, two members of the Victoriaville Tigres, both nineteen, were formerly charged with sexually assaulting a minor the previous June and filming this harm to share.[43]

Some perpetrators don't share their crimes on social media but still record them. In the summer of 2022, Canadian hockey fans were shocked by stories of alleged gang rapes involving members of the 2003 and 2018 men's World Junior hockey teams. Sources told TSN's Rick Westhead in July 2022 that a player referred to the 2003 atrocity as a "fucking lamb roast" before videotaping a group rape of an unresponsive woman.[44] The video is described as being six or seven minutes long and shows some six players taking turns sexually assaulting this woman who was lying face up on a pool table.[45] The 2018 incident was also videotaped, but, in July 2022, lawyers for seven unnamed members of the team showed *Globe and Mail* reporters two video clips recorded on June 17, 2018, which they claim prove that the sexual contact was consensual and that the woman was not scared, intimidated, or drunk.[46]

This book does not simply list all the incidents of misogynist behaviors committed by hockey players and other athletes that have transpired over the years. Definitely, more salient examples of people like Mailloux will be provided. But sound research shows that male athletes who participate in professional combative sports commit more crimes than nonathletes,[47] and it is our goal to explain why this is so. Drawing on extensive sociological research and Stu Cowan's rich experience as a sportswriter specializing in hockey-related issues (particularly those pertaining to the Montreal Canadiens), we delve deeply into the broader cultural forces that encourage and legitimate hockey players' violence against women.

Many people have asked, "What was Logan Mailloux thinking when he illegally distributed a photograph of his sexual relations with a woman?" The answer necessitates focusing on the social nature of behaviors like his and the reasons professional hockey culture accepts them. Professional hockey is an integral part of *rape culture*, in which sexual assault and other male attacks on women are normalized and women are blamed for their victimization. We are not the first people to make this assertion. Comb the internet and you will find many of the same or similar claims. Additionally, some feminist scholars and other researchers have examined patriarchal and misogynist beliefs expounded, supported, and propagated by participants in team sports, and they have attempted to link such beliefs to the harming of women in a broad variety of manners.

Journalists and academics have long argued that the pervasive misogynist language habitually used by some professional athletes can be connected to the sexual violence that they and others commit. There was a burst of creative investigation into sports masculinities and violence against women in the 1980s and 1990s, but this connection has been ignored in recent years. There are occasional attempts to reveal the deep-seated anti-woman culture in sports, such as the series of exposés about the behaviors of prominent people like Jon Gruden and Logan Mailloux, but as soon as the heat dies down the NFL and other leagues manage to sweep everything back under the rug.

It is time to go back and take this topic up again, and the key goal of this book is to do so by examining the connections between professional hockey, rape culture, and violence against women. But why focus primarily on this sport? Hockey, like other combative, professional male sports, has a culture of toxic masculinity and rewards men for their violent behavior on and off the ice. Yet, there are also certain features that are exclusive to hockey culture:

> [Hockey] thinks of itself as a sport that imparts positive values and creates better people, especially in making "boys into men." It champions respect, teamwork, niceness, and coachability. While these values are good, they are often twisted into something more sinister. These "values" are converted into actions that control and shape how players think, feel, and act.
>
> Hockey exists in its own bubble, literally and figuratively. It's composed mostly of boys and men who are white, cishet, straight, and upper-class. And those who play often become coaches and teach the same values to the next generation.[48]

What you will soon discover, if you haven't already, is that major cultural shifts have not happened in the last couple of decades, a conclusion confirmed by Jashvina Shah, a freelance hockey reporter and co-author (with Evan F. Moore) of the 2021 book *Game Misconduct: Hockey's Toxic Culture and How to Fix It*. She is also a sexual assault survivor, and her words below constitute a rallying cry:

> Nothing has changed. In some ways, it's gotten worse … hockey is still operating now the way it did twenty years ago … Organized hockey is too often a safe haven for predators. This isn't new. Convicted sex criminals have been signed before, as recently as 2018. But now feels worse than before. Now it feels like gloating in the faces of the survivors.[49]

If you don't believe her, consider these facts. On July 27, 2022, news sources reported that Hockey Canada had settled twenty-one sexual misconduct claims since 1989, paying out CAD$8.9 million in compensation. Nine victims were paid from Hockey Canada's National Equity Fund, which is partially funded by membership fees paid for by parents entering their children into the sport.[50] Then, there is, in the words of Jack Todd, "the mother of all hockey sex scandals, the Hockey Canada Eight and the decision made by hockey's national governing body to pay off the victim of an alleged 2018 gang sexual assault to settle a [CAD]$3.55-million lawsuit and buy her silence on behalf of her assailants."[51] Todd is referring to eight members of the 2018 Canadian men's World Junior team.

Within academia, the study of masculinities has continued to expand into new areas. Nonetheless, research on the specific relationship between sport and violence against women has stagnated over the past fifteen years. For example, in the 2018 *Palgrave Handbook of Feminism and Sport, Leisure and Physical Education*, only one of fifty-four chapters covering close to 900 pages was allotted to masculinities, and *none* were devoted to violence against women. Our book, then, reinvigorates interest in the relationship between male participation in male combative sports and various types of woman abuse.

The actions of Gruden and the aforementioned hockey players are not only symptoms of rape culture. They are also often indicators of what sociologist Michael Kimmel refers to as *aggrieved entitlement*, that is,

> the sense that those benefits to which you believed yourself entitled have been snatched away from you by unseen forces larger and more powerful. You feel yourself to be heir to a great promise, the American Dream, which has turned into an impossible fantasy for the very people who were *supposed* to inherit it.[52]

Aggrieved entitlement not only exists among those involved in professional combative sports but also fueled the 2016 election of former US president Donald Trump. Despite numerous progressive changes spawned by the feminist movement that have occurred over the past several decades, and even with 2016 US presidential candidate Hillary Clinton embracing parts of conservative policies, once again a man was elected president of the United States. Why not another man? One answer is that "the desire for a strong virile man in the White House runs deep in the American DNA."[53] Related to this point is that there remains an anti-feminist backlash in combative male sports organizations and other parts of society driven in part by a desire to return to the "good old days" when male superiority and privilege were normalized.

Many agree with *USA Today* sports columnist Mike Freeman's observation that Jon Gruden's emails exemplify the main ingredients of aggrieved entitlement:

> Gruden's emails hit all of these points. It's rare to peel back a public curtain and see unvarnished, white grievance bro culture in action, but that's what you see with his emails. Gruden hits all the familiar targets. He denounced the emergence of women game officials, hated the drafting of gay player Michael Sam and attacked Kaepernick and protesting players.[54]

It is difficult to miss that less than a handful of NHL and elite amateur hockey players are Black, and that they constantly endure racism on and off the ice. Think about what happened to Wayne Simmonds, now playing for the Toronto Maple Leafs. In September 2011, during a preseason game in London, Ontario, a "fan" threw a banana at him as he scored in a shoot-out. The next year, while playing in the Czech Republic during an NHL lockout, spectators yelled "Opice" at Simmonds and his friend Chris Steward. Opice, in English, means "monkey."

It is often said, "That was then, and this is now." Fast-forward to the present day and you will see that hockey's racist history repeats itself. P.K. Subban, a Black former NHL defenseman, recently asked, "When does it stop? This is happening every day in our game. EVERY DAY!" He also said that stories resembling this one are sent to him every day.[55] In late

September 2021, HC Kremenchuk player Andrei Deniskin was suspended for thirteen games and fined USD$1,800 by the Ukrainian Hockey League for making a racist gesture against a Black opponent during a game. Deniskin mimed peeling and eating a banana in front of Jalen Smereck, who is from Detroit. Simmonds reacted to this by stating:

> It's come to a point where it's sickening, it's disgusting. The way that guy did what he did without hesitancy, it makes me sick to my stomach. To know that I've got to play, and potentially have my children play hockey to face these types of incidents, I can see why people of colour don't want to play hockey. I can see why parents are completely afraid to put their kids into the sport. I'm the same way as well. I've faced a lot of these things myself, and I don't even know if I'd want my kids playing hockey to be quite honest.[56]

Kurtis Gabriel, one of Simmonds's teammates, was also angered by the light punishment given to Deniskin, declaring, "When you go light on racism, it just breeds … So, you got to come down hard on it. And there's no excuse for it anymore."[57]

But many NHL players apparently don't feel the same way about their white colleagues sexual harassing women, and excuses seem to be accepted. Note what Toronto Maple Leafs player Auston Matthews did in May 2019. In Scottsdale, Arizona, he and a group of his friends tried to enter a female security guard's car at 2:00 a.m. while she was sitting inside it. When she got out to confront them, some of Matthews's friends tried to get everyone to return to his residence, but as Matthews walked away, he pulled his pants down and "mooned" (with his underwear still on) the guard. In an incident report filed on May 26, 2019, the guard, who, incidentally, is a Black military veteran with PTSD, stated, "who knows what they intended to do," and that "it was more than one guy."[58] Some criminologists would label her experience an act of violence or, at the very least, sexual harassment.[59] When women like this guard are being followed, mooned, or harassed in other ways, they do not know how the event will end. It is only in retrospect that actions like Matthews's can be labeled as "minor."[60]

Even so, Matthews reportedly said that he thought it would be funny to see her reaction.[61] Charges against him were eventually dismissed, and in July 2020, the NHL proudly announced that Matthews was a Lady Byng Memorial Trophy finalist. Ironically, this trophy goes to a player who has "exhibited the best type of sportsmanship and gentlemanly conduct combined with a high standard of playing ability."[62] Even the popular media trivialized Matthews's actions. Now retired *Hockey Night in Canada* play-by-play commentator Jim Hughson, for example, downplayed Matthews's unacceptable conduct while praising accused rapist Patrick Kane (a current member of the New York Rangers):

> When I thought about that, I looked back to 2012 and thought about Patrick Kane ... (who) got into a little trouble with too many cameras around in Wisconsin that summer. And what did he do? He came back and was the Conn Smythe Trophy winner and won the Stanley Cup. And that's how you put a little problem behind you.[63]

How do people like Hughson and Matthews get away with their actions and comments? Chapter 3 provides a detailed answer to this question, but this is a suitable preamble to that part of our book. As Chris Baud writes:

> In such a predominantly white sport with a toxic, insular culture, it's easy to see how such a predominantly white, male media is going to cover up and enforce that status quo. Imagine how it feels to be a female hockey writer, having to put up with so many colleagues who are willing to overlook blatant sexual harassment because ... what? A player is cool and nice to them in the media room? The NHL keeps saying, "Hockey is for everyone," but it still doesn't know how to fix its obvious cultural problems, and ultimately ends up excluding almost everyone.[64]

Yes, how does it feel to be a female hockey writer? According to journalist Abbey Mastracco, sexual harassment "isn't just a problem with players, coaches and executives. Women face opposition and harassment from co-workers and other media members." She also said that her sexual harassment experiences in the worlds of professional hockey and baseball resulted in considerable trauma and her using avoidance strategies:

> I pulled back on my reporting, I only stuck close to players or coaches I was comfortable talking to, and I stopped trying to build sources. I hid in stairwells, I went up to the pressbox early and I didn't eat with anyone. I just withdrew. This is not an effective way to do the job. I moved to New York wanting

to make an impact and tell good stories, but by the end of the first season, I absolutely dreaded going to the ballpark every day. I cried some days before going to work. No one in any profession should be scared to go to work.[65]

Much more will be said about women's traumatic experiences in the world of elite hockey in chapter 2. In the meantime, mull over the fact that thousands of stories about sexual harassment and sexual assaults committed by men affiliated with professional hockey exist on a broad array of websites. As Velgey recently noted in a blog for *SB Nation*:

> Five minutes of searching would reveal allegations of several sports figures including players, coaches, and team managers embroiled in sexual harassment or assault allegations in the past few years. Those searchers would also reveal that, much like the cases brought against political and entertainment figures, legal cases are infrequently decided against the alleged harassers, if formal charges are made at all.[66]

Do a Google search using the words "sexual harassment in professional hockey." Our hunt in February 2022 uncovered 6,080,000 results in 0.48 seconds. Examples of story titles listed in our search include "New Details Emerge in Sexual Assault Allegations against Former Blackhawks Coach," "Canucks Place Jake Virtanen on Leave after Sexual Misconduct," and "Gods and Monsters – More Disturbing Stories about Hockey."

Despite the number of reports available on the internet about hockey players' abuse of women and the fact that a number of professional hockey players (all of whom are white) have been charged with violence against women over the past two decades, sports reporters, especially those based in the US, primarily turn their attention to acts of violence against women committed by NFL and National Basketball Association (NBA) players, most of whom are Black. These journalists often ask experts in the field, "What makes football or basketball players more inclined to abuse women?" Similar questions are rarely, if ever, asked about white hockey players.[67]

Most sociologists and criminologists who study violence in and around sport also focus exclusively on basketball and football. For example, in a recent issue of the widely read and cited peer-reviewed journal *Violence against Women*, James E. Sutton states, "I concentrate primarily on these sports because they are the most popular, the most profitable, and are where the most problematic cases tend to occur when reviewing the literature."[68] We hope Dr. Sutton will read this book.

Professional hockey is a sport where exceptional levels of very harmful behavior are generally seen as "just part of the game." In fact, hockey is the only professional sport that allows fighting. Though technically prohibited by the NHL rule book, two players fighting on the ice results in both receiving a five-minute penalty instead of a long suspension. To be sure, there are far fewer fights than there were ten years ago as well as far fewer "goons," or those *Montreal Gazette* reporter Pat Hickey describes as "one-dimensional players who picked up a paycheck for nights when they spent more time in the penalty box than they did on the ice."[69] Nevertheless, fighting is still very much a part of the game, and while the NHL has toughened its stance on body checks to the head, the league still tolerates punches to the head. Still relatively common are acts of ice-level interpersonal violence that occur "in the name of sport," which if perpetrated under any other banner short of warfare would be roundly condemned as heinous crimes.

One widely publicized example that still remains in the minds of many professional hockey fans, players, owners, and sportswriters is former Vancouver Canucks player Todd Bertuzzi's vicious attack on former Colorado Avalanche player Steve Moore on March 8, 2004. From behind, Bertuzzi grabbed Moore's jersey and punched him in the side of his head (an attack that is readily available to view on YouTube). Following this assault and Moore falling face-first onto the ice, several members of both teams, including Bertuzzi, piled on top of Moore. Moore suffered major injuries, including three fractured neck vertebrae, and never played professional hockey again. Many people obviously saw nothing wrong with what Bertuzzi did, however, as he was not given a criminal record and went on to play for Team Canada in the 2006 Winter Olympics.

Race definitely has much to do with the different societal reactions to the violent behaviors of hockey players compared to those of NFL and NBA athletes. To quote Jackson Katz, who is internationally known for his trailblazing work in the prevention of violence against women, especially in sports culture:

Parents who have sons playing youth hockey often worry about the example being set by players at the highest levels. But race is rarely part of the conversation. When was the last time you heard someone say with contempt that violence in hockey is a reflection of the lack of moral values in the white communities where the players come from? Yet when several Black NBA players during a game in Detroit in November of 2004 went into the stands and assaulted fans, league officials wondered aloud about the damage done to the "image of the league." This was widely recognized as a coded way of saying they were concerned that many white people believed the league had been taken over by a bunch of violent Black thugs with poor morals, who were setting a bad example for the youth of America. It is hard to avoid the conclusion that the key difference between the two phenomena is that Black men are typically held more accountable for their violence than are white men.[70]

As Katz further notes, regardless of whether they live in Canada, the US, or elsewhere, people who talk about the deviant behavior of male professional athletes are typically talking about famous Black men like O.J. Simpson, Mike Tyson, and Kobe Bryant. Katz goes on to direct us to the selective attention given to gendered wrongdoings by white hockey players like Patrick Roy. He is deemed far and wide, particularly in Canada, to be one of the greatest hockey goaltenders of all time. On October 22, 2000, he was arrested in Greenwood Village, Colorado, and was charged with domestic violence just a few days after setting the NHL record for most wins by a goalie. Not surprisingly, the charges were eventually dropped in the winter of 2001, and even most of his "hardcore" fans were unaware of this event.

Sometimes Black NHL players, and there are very few (97 percent of NHL players are white), are targeted by the press.

San Jose Sharks forward Evander Kane is one of them. Sports reporter A.J. Perez obtained court documents concerning a domestic violence restraining order application filed by his estranged wife Anna Kane on September 21, 2021, as part of her divorce case in California. It includes allegations that Evander sexually assaulted her and battered her multiple times.[71] One month later, the NHL announced that its investigation into these allegations could not substantiate them.

We do not put all the blame on professional hockey culture and the journalists who cover it, nor does our explanation for the harms covered in this book that is featured in chapter 3. Young men like Logan Mailloux enter the world of professional hockey already trained and primed to treat women as objects and often to commit sexual assault. For example, two Boston University (BU) male hockey players were charged with sexual assault in separate incidents in December 2011 and February 2012. The county prosecutor dismissed the charges against one player and accepted a guilty plea to a drastically reduced charge for the other. In this case, though, the president of BU, Robert Brown, took the uncommon approach of convening a broad-based and powerful task force to examine the hockey team, an important sports organization at BU, and the university's attitudes toward and procedures for dealing with rape and sexual assault. Many members of the BU community believed that the events that led to the arrests were part of a regular pattern.

In fact, the task force found that the team operated in a culture of sexual entitlement, which the task force defined, in a delicately worded passage, as "frequent sexual encounters with women absent an emotional involvement." The task force also said that not only hockey players but students generally needed sexual assault prevention training to protect the community.[72] Less circumspect findings in the subcommittee reports that were not made public, but which were obtained by the *Boston Globe*, outlined extensive group sex, drinking and sex parties in the locker room, and the conclusion that at least some of the team members had "the perception that they need not seek consent for sexual contact."[73]

Many male student athletes do not come to institutions of higher learning like BU as "clean slates" but, too often, as experienced abusers of young women. Innocent young men don't go to college or university and just happen to come under the influence of aggressive male athletes who teach them a brand-new set of values based on the exploitation and victimization of women.

For example, in the spring of 1989, something went terribly wrong in Glen Ridge, New Jersey, a place many people defined as a "paradise." It was frequently described as "an affluent, idyllic suburb, the kind of town that exemplifies the American Dream."[74] If you went there now, your first impression would probably be similar to that described by investigative journalist Bernard Lefkowitz over twenty-five years ago:

My first mental snapshot: Glen Ridge was a squeaky-clean, manicured town that liked to display its affluence by dressing its high school graduates in dinner jackets and gowns. What impressed me most was the orderliness of the place. The streets, the lawns, the houses – everything seemed in proportion. There were no excesses of bad taste, no evidence of neglect or disrepair.[75]

As is often said, "looks can be deceiving," and one should never "judge a book by its cover." On March 1, 1989, thirteen male student athletes (football players) who attended Glen Ridge High School (actor Tom Cruise's alma mater) lured a seventeen-year-old intellectually disabled girl into the basement of the home of two prominent "jocks" (Kevin and Kyle Scherzer), where four of them raped her with a baseball bat and a broomstick while the others looked on. It was weeks before anyone reported this monstrous crime to the police and years before the boys went to trial. Four of them – Kevin and Kyle Scherzer, Christopher Archer, and Bryant Grober – were eventually convicted of various crimes. Grober was convicted only of a third-degree conspiracy charge and received a sentence of three years of probation and 200 hours of community service. The other three were granted bail and remained free during the lengthy period until their appeals were decided. All three then went to prison.

This would not likely happen to a poor Black man arrested for allegedly committing similar crimes. Rather, as Lefkowitz points out:

> Most likely he wouldn't have been able to come up with the bail money when he was arrested. He would have to spend months, maybe years, locked up waiting to go to trial or to cop a plea. He wouldn't have been represented by the best legal talent that money could buy. He would have been represented by an underpaid public defender with a huge caseload. After he was convicted of first-degree sexual assault, he probably would have been jailed immediately.[76]

By allowing the three affluent white boys out on bail, the judge, as stated by Ron Scott, a reporter for the New York City CBS television station, gave the Glen Ridge community and the rest of the United States the message that "If you're White, it's all right." What's more, the community stood by the boys and attacked the media for covering the case, a boy of color who witnessed the rape and reported it to the authorities was ostracized by his peers, and the judge made it clear that he "didn't want to lock up all-American boys and throw away the key."[77]

Similarly, the judge in the Patrick Roy case mentioned earlier gave his Colorado community the impression that high-profile white athletes are exempt from harsh punishment for abusing women. CBC Sports reported that the judge dismissed the case, "ruling it fell short of the standard needed for misdemeanor criminal mischief during an act of domestic violence."[78] So, instead of spending a year in jail, getting a USD$1,000 fine, and possibly being deported, Roy left the court content with the knowledge that he would still be one of the starting goalies in the 2001 NHL All-Star Game that took place very shortly after the judge's decision.

The Glen Ridge rapists also engaged in less serious forms of deviant behavior and were not officially nor even informally punished for their conduct. Kevin Scherzer, for example, would frequently stroke his penis during classes, even in front of teachers and other students. As Lefkowitz notes, there was evidence of "odd behavior over such a long time. And no one in authority seemed able to stop it – or acted as if they were even aware it was going on."[79]

The Glen Ridge High School rapists were not hockey players, but there are a number of examples of similar problems with high school hockey players. In Boston in the winter of 2002, four seventeen-year-old Braintree High School students, including three members of the hockey team, were arraigned on charges that they raped up to three sophomore girls, all of whom were fifteen years old at the time. The police called this an ongoing scheme to have sex with underage classmates.[80] This might come as a shock to many readers, but two of the hockey players – Joseph Fratto and John J. Gould III – were sentenced to probation. Exacerbating the rape survivors' trauma was what the prosecutors did to these boys. They dropped seven counts of forcible rape of a child under sixteen against Fratto and three counts of the same charge against Gould. Four additional counts of statutory rape, five counts of possession of child pornography (Fratto videotaped one of the rapes), and a charge of indecent assault and battery on a child over fourteen against Fratto were also dropped, while Gould had a third count of statutory rape dropped against him.[81]

Though Logan Mailloux and the other recent examples of young, abusive, elite hockey players identified here did not play high school hockey, they were of high school age when they harmed women. And, like an unknown number of high-level high school hockey teams, major Canadian junior leagues prepare young men to abuse women when they become professionals.

Recent longitudinal evidence shows that boys' participation in high-contact sports like hockey in middle school increases their likelihood of sexually assaulting women in high school.[82]

Researchers affiliated with the Centers for Disease Control and Prevention and the University of North Carolina at Chapel Hill who uncovered this finding strongly suggest that middle school male hockey players who are at high risk for sexual assault perpetration in high school may be heavily influenced by their coaches and others in the sport whom they respect and admire.[83]

What do these people teach young boys? Coaches and other adults involved in managing sports teams are uniquely positioned to positively influence how adolescents think and behave in and out of hockey arenas, baseball parks, football fields, and other places where sports are played.[84] However, more than their fair share do the opposite, at least from the perspective of those struggling to end violence against women. This isn't a new phenomenon. Back in the late 1980s, Gary Alan Fine looked at the lessons sports teach preadolescent boys – that is, boys between the ages of nine and twelve. In his landmark study of Little League baseball, Fine found that boys are taught that failure is synonymous with anything feminine. Youth who on average have not yet begun puberty are taught that being sexually aggressive is their proper orientation and that being too friendly with girls will subject them to group ridicule.[85] In many cases, then, male athletes' sexist attitudes are solidly in place in elementary school, long before high school sports even begin to influence them.

It should also be noted in passing that many abusive Canadian men's earliest memories of violence center on minor hockey.[86] In a June 20, 2022, email sent to Walter DeKeseredy, Simon Jo-Keeling, who works for the Partner Assault Response program in a rural Ontario community, shared this perpetrator's story:

I played hockey as a child. One of the fights which broke out went on a long time and started involving more and more players. I stood back and watched. As things progressed, parents in the stands became more and more angry and some of them began physically fighting. It took a long time to calm down and end. I felt scared, but also confused, because, previously, I had taken hockey fights for granted and never felt much about them. I was also shocked at the behavior of the adults and didn't know what to think of them.

Laura Robinson's study of violence and sexual assault in Canadian hockey provides additional support for the assertion that coaches have a major influence on young players. Her statement below could easily be confirmed by thousands of youth hockey parents who hope that their sons will eventually play in the NHL:

> Young hockey hopefuls, facing a selection process ... have little chance of controlling their own futures in the sport, and probably have little understanding of how to begin to navigate a path that will take them closer to their dreams of playing in the NHL. The relationship between coach and player is, consequently, critical. The player has no choice but to depend on his coach entirely. Even if he plays his heart out, he still knows that he can always be replaced; there are plenty of excuses available to justify trading him off into the shadows ... The only way a player stands a chance to impress the coach is to become an irreplaceable part of the game.[87]

A key point developed further in chapter 3 is that coaches (former players/peers) are not alone in providing role models and support for hyper-aggression. For many hockey players and male youth who participate in other combative sports (e.g., football), some of the most important attitudes and lessons are taught by fellow athletes, who themselves have been carefully schooled through Little League or minor hockey, middle school, and high school to develop an aggressive masculinity that often bodes ill for women. The players themselves commonly use a discourse that emphasizes warfare, sexuality, and gender to encourage or embarrass others and in general to promote increased effort in games. The discourse and conclusions thus engendered later allow sexual assault to be treated differently by players and coaches. These people have a shared discourse that makes it seem logical and sensible to them to treat athletes differently when they are accused of sexual assault or other forms of aggression.[88]

What we are talking about here is *male peer support*, a concept developed by Walter DeKeseredy in 1988 and defined as the attachments to male peers and the resources that these men provide that encourage and legitimize various types of violence against women, including those committed by professional hockey players and other male athletes.[89] Male peer support is not only found in hockey culture. Over thirty-six years of rigorous sociological and social psychological research done by two of the co-authors of this book – Walter DeKeseredy and Martin Schwartz[90] – supports what criminologist Lee Bowker declared in 1983:

> This is not a subculture that is confined to a single class, religion, occupational grouping, or race. It is spread throughout all parts of society. Men are socialized by other subculture members to accept common definitions of the situation, norms,

values, and beliefs about male dominance and the necessity of keeping [women] in line. These violence-supporting social relations may occur at any time and in any place.[91]

Decades of research reviewed by DeKeseredy and Schwartz show that male peer pressure that legitimates the sexual objectification of women and their sexual and/or physical abuse is found among Black men in Chicago, among Puerto Rican drug dealers in East Harlem and poor Black boys in parts of St. Louis, among white students on North American university and college campuses and their immediate surroundings, in white rural Ohio and Kentucky, and in white rural New Zealand and South Africa. There are also pro-abuse male support groups in cyberspace, and many men who abuse women learn lessons by consuming pornography with their male friends.[92]

We wholeheartedly concur with the late Michael D. Smith's argument that the importance of peers as *reference others* must be recognized when trying to understand all kinds of violent subcultures, including those in professional hockey and other high-level male sports. Smith's influence on sociological studies of both hockey violence and woman abuse cannot be relegated to an endnote. In fact, his presence is felt throughout this book. Smith was Professor of Sociology and Director of York University's LaMarsh Research Centre on Violence and Conflict Resolution in Toronto. He passed away too soon, in late June 1994, but his death has not stopped sports sociologists and feminist scholars around the world from drawing upon his keen social scientific work on the key sources of male violence both on the ice and behind closed doors.

It is not only male peer support and other factors identified in this chapter that contribute to professional hockey players' violence against women. Chapter 4 identifies some of the broader social and cultural forces that influence them to abuse women. These include patriarchal structures in society that affect the socialization patterns of men and the ways they learn to do masculinity. Many men learn that there is nothing wrong with forcing women to have sex with them, an idea often married to the objectification of women, the acceptance of rape myths, and the lessons learned from today's violent and racist pornography.

The title of this chapter is "More Than a Few Bad Men." By now, some impatient readers are probably saying to themselves, "Enough already! Just tell us how many professional hockey players abuse women." There are studies showing that professional athletes have higher rates of violence against women compared to male members of the general population, but recent large-scale systematic research on the extent, distribution, sources, and consequences of hockey players' abuse of women is in very short supply. No one, to the best of our knowledge, has thus far conducted a representative sample survey of potential offenders affiliated with the NHL. Likewise, there are no surveys of women's victimization experiences in the professional hockey world, and there are no studies currently available that determine whether North American professional male hockey players victimize women more than those in other parts of the world (i.e., Europe and Russia). Most of the current data on professional hockey players' deviant and criminal conduct, in fact, comes from North American sports journalists or legal experts.

Of course, athletes are also victimized more often than others, mostly by other members of their athletic communities. A June 2021 digital survey of 800 US adults, both male and female, under the age of forty-five found that more than one in four current or former student athletes were sexually assaulted by someone in a position of power on college or university campuses, compared to one in ten of those in the general population. Athletes were nearly three times more likely to report such abuse, and coaches were most identified as the abusers.[93] Although we doubt it, we hope that the NHL will one day conduct a similar survey of its players. In the meantime, authors like us must primarily rely on secondary sources, such as news reports and legal documents.

The case study – "a qualitative research method involving a detailed analysis of a single event, group, or person for the purpose of understanding how a particular context gives rise to this event, group, or person"[94] – is another research method that is occasionally used in studies of athletes' wrongdoings. Case studies generally involve employing a variety of research techniques, such as archival research, interviews, and observations. Laura Robinson's pathbreaking 1998 book *Crossing the Line* includes rich case studies of violence and sexual assault in Canadian hockey, including the widely discussed and publicized victimization of Sheldon Kennedy. Between the ages of fourteen and nineteen, during his tenure with the Swift Current Broncos of Canada's WHL from 1984 to 1990, Kennedy was sexually abused 350 times by his coach Graham James.

The following short account of some of Kennedy's experiences helps to explain the contention that some coaches' influence on young male hockey players can have a dark side:

Kennedy describes his life as a lonely, living hell. He was sexually abused as a teen by Graham James, his coach and "father figure," who controlled his hockey career and his daily life from the time he was 14 to 19. Kennedy found he was unable to make friends. Unable to trust and unable to love. Unable to feel "normal" unless he was drinking. Unable to turn a junior career into a solid National Hockey League career. Suicidal at times because inner turmoil haunted him. "You feel people are looking at you. I put up a shield. I didn't let anybody in. It's a very lonely way to feel. You never feel normal. You know something is wrong but you don't know why it is like that," Kennedy said.[95]

When asked about the more recent Chicago Blackhawks case, Kennedy buttressed an argument made earlier in this chapter – nothing has changed:

This is all too familiar. And what's familiar here is the response has been archaic, and I mean, this is the way they would have tried to respond in 1998 when I came forward. Don't say nothing. That was how they addressed these issues. Don't say nothing. That's the familiar part, and that's what they tried to do.[96]

Robinson's work is still discussed today, particularly by people who are struggling to eliminate violence and sexual assault in hockey. Recently, Evan F. Moore and Jashvina Shah published *Game Misconduct*, a book that broadens the case study of crime and deviance in hockey to include not only issues covered by us and Robinson (e.g., sexism, heteronormativity, and violence) but also ableism and other inequalities in this sport. Their approach involved perusing relevant books, academic journals, videos and films, magazines, newspapers, periodicals, and websites, as well as conducting interviews with fans, players, journalists, coaches, administrators, siblings, parents, aunts, uncles, and cousins who have experienced exclusion or discrimination. These books, and ours, reinforce sports journalist Jack Todd's observation that it "sometimes seems that hockey is one long scandal, interrupted by the occasional game. On-ice assaults. Sexual assaults. Coverups. Financial shenanigans. Greedy players locked out by greedier owners. Player safety working to endanger players."[97]

Dated, like Robinson's offering, but still useful, is Jeff Benedict's case study of elite athletes and crimes against women. Presented in his 1997 book *Public Heroes, Private Felons*, Benedict's research did not exclusively focus on hockey players but is worth summarizing here nonetheless because of its major impact and Benedict's courage to challenge the status quo.[98] From 1992 to 1996, Benedict worked at Northeastern University's Center for the Study of Sport in Society, an institution created to uphold the integrity of organized athletics and that depended on the NBA, the NFL, and many National Collegiate Athletic Association (NCAA) departments for financial and political support. Benedict was placed in the unenviable position of gathering data to challenge the growing perception that athletes are major perpetrators of violence against women. He was required to monitor newspapers across the US for reports of athletes being charged with rape and domestic violence.

Benedict strayed from his assigned role by conducting a "first-of-its-kind" study of the prevalence of sexual assault and domestic violence committed by athletes at NCAA schools with basketball and football teams repeatedly ranked among the top twenty in the country. This study involved an examination of internal judicial affairs records of ten schools from 1991 to 1993. Benedict's research also involved researching hundreds of reported incidents of sexual assault and domestic abuse perpetrated by athletes and then selecting twenty-five for in-depth study. This component of his empirical work entailed over 300 interviews with professional and college athletes (mainly defendants and their teammates), survivors of sexual assault and domestic violence, criminal prosecutors, defense attorneys, plaintiff attorneys, judges, jurors, witnesses, police officers, victim witness advocates, medical personnel, rape crisis counselors, coaches, sports agents, and team and league officials. Furthermore, Benedict reviewed thousands of pages from criminal and civil case files, public records, and press reports.

Benedict took considerable "heat" for his pathbreaking research, as do most people who threaten the capitalist, patriarchal nature of professional and high-level amateur sports leadership. This heat comes from all kinds of directions, from fans, owners, employers, journalists, players, and a host of others. Consider caustic comments made by some people who read Stu Cowan's July 27, 2021, column on the case of Logan Mailloux. All comments in the *Montreal Gazette* that appear below stories like Stu's are, according to its publisher Postmedia, posted online for the purpose of "maintaining a lively but civil forum for discussion." Sometimes, though, the

word "civil" is arguably defined too broadly, as illustrated
by this man's statement:

> This woman or girl had consensual sex with this kid, a
> 17-year-old, and he put their pictures out here. Did she also
> make a mistake by having sex with a bozo? Of course ... and
> let's move on. This nanny culture which Cowan belongs to,
> this pc crap, this "oh, let's not offend anyone (except white
> males, btw)" culture has to stop.[99]

In another comment, one that responds to Brendan Kelly's
(BK) criticisms of Mailloux's image-based sexual abuse, the
same person again defends this player and the Canadiens
drafting him:

> It amuses me to see this holier than thou attitude towards
> hockey and sex. Who gives a damn about #metoo and all the
> complaining? BK and others in the media remind me of the
> Puritans in the early 17 century in the United States. Have
> any of you idiots heard of the sexual revolution that was first
> and foremost when I was a youth in the 1960s and 1970s?
> Reminds me of what people did to Trump during his four
> years in the White House. People in glass houses should not
> throw stones.[100]

Some readers may argue that we are "cherry-picking" to
make our point, and that the person quoted above is simply
"an army of one." If only this were the case![101] Not only is
he a member of the coalition of angry white men described
earlier, but he is also one of thousands of supporters of the

backlash against efforts to promote gender equity in sports and other sectors of society. Thirty-one years ago, journalist Susan Faludi popularized the term *backlash* in reference to the attempts throughout the media and popular culture to undermine the minimal gains made by the feminist movement. The backlash has always been with us, and it is, according to Faludi, "a sort of perpetual viral condition in our culture ... not always in an acute stage; its symptoms subside and resurface periodically."[102] The hostile male reactions to Stu Cowan's coverage of Logan Mailloux's treatment of the aforementioned Swedish woman personifies what Faludi refers to as an "episode of resurgence."

The chorus of denial starts with anti-feminists who claim that there just is not a tremendous amount of violence against women committed by hockey players and other types of men. Any claims that violence against women is a problem are just the cries of a group of feminist radicals, they argue. Such denials of the problem are not themselves the product of a "lunatic fringe." Rather, a large body of social scientific literature shows that resistance to reducing male violence against women and other highly injurious symptoms of sexism is a common feature of social life, whether in athletic organizations or elsewhere. The key elements of backlash and resistance to gender inequality on and off the playing field are "denial of the problem, disavowal of responsibility, inaction, appeasement, co-option, and repression."[103] Scattered throughout this book are examples of these components.

Another common tactic used by anti-feminists to challenge the overwhelming evidence of women's experiences with male violence is to say, "But women do it too," or, "Women are just as bad as men." Violence against women researchers are well aware that statements like these are some of the greatest obstacles to improving women's health and safety, regardless of how often they are refuted by research and statistics published in the world's leading scientific journals in the field.

The above claims are examples of the attempts of angry men – particularly angry *white* men – to reassert patriarchy, and their efforts have been strengthened, especially after the election of former US president Donald Trump.[104] One group deeply concerned about this is the Southern Poverty Law Center, which monitors racist hate organizations and now features men's rights groups in its annual survey of hate. It reports:

> Misogynists in the men's and fathers' rights movements have developed a set of claims about women to support their depictions of them as violent liars and manipulators of men. Some suggest that women attack men, even sexually, just as much as men attack women. Others claim that vast numbers of reported rapes of women, as much as half or even more, are fabrications designed to destroy men they don't like or to gain the upper hand in contested custody cases.[105]

That *some* women strike *some* men, sometimes with the intent to injure, should not be the subject of debate. Every competent survey of violence in private places has found battered men, some battered by other men, and some battered by women, including intimate partners. Nonetheless, decades of rigorous scholarly work consistently shows that women are far more likely to be physically and sexually abused in intimate, heterosexual relationships. Still, it is the voices of the men's rights community – people without data or research to back their claims – that get heard more by the general public. Of course, many people only hear what they want to hear, which is how a majority of US Republicans believe that the 2020 election was "stolen" despite a complete lack of evidence that can stand up in court. On the issue of hockey violence, the voices of people without supporting data are now prominent in the world of hockey journalism.

The reporting on former Montreal Canadiens forward Alex Galchenyuk's January 10, 2016, experience is a classic example of the exception that proves the rule. His then girlfriend Chanel Leszczynski was arrested following a "domestic dispute" at a party at his apartment. Charges were not filed, and she remained his girlfriend afterwards. Although this is an isolated incident in the context of professional hockey and other high-level sports, bloggers writing for *SB Nation* maintained that this episode shows that "men and women self-report perpetrating acts of domestic violence at similar rates."[106] Other anti-feminists saw Galchenyuk as a "poster boy" in their efforts to undermine attempts to hold male hockey players accountable for their crimes against women. The *Duquesne Duke*, for example, declared, "Galchenyuk could be a great spokesperson to bring domestic violence against men into the public eye and help other victims come forward."[107]

These statements are just but a few that reflect deep-rooted anti-feminist sentiments among fans and journalists, and they need to be taken seriously. People, especially youth, spend more time today on their computers than they do in face-to-face relationships, and social media sites such as Facebook, Twitter, and TikTok enable people to reach larger audiences. In this way, anti-feminists become aware of large "support groups" and become motivated to join what might be called the "Angry White Men's choir," whose members often dismiss female victims of male hockey player violence outright and who "whitewash" the perpetrators.[108]

Contemporary social media has joined the ranks of those who support and shape conceptions of masculinity. Of course, this runs a broad gamut, from the usual sports fans to what we just described as particularly toxic forms of anti-feminism. More than ever before, it is no longer necessary to leave the house to develop a cohort of peers who can mold and reinforce views that promote or excuse violence against women. As one example, a female reporter covering a 2019 sporting event (a race) was slapped and grabbed on the buttocks on live TV by a forty-two-year-old race participant – a youth minister and Boy Scout leader – as he ran past, an incident that went viral on social and broadcast media.[109] Most interesting were the comments on a variety of platforms. Some said it was the reporter's fault for standing where he could run off the course and molest her. The overwhelming majority said it was a minor incident and that she should just ignore it and move on, even though the police arrested and charged the man with sexual battery. He was later convicted.

Very similarly, but more broadly, Erin Ash and her colleagues analyzed thousands of Twitter posts on sexual assault, athletes, race, and class in response to various assaults reported in the press. They found that while numerous posts decried the violence, the majority of posts supported various components of rape culture. Most tweets attacked the victims of sexual assault, framed the offender as the true victim in a rape case, and in general provided support and reinforcement for attitudes commonly cited as indicative of rape culture.[110]

In their first major exposition of male peer support theory, Martin Schwartz and Walter DeKeseredy pointed out that one does not have to be on a sports team to be influenced by an online male peer culture that is anti-female and homophobic.[111] For instance, the more rabid followers of sports teams, whether they are hockey or NFL clubs, are often bound up in a culture that promotes the same hypermasculinity values among nonathletes. One such male peer support group centers around sports betting, where success in wagering brings high status in a world of alcohol, risk-taking, and loud group competitive social interactions before and during games.

Male peer support for sexual violence and other types of woman abuse is a common feature of this digital age,[112] but the power of voices involved in the online #MeToo movement cannot be underestimated. This recent development offers much hope and the possibility of major social change. To a certain extent, the #MeToo campaign was very successful and resulted in tangible action. Nevertheless, there are some serious problems with it. For example, despite the success in raising awareness about sexual harassment and workplace violence against women, the forum has been comparatively silent about male violence against women behind closed doors. Moreover, it ignores the plight of members of the LGBTQ+ community and has done very little for people of color. This is because #MeToo was initially championed by wealthy, white, heterosexual women with major public profiles and access to political, social, and economic resources that many other women do not have.[113]

Shortly after widespread allegations of sexual abuse against Hollywood producer Harvey Weinstein were released in October 2017 by journalists Megan Twohey and Jodi Kantor in the *New York Times*, white actress Alyssa Milano posted on Twitter, "If all the women who have been sexually harassed or assaulted wrote 'Me Too' as a status, we might give people a sense of the magnitude of the problem." Many other white US actresses including Gwyneth Paltrow, Ashley Judd, Jennifer Lawrence, and Uma Thurman promptly followed in her footsteps using the hashtag #MeToo.

Although arguably done unintentionally, many anti-sexual violence scholars and activists point out that Milano co-opted the words of Black sexual assault survivor and activist Tarana Burke, who actually started the "Me Too" movement in 2006. Burke did not take the co-optation of her work by white Hollywood actresses lightly, and rightfully so. This is reflected in a piece she wrote for *Time* in September 2021:

> None of what was happening in Hollywood felt related to the work I had been entrenched in within my own community for so many years. Seeing "me too," the phrase I had built that work and purpose around, used by people outside of that community was jarring.
>
> "This can't happen," I said through my tears. "Not like this! Y'all know if these white women start using this hashtag, and it gets popular, they will never believe that a Black woman in her forties from the Bronx has been building a

movement for the same purposes, using those exact words, for years now. It will be over."[114]

Except for a handful of cases, such as the 2019 firing of Toronto Maple Leafs coach Mike Babcock and CBC's *Coach's Corner* cohost Don Cherry for their unprofessional behaviors, the #MeToo campaign has done little to change the dominant toxic masculine and racist culture of professional hockey. Evidence disseminated throughout this book reveals an unsettling truth: the #MeToo moment in the NHL has passed. There are still no standardized sexual assault and domestic violence policies in this league.[115] This is not to say that all is lost and that a major cultural shift cannot occur in the NHL and other professional sports organizations. In chapter 5, we offer an evidenced-based recipe for meaningful and lasting changes, which, unlike the proposals offered by Jeff Benedict in the last chapter of his book *Public Heroes, Private Felons*, are intended to do more than simply "stop the bleeding."

We have no doubt that a sizeable number of fans, NHL team employees, journalists, and others will respond to this book in a myriad of negative ways. Some will declare that we are simply "social justice warriors" seeking to capitalize on a self-serving mission to destroy young men who made mistakes. Others will contend that in addition to doing this (which we aren't), we are creating what Neil Gilbert, Chernin Professor of Social Welfare at the University of California, Berkeley, refers to as a "phantom epidemic of sexual assault,"[116] while still others will continue down the well-worn path of declaring that "it only matters what happens on the ice." There will also be critics, such as Secoya Freedman, who will see us as both being "afraid of a real man like Brandon Prust" and as "leftists" who "are afraid of masculinity."[117] Certainly, other disparaging viewpoints besides these will be expressed, but this is something those of us in the struggle to make professional sports more equitable and safer constantly endure and come to expect. We know that the journey toward making hockey a better place will be arduous, but we are prepared for this strenuous trip.

Brandon Prust, by the way, is a former NHL player who used to play for the Montreal Canadiens as well as for the Calgary Flames, New York Rangers, and Vancouver Canucks. He is best known not for his goal scoring or defensive abilities, however, but rather for his role as an "enforcer." Prust did, and continues to, embody *hypermasculinity*, which is "the belief that ideal manhood lies in the exercise of force to dominate others – it is the prevalent ideology of manhood in contemporary society."[118] Recent evidence of this was seen during his rant in the summer of 2021 against people calling for mandatory COVID-19 vaccinations when he expressed his wish for one woman to be forced into the sex trade. He first laid out his argument against vaccinations on Twitter: "I'm going to be on the road tomorrow driving. If I see anyone else on the road I will lose it ... Also, everyone take their vitamins tomorrow because mine won't work if you don't take yours." A woman sarcastically replied, "Thanks in advance for driving safe." Prust then appeared to compare vaccine mandates to forced prostitution in his reply and stated, "So that means they can force me to do anything they want? I hope they force u into the sex trade so u can finally get laid u sheep. I paid more taxes for these roads than u could ever dream of money in ur account."[119]

Is this all just the bluster of a madman or the expressions of a person indoctrinated by a patriarchal hockey subculture? We have already presented our answer to this question, but we leave it up to you to make your own interpretation of Prust's Twitter tirade. Regardless of what accounts for it, we are not afraid of him, but we are very afraid of the type of masculinity that produces people like him. Hence, our goal is to contribute to the struggle to replace it with a different type of masculinity, one that promotes fairness, empathy, respect, and kindness within the world of professional hockey and other revenue-generating professional sports.

Many scholars and activists often see much of what is bad in our world as the product of men and masculinity. This is understandable seeing as men commit most of the predatory street and corporate crimes, take us to war, cause most of the world's environmental damage, and are the main perpetrators of violence against women. But we often forget an important point made many years ago by feminist criminologist Lee Bowker: "Much of what is good in the world ... has been contributed by masculine role players."[120] Much of what is good in professional hockey, too, has been contributed by men, but we need many more good men of this kind. Maybe, then, with the assistance of the policy initiatives featured in chapter 5, we will eventually reach a point where books like this are no longer necessary, and we will be able to think of hockey as a truly fun sport where the culture of violence against women has been eliminated, and where people from all walks of life are welcomed, valued, and appreciated.

2

In Their Own Words: Giving Voice to Survivors of Professional Hockey Violence and Sexism

I looked the worst after that Hawaii incident. I took a real beating there. [Bobby] just picked me up, threw me over his shoulder, threw me in the room, and just proceeded to knock the heck out of me. He took my shoe – with a steel heel – and proceeded to hit me in the head. I was covered with blood. And I can remember him holding me over the balcony and I thought, "This is the end, I'm going."

– Joanne McKay, ex-wife of Bobby Hull[1]

Does the man who almost ended his ex-wife's life resemble this glowing description of him?

Bobby Hull isn't just another hockey star. In fact, few athletes have had the impact on any sport that Hull has had on the game of hockey. Throughout the sixties, Hull was indisputably the number-one attraction in the game, a glamorous blond who brought fans to their feet with his daring rushes, who sent them home buzzing about his thunderous slap shots. And off the ice, well, there just wasn't anyone else like Bobby.[2]

Well, actually, off the ice, there are millions of men who behave like former Chicago Blackhawks star Bobby Hull.[3] Every day, women are beaten, raped, murdered, and violently victimized in many other ways "in numbers that would numb the mind of Einstein."[4] In fact, studies have shown that one in three women worldwide will be physically or sexually assaulted by an intimate partner in their lifetime.[5]

But what about Canada? Surely violence against women can't be a major problem in this reputable country where hockey is its national winter sport.[6] After all, the United Nations (UN) Human Development Reports have consistently ranked Canada as having one of the world's highest living standards since the early 1990s. This supports conventional wisdom and the self-image of almost all Canadians. Jeffrey Simpson, author of the book *Star-Spangled Canadians*, observes, "Canadians prefer to think of their country as virtue incarnate, its cup of tolerance running over. They endlessly recycle the cliché about Canada being the 'peaceable kingdom' in large part because it makes them feel good about themselves. Canadians are peacekeepers abroad, peaceful citizens at home."[7] Also worth mentioning is that the US News & World Report ranked Canada as the number one country in the world in 2021.[8]

Compared to residents of the US, Canadians are much less likely to be physically or sexually assaulted in public parks, streets, bars, and workplaces. This is one of the key reasons many Canadians passionately and publicly state "We don't want to be American" in response to attempts by businesses, political agencies, and other formal organizations to adopt various US policies and procedures, especially those that existed during Donald Trump's tenure as president. The mass media also contribute to Canadians' perceptions that their country is safer than the US. On any given day, violent acts committed by poor, Black, American men are central features of both fictional and nonfictional US television shows and movies that Canadians can easily and freely access.

Stranger homicides are unusual in Canada but are often reported on for weeks, and sometimes even years, in Canadian news media. On December 15, 2017, billionaire Barry Sherman, founder and chairman of the board of the generic drug company Apotex, and his wife Honey were found dead near their basement pool in one of Toronto's North York neighborhoods. This double homicide remains unsolved and is still being covered by the CBC and other major Canadian mainstream news outlets.[9] This is not to trivialize these deaths; they are deeply disturbing, and the Shermans' family and friends are living through immeasurable pain and suffering. Nonetheless, less sensational forms of what some criminologists define as "everyday" or "ordinary violence" often go unreported in Canada.

How often, for example, do the media report sexual assaults that repeatedly occur in Canadian institutions of higher learning? How frequently are male-on-female beatings in marital/cohabiting relationships featured on the evening news? And how often do the media and politicians address the plight of women killed by male ex-partners during and after the process of separation or divorce? Canadian female victims of lethal and non-lethal acts committed by current and former intimate male partners and acquaintances greatly outnumber the victims of predatory crimes that occur on the streets and in other public places. What's more, the Canadian rates of violence against women mirror those of the US. In spite of this, the media generally characterize male-on-female assaults in intimate heterosexual relationships as exceptional events or the result of some men's deep-rooted psychological problems. Only rarely are they headline-grabbing incidents.

Ironically, at a time when crime discussion, especially in the US, is dominated by "What about the victim?" discourse and calls for more prisons and more executions of convicted offenders, and despite ongoing feminist efforts to end violence against women and other destructive outcomes of patriarchy, there still remains a market for belittling and/or ignoring crime victims when they are tyrannized and assaulted by men behind closed doors. Recall the anti-feminist backlash described in chapter 1. The selective inattention given to female survivors of both offline and online male abuse parallels what Black sociologist W.E.B. Du Bois said about the United States' attitude toward the health and well-being of Black people at the end of the nineteenth century. He then observed that there had been "few other cases in the history of civilized peoples where human suffering has been viewed with such peculiar indifference."[10]

Some striking examples of peculiar indifference to the plight of women abused by men employed by revenue-producing athletic teams are provided in chapter 1, and you will soon read about more. Peculiar indifference, too, often leads to the *institutional betrayal* of female survivors. This involves insensitive responses by trusted persons in authority or leadership positions that "are experienced by victims as an especially acute form of disbelief and rejection because they come from social groups that victims often identify with and consider important parts of their self-concept."[11]

Sexual assault survivors will tell you that the criminal justice system symbolizes institutional betrayal. From an early age, they, and the vast majority of people throughout the world, are socialized to trust police officers, prosecutors, and judges. For most sexual assault survivors who have the courage to come forward with allegations, however, reality quickly sets in, and this trust is broken, rarely to be repaired. Before describing a story about a February 14, 2014, incident involving two former University of Ottawa Gee-Gees hockey players, it must be emphasized that only a tiny number of rapes reported to the police in North America are false allegations. Additionally, across North America one finds few local prosecutors who will take on sexual assault cases involving college students that are reported to the police. For those involving well-known famous athletes, the chances of a prosecution are even lower, no matter what the facts of the case may be.[12]

The evening of February 14, 2014, in Thunder Bay, Ontario, featured an alcohol-filled celebration of the Gee-Gees' overtime win against the Lakehead University Thunderwolves. A large party took place in a hotel that included adjoining rooms with connecting doors. A young woman (who cannot be named due to a publication ban) said that she met a roommate of Gee-Gee player Guillaume

Donovan on Tinder and that they arranged to meet at a local bar during the festivities. She said at the February 2018 sexual assault trial of Donovan and fellow player David Foucher that she and Donovan's roommate returned to the hotel room and started to have consensual sex. She also testified that their intimate relations were interrupted when Donovan and Foucher forced themselves on her in the hotel room.[13]

That Donovan and Foucher denied this allegation is not a surprise. Donovan testified that he intended to go to sleep when he returned to his hotel room after partying but that he became sexually aroused when he saw the couple having sex and thus approached them. He also said that his roommate asked the woman if Donovan could join them and that she agreed. Foucher, on the other hand, denied ever having sexual relations with the woman. He testified that he was with a group of Gee-Gees players who entered the hotel room with nothing on but their boots as a prank.[14]

In late June 2018, Donovan and Foucher were found not guilty because Justice Chantal Brochu doubted the woman's credibility, something that happens all too often in sexual assault cases. This explains why thousands of survivors never turn to criminal justice officials for help.

The famous legal case of Jian Ghomeshi, though he is not a professional hockey player, is briefly told here because (1) it, too, illustrates how negative perceptions of victim credibility influence trial outcomes, and (2) it generated a substantial amount of media and public attention due to Ghomeshi's international celebrity status. He was the host and co-creator of the CBC radio show Q, a job he held from 2007 to October

2014, when he was fired because CBC saw "graphic evidence that [he] caused physical injury to a woman."[15] Shortly after his dismissal, the *Toronto Star* published allegations by three women who said that Ghomeshi sexually abused them.[16] On November 26, 2014, Ghomeshi turned himself in to the Toronto Police Service and was charged with four counts of sexual assault and one count of overcoming resistance by choking after a police investigation that started on October 31. He appeared in court the same day and was released on CAD$100,000 bail with the conditions that he surrender his passport, stay in the province of Ontario, and live with his mother.[17]

Ghomeshi's trial began on February 1, 2016, and the judge delivered his verdict on March 24, 2016, one that is eerily familiar to the verdict of the Donovan and Foucher trial. Ghomeshi was acquitted based on Justice William B. Hopkins's interpretation that there was "outright deception" in the three complainants' testimonies. He relayed the following to the court:

> The success of this prosecution depended entirely on the court being able to accept each complainant as a sincere, honest and accurate witness ... Each complainant was revealed at trial to be lacking in these important attributes. The evidence of each complainant suffered not just from inconsistencies and questionable behaviour, but was tainted by outright deception.
>
> The harsh reality is that once a witness has been shown to be deceptive and manipulative in giving their evidence, the witness can no longer expect the court to consider them to be a trusted source of the truth.

I am forced to conclude that it was impossible for the court to have sufficient faith in the reliability or sincerity of these complainants. Put simply, the volume of serious deficiencies in the evidence leaves the court with a reasonable doubt.[18]

Three women who claimed Ghomeshi assaulted them made formal legal complaints and appeared in court, but a total of nine women publicly made terrifying allegations against him, ranging from workplace sexual harassment to choking without consent. Seven of them spoke to the *Toronto Star* under condition of anonymity, while *Trailer Park Boys* actress Lucy DeCoutere (who went to trial) publicly identified herself.[19]

Reading some of the nine women's revelations makes it plain that such events can enormously impact abused women's lives. Furthermore, these survivors, like those who were, and are, victimized by professional hockey players and other athletes, do not constitute a minority among Canadian women. Annually, thousands of women across Canada experience similar assaults.[20] Even so, hardly any of them report assaults and harassment for reasons like those articulated by a few of Ghomeshi's victims: fear of losing their jobs, intimidation, stigmatization, police and prosecutor insensitivity, and bullying on social media.

There are other reasons, too, for why most female survivors of harassment, physical violence, and sexual assault do not come forward. Whether they understand what happened to them may depend on whether survivors have supportive friends to turn to after being victimized. Those who ask the criminal justice system for help are frequently women with supportive friends and trauma therapists who reassure them that they have done nothing wrong, and hence these survivors define their victimization as sexual assault or rape.[21]

Was a wall of silence erected at CBC and in other social arenas in which Ghomeshi participated? There is no conclusive answer to this question, but some facts that emerged during investigations of his misogynistic behavior suggest that he had an alarming track record that was hidden from the general public. For example, a Q producer said that she complained to the show's executive producer in 2010 about Ghomeshi telling her that he wanted to "hate f---" her. This woman said that the executive producer's response was, "He's never going to change, you're a malleable person, let's talk about how you make this a less toxic work environment for you."[22]

Those who attack the CBC and other institutions for aiding and abetting Ghomeshi might first wish to discern the level and type of services provided by their own places of employment to the survivors of sexual harassment and other types of woman abuse, and they should ask about managerial efforts to find out who they are if they don't immediately self-report. What would be more shocking is to find a formal organization that *did* make such efforts. Do you think the CBC's insensitive response to Jian Ghomeshi's abusive behavior equivalent to what the Chicago Blackhawks did to Kyle Beach in 2010?

In his recent critically acclaimed book on lethal violence in Black communities in the US, Elliott Currie correctly notes that "communities that suffer the violence the most are those with the least voice or influence in the political arena."[23] As documented by the statistics presented at the start of this chapter, women, like young, Black Americans,[24] suffer an inordinate amount of violence, and male-dominated institutions, be they professional hockey teams or publicly owned broadcast corporations like the CBC, play a key role in silencing female abuse survivors directly or indirectly connected to them.

This is not to say that all survivors of violence committed by men affiliated with athletic teams (and by men in general) are simply passive victims. Many live through violent events that few people are capable of imagining. They are strong, brave women who have made great strides toward recovery and who plan futures free of fear, pain, and patriarchal tyranny. Much more legal, social scientific, and journalistic attention should be devoted to focusing on the incredible resilience of women who are, or were, abused by male athletes as well as their unique responses to the online and offline variants of violence they have endured.[25]

The women introduced to readers in this chapter and other parts of this book are "stronger than you know."[26] This fact rarely appears in media coverage of hockey players' intimate/romantic partners, regardless of whether or not they were abused. Peruse the internet and you will find thousands of sites that reinforce these and other sexist stereotypes of professional hockey players' wives and girlfriends:

- Barbara Blank (maybe better known by her WWE ring name, Kelly Kelly), former wife of retired hockey player Sheldon Souray, said that hockey wives constantly compete to see who looks best. She also said that designer clothes and makeup are essential, "especially on game day, when your No. 1 responsibility is to show up and support your man."

- Krista Ference, former professional snowboarder and wife of now retired player Andrew Ference, said that celebrating a Stanley Cup victory is "a messy affair, with champagne and beer spraying all over the locker room, so it is important to have a garbage bag to put the wives' designer handbags inside as protection."

- Emilie Blum, a former US Military Intelligence Specialist and wife of Jonathan Blum, a defenseman currently playing for Färjestad BK of the Swedish Hockey League, told reporters that she functions like a single mother and makes sure that all of her family's needs are met so that Jonathan can focus on hockey. She stated, "I feel like a maid, a massage therapist, an actual therapist."[27]

Seldom, if ever, revealed by the mainstream media is that many women abused by men affiliated with renowned amateur and professional sports teams fight back with their stories of resistance and triumph over adversity. Courtney Smith, ex-wife of former Ohio State University (OSU) assistant football coach Zach Smith, is one recent example. She underwent years of abuse, which led to Zach's firing from the OSU football program in late July 2018. She revealed her victimization in a televised interview with the sports network Stadium and disclosed that then OSU head football coach Urban Meyer[28] knew she was being beaten and did nothing about it. Meyer's wife Shelley and members of his coaching staff were also aware. In fact, Courtney texted Shelley photos and details. During her interview, Courtney recounted the following:

> Shelley said she was going to have to tell Urban ... I said that's fine, you should tell Urban. We can't have someone like this coaching young men. I believe that when someone is crying out for help, I believe the coach, along with the coach's wife have a duty to do something ... to help. Instead of worrying about winning games or who his mentor is and trying to protect that.[29]

It took much strength and courage for Courtney to break the silence on her ex-husband's violence and to reveal the legendary Urban Meyer's selective inattention to it.

The efforts of women's groups and feminist scholars to understand violence against women are firmly rooted in respect for real-life knowledge shared by survivors like Courtney Smith. The experiences of women who live with abuse or its memories are touchstones for people working to end woman abuse. Included, then, in this chapter are the voices of women who have been abused by professional hockey players and other types of male athletes. They reveal something about how they see life and professional sports, not only how they see abuse. Women who have been abused do not separate "the abuse" from the rest of their lives. This is a construct imposed on them by those who theorize about or try to stop violence against women. Therefore, the voices presented here were selected by the authors as those containing experiential theories of abuse.[30]

Not for lack of trying, we can't devote much space to the voices of women at the margins of the professional hockey world. The NHL, for instance, brags about its "Hockey is for Everyone" campaign (which also takes place during Black History Month), but the truth is that it is not for women of color. When was the last time you saw a Black or Asian woman provide play-by-play coverage of an NHL game? Do you know of any Black or Asian women commentators featured in live broadcasts of NHL games? Can you think of a regular, prominent newspaper column about NHL-related issues written by a woman of color? No such women come to mind because

> in the United States and in Canada, journalism, especially sports writing, is a predominantly white, male, suburbanite-driven profession. In America, newsrooms rarely reflect the demographics of the areas they cover. The *New York Times* and the *Wall Street Journal* are both 81 percent white, while the *Washington Post* is 70 percent white, according to numbers compiled by the Columbia Journalism Review.[31]

Further to this point, women of color are not only excluded from media coverage of hockey but also from coverage of other major sports like basketball. And, there is evidence that some privileged white women contribute to this problem. Rachel Nichols, longtime broadcaster for ESPN, is a recent example of such a woman. Nichols's Black colleague, Maria Taylor, took over her position as primary anchor for the 2020 NBA Finals pre- and postgame shows. A leaked video recording of a private telephone conversation on July 13, 2020, with Adam

Mendelsohn (longtime advisor to Los Angeles Lakers star
LeBron James and his agent Rich Paul) reveals that Nichols
took issue with Taylor's appointment and essentially labeled
her an unqualified minority hire. She said:

> I wish Maria Taylor all the success in the world – she covers
> football, she covers basketball ... If you need to give her more
> things to do because you are feeling pressure about your
> crappy longtime record on diversity – which, by the way, I
> know personally from the female side of it – like, go for it.
> Just find it somewhere else. You are not going to find it from
> me or taking my thing away.[32]

After hearing this conversation, multiple Black ESPN employees
told one another that it "confirmed their suspicions that out-
wardly supportive white people talk differently behind closed
doors."[33] Further confirmation of their suspicions is that Nichols's
statement was not a "one-shot" racist assault on Taylor during
her tenure at ESPN. Taylor received much attention for her on-
air comments about the May 25, 2020, murder of George Floyd
by a Minneapolis police officer, and another ESPN colleague
disparaged her for speaking out about this incident.

Shortly after Nichols's comments went viral, Taylor left
ESPN to join NBC Sports. She wrote in an email to ESPN
executives two weeks after this incident, which was obtained
by the *New York Times*: "I will not call myself a victim, but
I certainly have felt victimized and I do not feel as though
my complaints have been taken seriously ... Simply being a
front facing Black woman at this company has taken its toll
physically and mentally."[34]

The case of Rachel Nichols speaks to us on many levels. One key takeaway point is that some women, particularly those who are white, have more privilege in the world of male-dominated professional sports than others. Some would even go so far as to describe women like Nichols as *exonerators*. In other words, they turn women against each other.[35] One thing that we do know for certain is that all women who work for big media companies like ESPN (and other major corporations) have little power relative to men, but there is a constant struggle for power between different groups of women within these organizations.[36]

The voices of non-white female survivors of male hockey players' violence are also conspicuously absent from this book because, except for rare incidents such as that involving Auston Matthews (see chapter 1), there are no published stories about the atrocities that these women have experienced at the hands of "ice men." The same can be said about Indigenous women.

Additionally, you will not read about the experiences of women who kill hockey players who abused them because there are no officially recorded cases of this type of homicide. Returning to the horrors experienced by Bobby Hull's second wife Joanne McKay, it is truly disturbing that so many women have had similar experiences. Bobby's beatings did not stop after the aforementioned incident in Hawaii, which motivated Joanne to file to end their marriage in 1970. They reconciled for a short time until Bobby threatened her with a loaded shotgun in 1978. He remarried in 1984, and he also hit his third wife Deborah.[37] Cases like these prompt some people to say, "It is amazing that so few women kill the men who batter them." This is not an odd statement considering the staggering amount of violence against women briefly described earlier in this chapter.

Leaving an abusive man, whoever he is, is never easy, and a woman's decision to get away may be long and complex. The overwhelming majority of battered women *do* leave, but there are many reasons a woman might choose to stay. Some women are simply afraid to leave – often with excellent reason. They have become convinced that they will be beaten if they stay but killed if they try to leave. After living with abusive men for years, they are often much better judges than we of what such men are capable of doing. Other women are afraid of being on their own. This may be an economic issue; they do not believe they can house and feed their children, for example. Or it may be a problem of self-esteem; after years of being belittled, they have come to believe that they are not capable of making decisions for themselves.[38]

Lenore Walker notes that some women tyrannized by their current or former male partners are "pushed to the edge out of fear for their own or their children's lives" and "kill their abusers ... as a last resort."[39] Ms. Melzena Moore is one such woman. Walter DeKeseredy came into Ms. Moore's life in the spring of 2021 when her Laurel County (Kentucky) public defender asked him to serve as an expert witness. She killed her boyfriend Raymond Jackson on Saturday, May 23, 2020, and was charged with first-degree manslaughter.

Why did she kill him? Put simply, she feared for her life. Women like Ms. Moore who kill their current or ex-partners typically do so after years of physical, sexual, and psychological abuse. Ms. Moore was intimately connected to Mr. Jackson for three years and was savagely abused in the last two years of their relationship. Consider that Mr. Jackson had a coffin in a closet in his home and wrote "Zeke [her nickname] Rest Here" on the side of it. He repeatedly threatened to put her in the coffin and nail it shut. This, arguably, is just the "tip of the iceberg," given the other abusive events Ms. Moore revealed to Walter during his Zoom interview with her on April 30, 2021, information her criminal defense lawyers provided him, and Ms. Moore's responses to questions included in the Danger Assessment (DA).

Developed by Dr. Jaqueline Campbell (Johns Hopkins School of Nursing), one of the world's leading experts on *intimate femicide* (killing of a current or former intimate female partner), the DA is a tool to help determine the level of danger that an abused woman has of being murdered by her current or former partner.[40] The version Walter used includes twenty questions, and the scores are classified into four categories that reflect a woman's risk of being murdered: less than 8 = variable danger; 8–13 = increased danger; 14–17 = severe danger; and 18 and over = extreme danger. Ms. Moore's total score was 31. She answered "yes" to seventeen of the twenty questions. What is more, Walter only asked her about abusive events that occurred during the year prior to the shooting. She did, however, tell Walter that she experienced a large amount of abuse during the last two years of her relationship with Mr. Jackson.

The number one risk factor for intimate femicide is a history of male violence against women. Raymond Jackson had such a history. He physically, sexually, and psychologically abused Ms. Moore over a two-year period and beat and raped his previous wife. Another major example of Mr. Jackson's violent past is that he sometimes choked Ms. Moore until she passed out. He would then blindfold her, tie her to a bed, and would let drug dealers rape her in exchange for them giving him drugs. What is more, he threatened to kill her each time she left him on several different occasions. Note that a woman's risk of being killed by an abusive man increases six-fold after she leaves.[41]

Mr. Jackson had these and other characteristics that put him at an elevated risk of killing Ms. Moore (some that were shared by Bobby Hull, who had a well-documented drinking problem[42]):

- possession of weapons (Jackson owned throwing knives),
- stalking behavior,
- jealousy and possessiveness,
- heavy use of alcohol and illegal drugs (e.g., methamphetamine),
- male friends who abused women, and
- unemployed.

Again, women like Ms. Moore kill men in their own homes during periods of great fear, and the evening of the shooting was very fear inducing. She had a reasonable apprehension of death or serious bodily harm. A few hours before Mr. Jackson died, he raped a woman named Brittany in front of Ms. Moore and then asked her to kill Brittany with a knife. When she refused, Mr. Jackson raped her. Mr. Jackson eventually fell asleep and Ms. Moore helped Brittany escape to the hospital. Ms. Moore then returned to Mr. Jackson's house to confront him about what he did to Brittany. He was enraged that she helped Brittany flee his house of horrors and punched her in the face, which knocked her out of the house and onto the front porch. He then reached for a throwing knife and she quickly grabbed her gun out of her backpack that was sitting on the porch to scare him. He grabbed the barrel of the gun and pulled it toward himself. Then she shot him.

Ms. Moore's relationship with Mr. Jackson began in 2017. Over a two-year period (2018–20), Ms. Moore was terrorized to the point of feeling trapped, vulnerable, and worthless. She felt that she was unable to escape the relationship. The shooting was the desperate act of a woman who sincerely believed that she would be killed that night.

Why did she return to Mr. Jackson's house the night of the shooting? Why didn't she just leave? Why did she stay with an abusive man for two years? For reasons presented earlier, these questions should be replaced with "What kept her from leaving?" She didn't want the relationship to end; she wanted the violence to end and thought that pointing a gun at him would influence him to stop hurting her and other women. Furthermore, Ms. Moore told Walter that she had low self-esteem, whereby after two years of being degraded, belittled, beaten, and sexually assaulted, she came to believe that she was not capable of deciding on her own to leave.

With any luck, no woman affiliated with professional hockey will ever go through what Ms. Moore did, although the more than four years of physical and psychological abuse experienced by Hull's second ex-wife Joanne is strikingly similar. What happened to Joanne must never happen again, and chapter 5 provides a roadmap to help us meet this objective.

We hope, too, that we will never hear about another case like the murder of Kelley Clayton in late September 2015. It is exceptionally unusual for a man to kill a woman he wants to leave, yet this is what Thomas Clayton, former player for the semi-pro Elmira Jackals, did to his wife Kelley. More precisely, Tom paid Michael Beard, a former employee at one of his companies, USD$10,000 to kill her, which Beard did by beating her with a fiberglass maul handle. Donald Lewis, an investigator for the Steuben County (New York) Sherriff's Office, told ABC News reporters that this "was an extremely brutal attack, a very gruesome situation … This is probably by far the most interesting and the most complicated case that I have ever been a part of."[43]

Sources say that Kelley Clayton was a beautiful wife and loving mother of two small children, but this meant little, if anything, to Tom. Kelley's sister, Kim Bourgeois, strongly believed that Tom "wanted his freedom." Related to her interpretation of his murder-for-hire, authorities claim that Tom was romantically involved with other women, wanted to end the marriage, and didn't think divorce was an option. Lewis said, "He made comments to some of these women … that if he was to divorce Kelley, 'she would take everything from me.'"[44]

Again, it is atypical for a man to kill an intimate partner whom he wants to leave or has left. On the other hand, numerous men, such as Raymond Jackson, are pathologically determined to prevent their partners from leaving. They use a variety of means to try to "keep them in their place." Sometimes these methods are lethal, and the motivation is mixed with some notion of "if I can't have you, then no one can."

What compels men to murder their estranged wives and/or lovers? Certainly, it is easy to dismiss them as sick or "mentally disturbed." Some male killers have serious mental health problems (just as there are such people in all walks of everyday life), but the truth is that most men who engage in both lethal and nonlethal violence against women are "less pathological than expected."[45] Men with serious mental disorders, in fact, account for only about 10 percent of all incidents of intimate violence.[46]

Much more will be said about why many professional hockey players and other groups of men abuse women in chapters 3 and 4. As a lead up to these chapters, it is first necessary to continue to debunk the myth that men who hit, rape, kill, and hurt women in other violent ways are mentally disturbed. If only a handful of men assaulted and/or killed women, it would be easy to accept non-sociological accounts of their behavior: they must be disturbed individuals. Unfortunately, male-on-female violence in intimate relationships is deeply entrenched in our society (and in many other societies). Given the widespread nature of domestic crimes around the world, how can we maintain that they are committed mainly by pathological individuals? We cannot completely reject individualistic explanations, which do help make sense of criminal acts committed by *some* people. As stated above, there are those whose biological or psychological problems are factors in their decisions to assault women, and some of them have been stopped from committing future crimes through the use of therapy, psychotropic drugs, and other psychologically and biologically informed treatments.[47]

Prior to the late 1970s, social scientific theories of violence against women centered mainly on "wife beating," were grounded in psychology, and focused on the characteristics and behaviors of female survivors instead of male offenders. Psychiatrist J.J. Gayford, for example, claimed that abused women themselves can be seen as deviant or mentally ill and thus bring the violence upon themselves.[48] As well, there were (and still are) psychologists who asserted that many men beat, kill, and sexually assault women because they are mentally ill, suffer from personality disorders, or consume large quantities of alcohol.

Due in large part to the pioneering scientific efforts of feminist sociologists,[49] there was a major shift in the late 1970s from trying to explain, "What is wrong with women who are abused?" and, "What's wrong with men who abuse them?" to, "How do our society's gender norms contribute to high rates of violence against women?" and, "Does the differential power that males and females have in our society contribute to the problem of woman abuse?"[50]

Sociologists with vast experience studying various types of violence against women call for what the late C. Wright Mills referred to as the *sociological imagination*.[51] This perspective seeks an understanding of how *personal troubles* are related to *public issues*. Personal troubles are just what you might think. If you are raped, robbed, beaten, or cheated, you have a problem and you have to deal with it. You may need medical attention, comfort from friends or family, financial help, or some other form of aid. Sometimes, though, many people are suffering individually from the same personal problem at the same time. If a hundred women are raped in one year on a university campus, each one of these women has a personal problem. At the same time, broader structural or cultural forces – such as patriarchy or capitalism, Mills would argue – allow for so many women to be victimized. To look beyond the personal troubles of one or two female students who have been sexually assaulted and see the broader problem of rape on campus and its causes is to possess the sociological imagination. Before having a chance to carefully examine the reasons for his violence, we might assume that a man who sexually assaults someone he knows well or whom he is intimately involved with must be suffering from stress or be mentally ill. That may seem an adequate explanation for the two or three cases that we know personally. Still, when we look at the fact that nearly one out of every four female undergraduates will be sexually assaulted on North American college/university campuses and their immediate surroundings during their academic careers, we have an indication of a structural issue having to do with patriarchal gender relations in institutions of higher learning. A few US studies have uncovered even higher sexual assault figures, some as high as 34 percent.[52]

Though sociological factors best account for the high rates of male-on-female violence committed by hockey players and other groups of men, we would be remiss if we didn't emphasize that if you choose any form of violence and look at international statistics on its key correlates, you will always find a severely unbalanced age ratio. Younger people, especially adolescents and young adults, are disproportionately involved in violent crimes as both perpetrators and victims compared to older people.[53] The online and offline victimization of women is no exception. Young men (especially those eighteen to twenty-nine years old) are much more likely to assault their wives/cohabiting partners, dating partners, "hookups,"[54] and female acquaintances than are older men. Partially explaining this correlation is the fact that younger men have stronger associations with highly influential deviant peers than do their more senior counterparts.[55] This is certainly the case with professional hockey players, and there is a large anthropological cross-cultural data set – the Human Relations Area Files – showing that pro-abuse peer relations often breed in cultures where men band together and sleep in hotels and other residences apart from women.[56] This is what hockey players do when they are on the road. Their wives and girlfriends typically do not travel with them to regular season and playoff games played away from home. The abuse of women, of course, is not the behavior of all, or even most, men. Yet, in her now dated analysis of hockey players' violence against women, Laura Robinson warns us that "it is the behavior of certain men who travel in groups and have a great deal of power."[57]

Related to being at high risk of having young abusive peers is that many professional hockey players marry young, which also increases their likelihood of assaulting women. Noureen DeWulf, actress and wife of former NHL goaltender Ryan Miller, supports what hockey sportswriters like Stu Cowan have known for years:

I was shocked when I came into the hockey world and would see my husband's much younger teammates, at 23, 24, married, and then with two or three children by 26, 27 ... For me, having lived in Los Angeles, where everybody holds out as long as they can to do everything, I was shocked ... I always asked Ryan, "What compels these guys to get married so young?" I really don't have the answer.[58]

In most parts of North America, divorce rates are highest among couples in their twenties,[59] which in part explains why young men are more prone to assault female intimates. Abuse, too, is one of the key reasons women are the ones who most often file for divorce.[60] The precise divorce rate among NHL players is unknown, but NHL Alumni Association executive director Glenn Healy claims, without presenting his data source, that 75 percent end up divorced.[61] According to *Sports Illustrated Vault* reporter Pablo Torre, athletes and their agents frequently claim that the divorce rate ranges from 60 to 80 percent.[62] This is plausible for two reasons: (1) most pro-athletes, including hockey players, are young; and (2) 40 percent of marriages in Canada and between 40 and 50 percent of marriages in the US will eventually end in divorce.[63]

This should not surprise many female readers, but numerous pro-athletes blame their ex-partners for the termination of their marriages and often attribute these women's exits as motivated by financial reasons. Some men contend that their partners left them because their incomes dropped considerably during retirement, which causes radical lifestyle changes and considerable stress. Stu Cowan often hears this statement bitterly uttered in hockey arenas and other contexts where pro hockey players socialize: "First the legs go, then the career goes, and then the wife goes."

Other pro athletes assert that their ex-wives are simply "gold-diggers" who only married them for the purpose of getting a substantial sum of money after a divorce. This claim is regularly buttressed by sportswriters like the ones who made these statements about some NBA stars' wives:

The women are ... constantly tempted since the husband is constantly out and she's left alone with all that money. What's she supposed to do? Knowing what kind of lifestyle they're signing up to, the women may eventually marry the money and not necessarily the basketball player. Since he's nowhere to be found, he might as well be anybody, right? If things go bad, there's always a chance to get some more money during the divorce.[64]

What is hardly ever mentioned by pro-athletes as a prime reason for their wives leaving them is what Jeff Benedict coins as their "brazen adultery and callous disregard for family responsibility."[65] How many hockey players do this and who are they? It is not the purpose of this book to reproduce unsubstantiated rumors, and thus answers to these questions are not provided. Nevertheless, there are numerous substantiated and widely publicized examples of celebrated professional athletes who have had extramarital affairs. An unknown number of them engaged in a myriad of deceitful behaviors like these reported by an ex-girlfriend of a former Montreal Canadiens player:

I always had a hunch, I heard rumours about him cheating, but I chose to believe him. It wasn't until I decided to look through his phone that the truth really came out ... He had stored different girls under his alias male names, after I opened a text message from someone named "Paul" I discovered the man I was in love with was cheating on me every chance he got, it broke me.[66]

There is reason to believe, however, that hockey players are not as prone to cheating as are baseball players, for example, because ice men don't spend much time in each of the cities included in their road trips. Baseball players, on the other hand, spend between three and five days in each city they visit. Stu Cowan frequently heard about certain "boys of summer" having "road girls" whom they flew into visiting cities. These women typically live near the players' residences. Cowan was, for example, privy to stories about married Montreal Expos players meeting women in Montreal and then flying them to Los Angeles or some other city on a road trip so they could spend time together without having to worry about their wives catching them.

Today, the public is indifferent to, or more accepting of, pro athletes' extramarital sexual activities, even if they involve violence. Bear in mind that the late NBA star Kobe Bryant suffered little for his behavior on the night of June 30, 2003, at the Lodge & Spa at Cordillera in Colorado. He was charged with the sexual assault of a nineteen-year-old front-desk employee, but he never went to trial. On September 1, 2004, one week before opening statements were to be made, the case against Bryant was dismissed after the accuser (who was ruthlessly stigmatized by the media and Bryant's defense team for months) told the court she would no longer testify. She filed a separate civil suit against Bryant and agreed to the dismissal of the sexual assault charge if he issued an apology to her that was read in court by Bryant's attorney. The civil suit was settled in March 2005, and the accuser received an undisclosed amount of money. Meanwhile, Bryant continued to flourish as a basketball player and later as a "Hollywood and tech mogul" until he died in late January 2020.[67]

Conversely, infidelity is defined by numerous violence against women scholars, practitioners, and activists as a highly injurious type of psychological abuse. Women harmed by adultery live through serious physical and mental health problems including substance abuse, depression, anxiety, feelings of betrayal, lowered self-esteem, and the feeling that they could not measure up to their partners' lovers.[68] Nonetheless, many promiscuous men vehemently deny that they abused their wives, girlfriends, or cohabiting partners, and they attempt to justify their actions with words like these: "After all, [I] only had an affair (or two) and [didn't] strike her or otherwise lay a hand on her."[69]

When most people think of abuse, they think of physical brutality. They also automatically think of cases of forced sexual penetration. But female targets of any type of male physical violence regularly say it is the psychological, verbal, and spiritual violence that hurts the most and longest. Infidelity, then, should be considered part of any definition of violence against women. Moreover, physical abuse, sexual abuse, psychological abuse, and other types of assault on women are not mutually exclusive. Many abused women, in fact, experience *polyvictimization*, which is multiple victimizations of different kinds.[70] As well, there are plenty of recent examples of how, in the words of Benedict, "an athlete's sexual irresponsibility breeds neglect and violence at home."[71] The case of Kelley Clayton is but one of many that could easily be identified here, but her views on this correlation will never be heard.

Even if female survivors of male abuse live to tell their horrific stories of victimization, no concrete steps to curb the harms done to them and others like them are promptly taken by prominent members of the hockey world, if ever, no matter how far and wide these women's narratives may travel. Consider the response of Sidney Crosby, captain of the Pittsburgh Penguins, to Chinese tennis star Peng Shuai's November 2021 allegations that Zhang Gaoli, a former high-ranking Chinese government official, sexually assaulted her. She wrote a 1,500-character social media post accusing Gaoli of forcing her to have sex despite her repeatedly saying no. Peng's post went viral and her accusations received substantial media coverage around the world.

To be expected because of its long history of censorship and totalitarianism, the Chinese government deleted Peng's post, and searches for her name and the word "tennis" were blocked on the government-operated internet in China. Here is an excerpt of what she posted on Weibo:

> I know that for someone of your eminence, Vice Premier Zhang Gaoli, you've said that you're not afraid. But even if it's just me, like an egg hitting a rock, or a moth to the flame, courting self-destruction, I'll tell the truth about you.[72]

While Peng has not posted on Weibo since the removal of her post on November 2, 2021, and has not been seen in public or answered attempts by the Women's Tennis Association (WTA) to reach her, many influential people did not stand idly by. Peng received public support not only from the WTA, which, as of December 3, 2021, suspended tournaments in China due to concerns about Peng's well-being, but also from tennis champion Serena Williams and the White House. Steve Simon, the chairman and CEO of the WTA, issued this statement a few weeks before the start of the suspension:

Peng Shuai, and all women, deserve to be heard, not cen-
sored. Her accusation about the conduct of a former Chinese
leader involving a sexual assault must be treated with the
utmost seriousness. In all societies, the behavior she alleges
that took place, needs to be investigated, not condoned or
ignored.[73]

Then White House press secretary Jen Psaki said that the
Biden administration was "deeply concerned" about Peng's
health and well-being and called for the Chinese government
to "provide independent and verifiable proof of her whereabouts and that she is safe." Psaki also told reporters:

Any report of sexual assault should be investigated and we
support a woman's ability to speak out and seek accountability,
whether here or around the world. Second, we'll continue to
stand up for the freedom of speech, and we know that the
PRC [People's Republic of China] has zero tolerance for criticism and a record of silencing those that speak out and we
continue to condemn those practices.[74]

As noted, Serena Williams was among a group of world-renowned
athletes, including fellow tennis champion Naomi Osaka, who
publicly expressed their worries about Peng. On November
18, 2021, Williams posted this message on Twitter:

I am devastated and shocked to hear about the news of my
peer, Peng Shuai. I hope she is safe and found as soon as possible. This must be investigated and we must not stay silent.
Sending love to her and her family during this incredibly
difficult time. #whereispengshuai[75]

Even the UN voiced concern about Peng. It called for an investigation into her allegations against Gaoli and asked China for evidence of her whereabouts.[76]

What was the NHL's official response? Radio silence. Based on his investigation into the NHL's reaction to Peng's situation, *Toronto Star* reporter Chris Johnston concluded the following on November 22, 2021:

> There's little evidence yet that it's caused a stir among those most invested in seeing the NHL's commitment to participating [in the Olympics] actually happen. Hockey players tend to be notoriously strong compartmentalizers and appear to be placing their faith in the process.[77]

Sidney Crosby is obviously one such hockey player. He can be considered, because of his stature and stellar performance record, the Serena Williams of professional hockey, a player with the potential to sway many hearts and minds. Unlike Colin Kaepernick and LeBron James, who have no problem taking a stand against social injustices, Crosby took a passive bystander approach to the rapidly growing calls to cancel Canada's participation in the 2022 Olympic Games in Beijing because of China's disturbing response to Peng's allegations and the health risks posed by variants of the COVID-19 virus. More specifically, he said:

> From my experience with this stuff, I try not to follow it too (much) day to day. There's a lot of different storylines and a lot of different things could happen. I think everyone feels pretty strongly they'd like to be there, but I try not to think too far ahead and get too caught up in it.[78]

We are not, by any means, saying or suggesting that Crosby intentionally or directly condones violence against women or supports governments purposely ignoring it. We know nothing about his personal life and his relations with women, but it is fair to assume that, like most men, he is what Tony Porter, CEO of A Call to Men (a nonprofit organization that works to promote healthy, respectful masculinity), refers to as a *well-meaning man*. Such a man is one

> who believes women should be respected. A well-meaning man would not assault a woman. A well-meaning man, on the surface, at least, believes in equality for women. A well-meaning man believes in women's rights. A well-meaning man honors the women in his life. A well-meaning man, for all practical purposes, is a nice guy, a good guy.[79]

Whether or not they are aware of this, well-meaning men also contribute to woman abuse by remaining silent because

- they feel that it's none of their business;
- they don't know what to say;
- they don't want to make things worse; and
- they don't want to "get involved with politics."[80]

Based on his close involvement with Set the Expectation (STE), a US-based nonprofit organization that raises awareness and provides resources to prevent violence against women, Washington Commanders player James Smith-Williams agrees that "good guys" who remain silent are complicit. He says, "being silent on things you know to be wrong is almost as bad as committing the act yourself ... There is much work to be done in every walk of life, but especially our industry, and it isn't just one [man's] responsibility, but all of ours."[81]

What, then, can elite male athletes do? Jeffrey O'Brien, vice president of the Institute for Sport and Social Justice, told the authors of *Game Misconduct* that one way of ending the silence identified here is to teach hockey players how to identify abusive behavior and provide them with the skills to intervene and prevent the harms covered in this book.[82] Alyse Nelson, president and CEO of Vital Voices, likewise contends, "Young men look up to sports icons ... To see that you can be a strong male athlete and icon and you can also care about the rights of women and being a voice of solidarity, I think that's profound."[83] We couldn't agree more, and effective techniques of transforming well-meaning men into responders are featured in chapter 5.

It is also essential to change how women are viewed within hockey's governing structures and to treat them as equals instead of simply as accessories to male executives. Mull over the Montreal Canadiens' male-dominated management team. On November 29, 2021, President and CEO Geoff Molson held a press conference to provide more information about his rationale for firing Marc Bergevin, Trevor Timmins, and Paul Wilson on November 28. He said that one of the top priorities for his new management team would be to add "diversity and support." This is admirable, but at that time, Molson was unable to define exactly what he meant by "diversity," but he made it clear that his new general manager (GM) would have to speak French.[84] This goal was achieved by naming Kent Hughes as the new GM on January 18, 2022.

Women's rights advocates hope Molson's plan does not entail following in the NHL's recent footsteps by featuring Calvin Cordozar Broadus Jr. (aka Snoop Dogg) at major hockey-related events. The American rapper makes regular appearances at annual NHL awards ceremonies and was "treated like royalty" when he attended a December 9, 2021, Los Angeles Kings game. *Montreal Gazette* sportswriter Pat Hickey's concerns about the "NHL's love affair with Snoop Dogg" are well founded:

> I know the NHL is on a diversity kick and it may seem like a good idea to hook up with a popular black entertainer who has sold 13 million albums, but if you're concerned about your image, he's not the guy.
>
> He has been arrested multiple times on weapons and drug charges, he has boasted about how much he enjoyed working as a pimp, he has made a pornographic movie, he has been barred from entering at least two countries and he joins O.J. Simpson on the list of people who have beaten a murder rap with the help of Johnny Cochran.[85]

Molson has made it abundantly clear that he wants French-speaking people, particularly men, to be treated fairly and adequately represented in his organization. Yet, prior to the hiring of Chantal Machabée in early January 2022, it seemed that he was not equally interested in increasing the number of women and people of color in high-profile positions. Things are now somewhat better. There are, for instance, six white men and four white women in the hockey administration department, one of whom is Machabée, who replaces Paul Wilson as vice president of communications. Prior to her appointment, there were seven men and three women. Though this is an obvious progressive sign of change, people of color remain shut out of high-level NHL administrative positions, just as players of color continue to be shut out of playing center in the NHL.[86] Thus, plans to accelerate efforts to improve racial/ethnic diversity in professional hockey need to be shifted into overdrive. Going "beyond traditional thinking when it comes to diversity" should also involve hiring members of the LGBTQ+ community at all levels of the sport.[87]

Here is something else to chew over. On September 15, 2021, in response to intense criticism of the Canadiens selecting Logan Mailloux as a first-round draft pick, the organization launched its Respect and Consent Action Plan. The program is designed to enable the Canadiens organization to "act both internally and externally to raise awareness and educate its employees and the public about respect and consent and the seriousness of sexual cyberviolence."[88] That Geneviève Paquette, the Canadiens vice president of community engagement, was put in charge of this program is a very positive sign of progressive change. However, some commentators, such as *Montreal Gazette* journalist Jack Todd, see her appointment as an example of "yet another woman charged with cleaning up the mess the men have made." During her Zoom press conference to discuss her role in the Canadiens' attempt to rescue "something positive from a near catastrophic draft decision," Paquette said that she was not consulted on the decision to draft Mailloux: "my reaction ... I was surprised."[89]

Will the Respect and Consent Action Plan work? Briefly described in chapter 5, it seems to have had a positive effect on Logan Mailloux as of July 2022. Leading experts on violence against women, in fact, repeatedly find that education and awareness programs, such as videos, workshops, presentations, and classroom discussions, are potentially effective prevention strategies. Collectively, they help provide an atmosphere wherein people show more respect for each other, and they can change attitudes, increase knowledge, and change behavioral intention.

Yet, in an interview with Global News reporters Kalina Laframboise and Dan Spector, Walter DeKeseredy raised some well-founded concerns about the Action Plan that are consistent with those of others with much expertise in sexual assault prevention program evaluation: "Is it a one-shot initiative? … Are they just going to do it at the start of the season and then not do anything else after that?"[90] Part of the problem with programs that have not worked in the past is that they operated on a "haphazard, one-classroom-at-a-time approach."[91] We will not know if history is going to repeat itself here until the Canadiens' Action Plan is up and running.

Jack Todd also has some doubts about the effectiveness of this program. While he makes it clear that he has much respect for Paquette and maintains that "if anyone can turn a disaster into a positive, she can," he also states:

> Given the toxic male response I've received to commentary on the decision to draft Mailloux in the first place, Paquette has a tall task ahead. There has been a whole lot of boo-hooing from the fan base over the poor, misunderstood athlete and the "redemption" to which he is supposedly entitled – and a bare minimum of concern for the young Swedish woman who was the victim of Mailloux's nasty cyber stunt.

Can Paquette make a difference? Will the organization give her the backing that she needs? Will fans and media who have been highly critical of the pick accept both this effort and Mailloux's attempt to rehabilitate himself and his reputation?[92]

Paquette is, as Todd observes, "self-possessed, articulate in both official languages, highly intelligent and possessed of an inherent wisdom about the hockey club and the world in general." Even so, she faces major obstacles, one of which should now be obvious to most readers if it wasn't before: sexism is ubiquitous and "is threaded through hockey."[93] Likewise, despite being highly qualified as trainers, administrators, or other types of professionals involved in hockey, women are often perceived as little more than add-ons to men. Related to this problem is the fact that women like Paquette who want to eliminate the harms caused by people like Mailloux risk being ostracized from the hockey world altogether.[94]

Paquette belongs to a tiny group of female hockey executives who publicly express a desire to change the status quo, something that is met with much resistance by the vast army of men who exonerate sex offenders like Mailloux. As well, profit is one of the most powerful (if not *the* most powerful) determinants of corporate decision-making in professional sports contexts. Therefore, it is far from clear that "replacing some people with penises with others with vaginas" would, at this point in time, do much to push the NHL into confronting rather than ignoring the sexual abuse and sexual harassment of women, as well as other types of male-on-female violence, if the players who engage in such behaviors perform well on ice and stimulate both high ticket sales and broadcast revenues.[95]

The skeptical points made here should by no means be viewed as criticisms of the skills that Paquette and other women in executive positions bring to the hockey table. Yes, they continually face sexism and institutional resistance to change, but they all deserve considerable recognition for their achievements, and there is undisputable evidence that they were hired for reasons other than their employers being primarily concerned about ticking off diversity, equity, and inclusivity checkboxes in the easiest and quickest way possible.

Three examples, besides Paquette, that immediately come to mind, especially because Stu Cowan knows them well in his role as a member of the *Montreal Gazette* sports department, are France Margaret Bélanger, Chantal Machabée, and Marie-Philip Poulin. Geoff Molson named Bélanger president (sports and entertainment) of Groupe CH on August 24, 2021. She first joined the organization in 2013 as senior vice president and chief legal officer after eighteen years at the Stikeman Elliott law firm. In 2014, Bélanger was promoted to executive vice president and chief legal officer. In 2017, Bélanger became executive vice president and chief commercial officer as her scope was expanded to lead the hockey commercial strategy. In 2020, her scope was further broadened to lead the entertainment group, as she continued to oversee legal and public affairs and community relations.

Bélanger is the first woman to serve on the executive committee of the Montreal Canadiens in its 104-year history. She also serves, alongside Molson, as an NHL alternate governor for the Canadiens. In 2020, she was chosen by NHL commissioner Gary Bettman to sit on the NHL's Executive Inclusion Council. "With her mobilizing leadership and expertise, France Margaret will continue building on successful partnerships and leading our one-team approach across the organization," Molson said in a press release.[96]

These are, indeed, impressive credentials. So are Machabée's. As Cowan puts it, the Canadiens "scored big" by hiring her away from RDS, which is a Canadian French language Category A digital cable 24-hour sports channel. After thirty-two years at RDS, Machabée left television and her job covering the Canadiens to work for the team in late 2021. One of her main objectives is to improve the Canadiens' relationship with the media, which was seriously frayed during the last three years of Paul Wilson's tenure as senior vice president in charge of public affairs and communications.

In his January 5, 2022, column, Cowan offered his perspective on her skills, one that is shared by many:

> I can't think of a better person than Machabée for the job. She understands the demands of the media and I believe she is liked and respected by everyone who covers the team since I have never heard anyone say a bad word about her. She is an intelligent, thoughtful woman with great communications skills. The players and the coaches also know her well. I believe she will be honest and fair – and as a member of the media that's all we ask for.[97]

Machabée was first approached about the job on November 30, 2021 – two days after Wilson and Bergevin were fired – by France Margaret Bélanger. It was unexpected, and Machabée wasn't looking to change jobs, expecting to finish her career with RDS. But two more calls convinced Machabée to change paths.

Machabée started her career in hockey as a statistician with the QMJHL's Laval Voisins, and Mario Lemieux kept her busy during the 1983–4 season when he posted 133 goals and 149 assists in 70 games. She was also attending the Promedia TV-Radio School, and one of her teachers was Pierre Houde, a Canadian play-by-play announcer for RDS who had been announcing broadcasts of Canadiens games since 1989. Machabée and Houde were among the first people hired by RDS when it was launched in 1989. Machabée was only twenty-four at the time.

Over the years, Machabée has been both an inspiration and a role model for young women looking to break into the sports media business. She was a pioneer in Quebec in that respect. Jessica Rusnak, a radio sports reporter on CBC's *Daybreak* and regular panelist on the *Montreal Gazette*'s weekly Hockey Inside/Out Show, told Cowan:

> Even though I'm English and she's in the French media, she's someone that everyone in Quebec knows and one of the most trusted reporters when it comes to the Montreal Canadiens and how to handle yourself.
>
> I remember when I first started covering the Canadiens and seeing her there, I was just so in awe of her. I went up and introduced myself to her and she was the nicest person ever. She told me, "If you need anything I'm happy to help you." I think a lot of times there's this misconception that people like to say women don't want to help other women, but that's not the case in real life and Chantal Machabée is

a perfect example of that. She's someone who has helped every single woman who has come into this business. She's always there to listen, to help, and she always spoke about having to put in that extra work.

On June 21, 2022, the rebuilding Canadiens named Marie-Philip Poulin as a player-development consultant. For the next four years, it will be a part-time position for the thirty-one-year-old Beauceville native as she also continues her stellar playing career with a goal of winning a fourth Olympic gold medal at the 2026 games in Italy. Not only has Poulin won three Olympic gold medals, but she has also scored three "golden goals" for Team Canada, earning the nickname "Captain Clutch."

"She's a winner, she knows how to win. Our players are young, and they need to learn that as well," owner/president Geoff Molson said during a June 7, 2022, news conference with Poulin at the Bell Sports Complex in Brossard, Quebec. "I think that's probably the biggest priority. But at the same time, we tick many boxes with Marie-Philip. We not only get somebody who is very competent in hockey development, player development, but who also is passionate about analytics and who is also a woman. Having all three in our organization is a big win for us."[98]

Poulin's other credentials include being captain of the women's hockey team at Boston University, graduating in 2015, and ranking third in the school's history in goals (81) and points (181). She won two Clarkson Cups while playing for the Montreal Stars in the Canadian Women's Hockey League (CWHL) and was named the league's most valuable player three times. She has also won fifteen medals during her international career with Team Canada (five gold, nine silver, and one bronze).

In January 2022, the Canadiens were in the process of recruiting a new general manager to replace Marc Bergevin. While Kent Hughes ultimately got the job, two highly qualified women were seriously considered: Émilie Castonguay and Danièle Sauvageau. Their candidacy reflects the need for more diversity in the Canadiens hockey operations department, which then consisted of ten men and one woman, all of whom are white. Other NHL teams at that time were well ahead of the Canadiens, including the Toronto Maple Leafs, who have Hayley Wickenheiser as their senior director of player development and Danielle Goyette as director of player development. Note, too, that Cammi Granato is a scout for the Seattle Kraken, and Alexandra Mandrycky takes care of advanced statistics for this new franchise.

It is often said, "Better late than never," and in January 2022, there was serious talk on the street about the Canadiens hiring Castonguay as assistant general manager and Sauvageau as a player development coach. Castonguay joined Momentum Hockey in 2014 and, two years later, became the first NHLPA-certified agent in Canada. She has represented a half-dozen NHL players, including Alexis Lafrenière, the number one overall pick by the New York Rangers at the 2020 NHL draft. Castonguay also played four years of NCAA Division I hockey at Niagara University, graduating with a bachelor's degree in finance in 2009 before going on to earn a law degree from Université de Montréal.

The Vancouver Canucks fully recognized Castonguay's outstanding qualities, and on January 24, 2022, she became the team's first female assistant general manager. She is a trailblazer since she is only the second woman to be named an assistant GM in NHL history. Rarely mentioned until this momentous event, however, is the fact Angela Gorgone paved the way for Castonguay by being promoted to assistant GM of the then named Mighty Ducks of Anaheim at the start of the 1996–7 season. She is no longer connected to the NHL, but all thirty-two teams affiliated with it should pay careful attention to what she said in late January 2022 about the role of women in the world of professional hockey:

> From what I heard, [Castonguay] is highly respected and experienced in the world of hockey ... It's not easy to get a similar position in the National League, and especially not for a woman. I congratulate her on this achievement.
>
> I can't speak for Emilie or any of these women, but I don't think it was the goal for any of us to become the first woman to hold any position in the league. As men, we are passionate about this sport. We have the determination to make it our career. Our goal is not to gain recognition as a woman, but to have the chance to prove that we can do the job.[99]

Sauvageau was head coach of the Canadian women's team that won a gold medal at the 2001 International Ice Hockey Federation (IIHF) World Championship and again at the 2002 Olympics in Salt Lake City. She has also been general manager and a coaching advisor with the national women's team, involved in six Olympic Games and several World Championships, and worked as an assistant coach with the QMJHL's Montreal Juniors before cofounding the women's hockey program at the Université de Montréal. Sauvageau also worked twenty-four years as a police officer. We hope that Danièle Sauvageau will be – sooner rather than later – a much-needed member of the Canadiens' organization.

The moral of the story is that hockey can, and will, change, but the transition to a more equitable place for all walks of hockey life can only begin with *effective listening*. This entails high-ranking professional sports officials, athletes, journalists, fans, and others "actively absorbing" the information given to them by those they have historically blocked out and discriminated against.[100] Effective listening and transitioning from a "well-meaning man" to an active bystander go hand in hand. James Smith-Williams exemplifies our line of reasoning. This is what happened to him after hearing sexual assault survivor and STE founder Brenda Tracy speak a few years ago:

The auditorium on the first floor of North Carolina State's James B. Hunt Jr. Library, with its rows of seats that rise to the back wall, can make for an intimidating platform. From that stage one day in April 2019, Brenda Tracy, a 5-foot-10 stranger to most in the room, shared her story with close to 400 of the school's male athletes.

She told them of the night in 1998 when she was 24 and she and a friend attended a party. She told them how she was drugged and gang-raped by four men, two of whom were Oregon State football players …

As she shared her story that day in 2019, Tracy's recollections made a particularly strong impression on one football player seated in the front row.

"I was in shock thinking about everything she said, reflecting on her story and what I could do to make a difference where I am," said James Smith-Williams, then a senior defensive end for N.C. State. "She had a call to action and was like, 'If you're a good man, what are you doing to be a good man?'"

Shortly after learning Tracy's story, Smith-Williams took action. And over the last two years he has become an ambassador – the first and only NFL ambassador – for her organization, Set the Expectation ...

The cause has become a passion project for Smith-Williams, and since leaving Raleigh for the D.C. area after he was drafted by the Washington Football Team in 2020, he has expanded his efforts to help both communities while also trying to initiate a broader change – locally, nationally and within the NFL.[101]

Smith-Williams is one of "a few good men,"[102] and more will be said about men like him and the work they do in chapter 5. He proves that meaningful change occurs when we listen to female survivors of male violence, regardless of whether the men who harmed them are athletes or not. Too many women suffer in silence, and when they do ask for help, rarely are people like Smith-Williams around to respond. As one rural Ohio survivor of separation/divorce sexual assault told Walter DeKeseredy and Martin Schwartz, "People have to be, you know, listen, and um, be sympathetic in relation to what exactly happened." Many other rural Ohio women interviewed in this same study emphasized the importance of listening to survivors' voices and developing sensitivity to women's needs and pain. For example, Jane's advice was direct: people need to listen. "Listen to what they [the women] have to say. Don't jump to conclusions and tell them that they're liars or it will be okay, to get over it."[103]

Possibly, the Pittsburgh Penguins organization will now carefully heed Jane's advice and engage in effective listening the next time a woman reports being assaulted by one of its employees. Ponder this case. In November 2020, former Wilkes-Barre/Scranton Penguins (the American Hockey League affiliate of the Pittsburgh Penguins) assistant coach Jarrod Skalde and his wife Erin filed a lawsuit against the Pittsburgh Penguins, its ownership, and former head coach Clark Donatelli for "negligently retaining a known serial harasser ... as a head coach, allowing him to harass and sexually assault women," and then retaliating against Skalde after he reported Donatelli's November 2018 assault on his wife. The Penguins dismissed Skalde on May 5, 2020, and he contends in the lawsuit that he was let go as retribution for reporting Donatelli, who resigned as head coach on June 28, 2019.[104]

The lawsuit alleges that after a road game in Providence, Rhode Island, when Skalde left to schedule a car ride back to the team's hotel, Donatelli pulled Erin close to him, put his arm around her, and called her "sexy." The lawsuit also alleges that when she pushed him away, he reached under her shirt, grabbed her breasts, and attempted to reach into her pants. Skalde then returned and the three of them got into a car with Donatelli telling Jarrod Skalde to sit in the front seat.

The lawsuit reads, "Still in shock and uncertain what to do in response to her husband's boss sexually assaulting her, Mrs. Skalde fearfully entered the backseat of the car, trying to put as much distance between herself and Mr. Donatelli as she could, to avoid him again sexually touching her." Donatelli, though, again sexually assaulted Erin in the backseat. Also stated in the lawsuit, "Mrs. Skalde was in shock and began to cry ... Only later did Mr. Skalde find out what happened to his wife that night shaking him to the core to learn that he sat unknowingly in the front seat as his boss sexually assaulted his wife."

The lawsuit also alleges that Donatelli was a serial sex offender who had assaulted other women, including the Skaldes's friend who was visiting from out of town. It claims that he tried to pull up her skirt and grope her in a Pennsylvania bar in November 2018. Additionally, the lawsuit declares that the Pittsburgh Penguins' handling of the incident

> included Jarrod being told to keep quiet by the organization management, Erin being called a liar and never being interviewed as part of the team's investigation, along with Jarrod being fired from the organization ... Additionally, the Penguins organization has made public comments that show an utter disregard for the experience of a sexual assault victim and have retraumatized her multiple times.

On November 9, 2021, the Penguins organization announced that it reached an agreement with Skalde and his wife Erin: "Through this resolution, the Penguins hope to bring closure to the Skaldes, provide some measure of peace, and continue to encourage and promote a culture of openness, accountability, and respect at all levels of professional sports."[105] Our cynical response to this press release is, "One can only hope."

We would not have known about the Skaldes's trauma had it not been for a close male friend of Walter DeKeseredy. His wife's brother and Skalde both played for the OHL team the Oshawa Generals, and they continue to stay in touch. This is how the Skaldes's case came to the attention of the wife of DeKeseredy's friend, and we thank them for directing us to public information about it.

Perhaps the Skaldes can derive some small comfort from the fact that on top of having their lawsuit settled, a Rhode Island state-wide jury charged Donatelli with four counts of second-degree sexual assault in connection with his assaults on Erin. The Rhode Island attorney general's office reported that Donatelli was arraigned on November 10, 2021, and the incident that led to the charges "occurred in the city of Providence sometime on November 1, 2018." Donatelli entered a plea of not guilty and was released on USD$10,000 bail prior to a December 15, 2021, pretrial conference in Providence Superior Court.[106] He was cleared of all four counts of second-degree sexual assault on June 21, 2023.

We can't speak for Erin Skalde, but we are sure that she and other women who have had similar horrifying experiences would unequivocally agree with Rita, a rural Ohio woman who shared her violent experiences with Walter DeKeseredy and Martin Schwartz. She said one of the hardest things is simply getting listeners to "believe what it is you're telling them. Sometimes you'll tell somebody what exactly happened, it's like, oh no, it didn't happen that way. But that is the way it happened. Why would you make up something like that? I mean, trying to come up with a story like that, it's not, it wouldn't be easy."

Following an approach taken by sociologist Dr. Ann Goetting, the women's stories briefly described in this chapter are included for the purpose of "breathing life" into the patterns of sexism, violence, and harassment that women involved in professional male sports, especially hockey, routinely experience. In the words of Goetting, "They invite you to slip into the skins of these women and to witness, through their eyes, their tempestuous journeys to hell and back."[107]

As painfully observed by feminist writer, historian, and activist Rebecca Solnit, "The entitlement to be the one who is heard, believed and respected has silenced so many women who may never be heard in so many cases." Now that you have read this chapter and the experiences of the women included in it, keep these words expressed by Solnit in mind: "As these stories come to light, you have to remember how many more never will, in cases where the victims died silent, as they have over generations, or have not yet found an arena in which they dare to come to voice, or have spoken up and only been mocked, shamed, or attacked for doing so."[108] Hence, in the struggle to end the atrocities covered in this book, we should always be mindful of the women who did not, or could not, speak to us and that we are not getting their perspectives and insights.[109]

3

With a Little Help from Their Friends: Male Peer Support and Violence against Women

There is a truly disturbing acceptance of sexual assault by claiming that it is a matter of "boys will be boys" among other inane tautologies.

And while this should certainly enrage women, it also comes across as deeply offensive toward men. This long-perpetuated notion that men are dumb, testosterone-fueled sex hounds is – as a man – profoundly insulting for several important reasons.

First, it implies that men can't control themselves – if we see an opportunity for sex, we will unerringly pursue it, regardless of morality. After all, we can only think of our penises, right? This type of thinking exempts male sex criminals from being held responsible for their misbehavior, treating such acts as merely the result of a natural state ("he couldn't help himself").

And this directly leads into the next implication: Women are solely responsible for not being sexually assaulted or harassed. How many times have we all heard things said about a survivor such as "she shouldn't have drunk so much" or "she shouldn't have been wearing revealing clothes?" These absurd assertions are also outrageous as a man – it necessarily implies a man can't see some skin or an inebriated woman without losing control and harassing or assaulting them.

– Llowell Williams[1]

Why do men engage in violent acts against women similar to those committed by Bobby Hull? In chapter 2 we noted that outside of sociological circles, the most common answer is that they must be "sick" or mentally ill. How could a normal person do what Hull and Thomas Clayton did to their wives? Certainly, the media help to build that myth: violence against female intimates is commonly portrayed in novels, television shows, offline and online news reports, and films as involving a drunken, pathological, sexually deviant, foreign, or criminal assailant.[2]

Even for sociologists like Walter DeKeseredy and Martin Schwartz, it is difficult sometimes to see men who rape or kill women as anything other than sick. Try to grasp what happened to this rural Ohio woman they interviewed in June 2004. She was coerced into having group sex and beaten after going through brutal degrading rituals:

He ended up bringing someone into the relationship, which I didn't want, but he told me that if I didn't do it he would leave me. And I ended up staying with him. He was more into group sex, and uh, trying to be the big man. He wanted sex in a group thing or with his buddies or made me have sex with a friend of his. See one time, he made me have sex with a friend of his for him to watch, and then he got mad and hit me afterwards. I mean he tied me up so I could watch him have sex with a thirteen-year-old girl. And then he ended up going to prison for it. So, I mean it was nasty.[3]

Many agree that this man is not sick, but they offer other flawed explanations for his actions like those included at the beginning of this chapter. One of these faulty, albeit popular, accounts is that man's evolution was violent, which is why there is so much male violence in the world today. Related to this erroneous theory is the still current claim that, in sharp contrast to the "natural" meekness of women, men are "naturally" violent, "with uncontrollable voracious sex drives."[4]

The reality is that male aggression has little to do with biological makeup or factors identified by evolutionary psychologists who maintain that male violence is the result of competition for sexual access to women.[5] Using a wealth of scientific evidence, zoologist Ann Innis Dagg and biologist Lee Harding challenge the evolutionary argument by demonstrating that humans' early ancestors were basically peaceful and that serious human aggression only emerged less than 12,000 years ago.[6]

There are other problems with evolutionary theories of male aggression, including, as stated at the start of this chapter, that it is often used to legitimate men's sexual assaults.[7] A popular notion is that evolution favors strategies that promote the reproduction of the group. However, as one sociological critic puts it, "To murder or assault the person you are trying to inseminate is a particularly unwise reproductive strategy."[8]

As well, while males are biologically similar with the same evolutionary patterns, male violence is not universal, with Nordic societies, for example, having lower rates of violence than those of Columbia, the Russian Federation, and the United States.[9] Definitely, some societies are much more likely to teach violence to men than are others. The lesson here is that, in the words of Dagg and Harding, "faulty reporting and interpretation of biology were the bases of the pervasive notion that humans and many other primates are inherently aggressive; and the cooperative and affiliative behaviors more accurately characterize most primates' daily lives, including humans."[10]

The myth that men who abuse women have biological, testosterone-driven violent tendencies is deeply embedded in mainstream society and is perpetuated and legitimated by people with strong academic credentials. For example, Walter DeKeseredy attended a 2008 World Health Organization conference on injury prevention and safety promotion in Merida, Mexico. At the start of his journey home to Ontario, he met by chance another attendee at the Merida airport. He is a prominent, world-renowned civil engineer and a professor emeritus still affiliated with one of Canada's most prestigious universities, but he knows little, if anything, about the reality of sexual assault. He inquired about Walter's research, and Walter said that he had spent close to twenty-five years studying various types of violence against women in intimate relationships. The engineer then voiced his "theory" of rape, one that is heavily informed by a highly problematic interpretation of evolutionary theory.

He said men rape because they are biologically compelled to "spread their seed." When Walter asked if he was serious, he snapped, "I am, and your research is biased by a feminist perspective." There was no point in continuing the discussion and telling this man that, as Dagg and Harding have conclusively shown, rape among primates is a rarity and is definitely not a male technique of increasing reproductive success. Rape rates differ across societies, and this gendered harm is not a sexual behavior – it is an act of power and control.

Many theories attempt to lay out the factors that best predict acts of male violence against women, including those committed by professional hockey players, but one of the most robust determinants of who beats, rapes, and assaults women in other ways is whether the offender receives male peer support, a problem briefly discussed in chapter 1. This chapter highlights the value of our male peer support (MPS) theory – one of the two most commonly used theories of masculinity and violence against women[11] – in explaining the connection between playing professional hockey, masculinities, and violence against women

Why offer a theory? Aren't we stating the obvious? Yes, "social scientists have known for decades what parents have known for thousands of years – that kids get into more trouble when they are with other kids."[12] So, by advancing a theory, aren't we just eating up space by including "an irrelevant antonym of fact," engaging in "mental gymnastics," and reciting "fanciful ideas that have little to do with what truly motivates real people."[13]

Many, if not most, members of the general public call social scientific theories "bad words." So do numerous other people, including male populist talk show hosts (e.g., the late Rush Limbaugh) who use AM radio airwaves to reach millions of mainly male listeners each week.[14] For instance, in Ottawa, Ontario, in the late 1990s, Walter DeKeseredy was interviewed about women's use of violence in intimate, heterosexual relationships by such a radio personality. DeKeseredy offered what he considered to be a highly intelligible, theoretically informed account for this behavior, but this well-known morning talk show host called his explanation nothing but "psychobabble." Like one of the detectives in the once popular fictional television series *Dragnet* (1951–9, 1967–70), he wanted DeKeseredy to give him "just the facts."

"Facts" or data do not speak for themselves; they must be interpreted. What is more, while we know that there is much truth to the old saying "birds of a feather flock together," most people actually "know very little about exactly what happens in the context of friendship groups that seems to promote bad behavior."[15] MPS theory addresses this knowledge gap and offers a more nuanced account of what social scientists refer to as the *causal mechanisms* that explain the correlation between professional hockey players' peer influence and violence against women.[16]

What makes the crude "birds of a feather" theory flawed is that it, like the *intergenerational transmission* (IT) or *social learning* theory of violence against women, assumes that people are simply "hollow" beings who just do what they are told by significant others (e.g., parents and peers) or emulate whatever they see. Proponents of IT theory maintain that male children are more likely to grow up to assault female intimates if their parents abused them or if they observed their fathers assaulting their spouses. "Craig," a violent husband, provides an example of this learning process:

> I was a product of seeing my mother being beaten up. I also was beaten up, whipped with a belt. I thought once that maybe my mother died to get out of that relationship with my father. I mean, I know she died of cancer ...
>
> That's the ironic part: I remember wanting to dial the police when they were arguing, to protect her, and yet it's funny how I did the same thing as my father.[17]

The IT theory has some empirical support and is widely accepted across the political spectrum. Yet, the family is not entirely responsible for the actions of people like Craig. Many men raised in relatively nonviolent homes abuse their wives and children. And conversely, research consistently shows that the majority of children who have experienced child abuse or have watched their fathers beat their mothers never grow up to abuse their marital/cohabiting partners or children.[18]

While many children's violent fathers may indirectly or directly teach them to abuse their wives, studies consistently find that abused mothers may spend a substantial amount of time and effort teaching their male children that abusing women is wrong and that their future wives/cohabiting partners deserve to be treated much better than them. Lots of children, too, fully recognize that violence against women is a cruel and destructive behavior, and they often do whatever they can to protect their mothers.[19]

This is not to say that the family is not a key "training ground" for violence against women and children;

however, men learn violence and other forms of intimate abuse from external sources such as their male peers. Still, close to four decades of international research done in a variety of social contexts shows that most men, including professional hockey players, are also not merely hollow individuals. They don't naively come into contact with patriarchal, abusive teammates or other types of sexist peers and then go through a "transformation of consciousness," "yield themselves to the group," and "gain a new self."[20] Data presented in chapter 1 strongly indicate that a sizeable portion of violent adult professional hockey players were highly trained as far back as middle school to treat women as sexual objects and to use women as purely things to achieve their own desires: "scoring," or engaging in sexual activity. They do not need further instruction when they arrive in the NHL.

Household childhood socialization, however, is sometimes connected to male peer support for violence against women. In an unknown number of families, Lee Bowker points out, there exists a social psychological process in which males develop *standards of gratification* that promote a belief that they should dominate women and children. These standards are developed through children exposed to their mothers being dominated by their fathers and by boys themselves being dominated in their family of orientation. In other words, they learn that both women and children are subordinate to the man of the family. When these men find that their patterns of domination are threatened, or even get the impression that there is a challenge to such domination, they suffer from psychological stress. They react to this stress with a contrived rage, designed to reestablish domination patterns that meet their standards of gratification. Some MPS theorists argue that standards that lead men to abuse women are fully developed in men who are heavily integrated in male peer groups that continually reinforce standards of gratification through dominance.[21]

John (a pseudonym) embodies Bowker's standards of gratification perspective. He was a star player on a professional hockey team and periodically physically assaulted his girlfriend Marcia (also a pseudonym). When asked about what he perceived to be the cause of his violence, his answer was, "I guess I am just that kind of guy." He recalled seeing his father and older brothers abuse women and he said that "they really deserved it" in a few cases because the women "were too aggressive."

John was socialized to hit women like Marcia if his masculinity was threatened, and his violence was reinforced and encouraged by his teammates who were "cultivators" of his aggression. Based on his case study of John, Columbia University professor Derek H. Suite offers this conclusion that supports Bowker's theory:

> From the case illustration, it is not difficult to see that John's masculine identity was deeply influenced by his upbringing as a traditional male in Western culture, amid all of the social pressures and cultural cues to be identified and perceived as a "man." Indeed, John's training started in childhood, well before he got into sports, as he witnessed displays of masculine aggression modeled within his own family by older males. The underlying notions of power and control, imbibed and imprinted on his subconscious through family experience,

were perhaps amplified in the context of assuming the "alpha male" role on the team – a role that exalts power and control.[22]

There are more than valid scientific reasons for examining the complexities of male peer support and for featuring MPS theory in this book. In the words of Kurt Lewin, the founder of modern social psychology, "there is nothing so practical as good theory."[23] To both prevent and control violence against women in the world of professional hockey and other social contexts, more than accurate data or "facts" is required. We need to explain the problem. We first briefly trace the history of our MPS theory depicted in figure 3.1 because it has roots in the work of the late Michael D. Smith (see chapter 1), one of the world's pioneering experts on violent hockey subcultures.

During the mid-1980s, there was a conspicuous absence of Canadian sociological data on violence against women in dating relationships. Walter DeKeseredy was then a PhD student in York University's Department of Sociology and he wanted to fill this research gap. DeKeseredy initially intended to only collect self-report survey data from potential male undergraduate perpetrators, but his supervisory committee, consisting of Drs. Demond Ellis, Michael (Mike) D. Smith, and Clifford Jansen, said that this was not good enough. They declared (and rightfully so) that an original doctoral dissertation requires a theoretical framework that can be tested. So, from November 1985 to the early part of 1986, DeKeseredy plugged away in York's enormous Scott Library looking for theoretical guidance, and his frustration grew with each passing day.

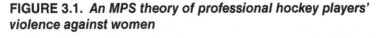

FIGURE 3.1. *An MPS theory of professional hockey players'*
violence against women

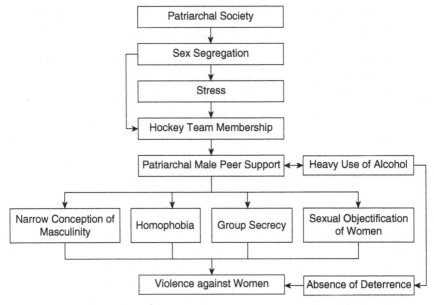

Then, in the fall of 1986, while drinking his morning coffee at York's Cock and Bull Pub and preparing for an undergraduate tutorial that he was about to lead, one of the most important events in his life transpired that would eventually lead him to coauthor this book. At a nearby table sat a group of six undergraduates, and DeKeseredy overheard them trying to solve one group member's dating problems. The advice recipient was very upset because he took a woman out for dinner and she refused to have sex with him at the end of the evening. Some of his peers suggested that he stop seeing her, while others stated that he should have physically forced her to have sex with him.

At that moment, DeKeseredy remembered Eugene J. Kanin's *reference group theory*.[24] Kanin was the first North American sociologist to tackle this important question: How do all-male groups make sexual abuse in courtship legitimate to their members? Furthermore, how do they perpetuate this problem over time? Applied to Logan Mailloux's abusive behavior, for example, Kanin would argue that Mailloux's Swedish teammates constitute a *hypererotic* subculture that generates very high levels of sexual aspiration. This fraternity member's description of life in a New England state university "frat house" provides a vivid example of this socialization process:

> I'll say this, at a fraternity, I'd be a liar if I didn't tell you that just the atmosphere of a fraternity or any group of guys in general is they promote how many girls can you have sex with, how many different girls can you have sex with. I hear it every day. At Friday morning breakfast [fraternities on his campus had big parties Thursday night], guys all have stories.
>
> *Interviewer*: And one common goal is "scoring?"
>
> [*Response*:] Well, yeah, basically. There's individuals for who it's not, but overall, I'd say yeah.[25]

Hypererotic subcultures teach men to see sex as an "achievement of a valued commodity: that is gaining possession of a woman."[26] One of the problems for these men, however, is that the goals they have of extensive sexual conquests are almost impossible to achieve. Some men experience *relative deprivation* or sexual frustration because they fall short of what they see as their peers' high expectations. Put another way, if members of these subcultures feel they are not getting as much sex as their friends say they are getting, they are more prone to engage in behaviors like Mailloux's.

In an interview with Stu Cowan on July 27, 2021, in which he shared his thoughts about the Canadiens drafting Mailloux, Walter DeKeseredy, drawing from Kanin's perspective, argued that Mailloux's non-consensual sharing of the picture of him having sex with a woman who consented to have sex with him was mainly about gaining status among his teammates at the survivor's expense.[27] The same, according to Laura Robinson, can be said about hockey players who commit gang rapes, which are frequently described by them and gang rapists who play other types of male contact sports as "shows," "rodeos," or "pulling train":

> A player who engages in group sex, who long ago shut down the voice inside him that questions if the woman has really consented, does so because he needs to meet his own standards of masculinity and gain the approval of his teammates, who will judge him not as a compassionate human being, but as a hockey player. His actions have nothing to do with providing sexual pleasure and respect for a woman and everything with being seen as a man in his world. He does this because being a "team player" is good for his game, his bank account, and his future worth in hockey.[28]

It becomes more important to be part of the team than it is to do the right thing. This is why, many argue, numerous essentially "good" kids take part in a gang rape or stand by and watch a screaming woman being held down and raped in a basement, or just brush off hearing about such an event the next day without even considering taking any action against it.

One problem with both Kanin's formulation and DeKeseredy's interpretation of the factors that motivated Mailloux to secretly photograph a sexual act and share the picture and his partner's identity with his SK Lejon teammates is that it is impossible to believe that men with high sexual expectations who act like Mailloux did can somehow justify their behavior as legitimate "conquests" when this behavior is (and was in Mailloux's case) officially defined as criminal. For Kanin, this is one more area where male peer support groups provide a service to their members. They supply what sociologists call a *vocabulary of adjustment*. Those men who might feel guilty, conflicted, or stressed learn a language that defines victims as legitimate objects of abuse.

In the world of hockey, offenders and their teammates sometimes label sexual assault survivors as "puck bunnies," a derogatory term implying that they are "inauthentic," not "dedicated in their support of the game" and more interested in having sex with players than in the sport itself.[29] Men who adopt and come to internalize this group-based justification for their abuse of "deviant" females convince themselves that these women deserve to be treated this way. Hence, the players who commit these acts can convince themselves that they are not criminals. They can maintain their image of themselves as normal, respectable, elite athletes, even if they participate in gang rapes.[30]

It is not only teammates who provide perpetrators with a vocabulary of adjustment. Some young players, as reported by Laura Robinson, learn much about the justification of sexual assault and other types of violence against women from their parents. For example, on March 14, 1992, seventeen-year-old Cindy Green attended a party held at the billeting house of a young man who played for the Ontario major junior hockey team the Guelph Storm. She was orally and vaginally penetrated against her will by three players who said that she was a "willing partner." On March 18, she went to the Guelph police, who charged these boys with sexual assault six days later. The case soon went to court, but the charges were dropped on the trial date because the Crown attorney believed he didn't have strong evidence against the defendants. A few minutes after his announcement, a mother of one of the defendants said, "He's not capable of anything so horrendous. Those girls just want to be stars, and they think if they sleep with the boys they will get lots of money when they play in the NHL."[31]

Robinson uncovered that there were other adults connected to the Guelph Storm who supported this woman's framing of the case, including the mother of a player who videotaped part of the party and then later passed out from excessive alcohol consumption. She called Green "a vindictive little slut." She also remarked, "If it was one of my girls, I'd break her neck. But the boys are nice and polite to everybody. They're not going to tell a kid to take a hike. She stayed because she wanted to. She crashed it; she wasn't invited. She just wants to make a quick buck when the boys turn pro."[32] Truth be told, less than 1 percent of youth hockey players end up playing in the NHL.[33]

With Kanin's work in mind and a much-improved outlook on his academic future, DeKeseredy went to his tutorial that

FIGURE 3.2. *Original male peer support model*

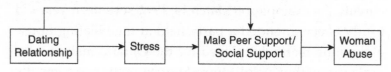

day in 1986 and immediately after told Mike Smith about his pub experience. Mike had a keen interest in the *violent subculture hypothesis* derived from criminologists Marvin E. Wolfgang and Franco Ferracuti's 1967 classic book *The Subculture of Violence*, and he tested it using data provided by 740 amateur hockey players. Mike was also familiar with the sociological literature on what was then referred to as "wife beating," and he asked DeKeseredy to read Lee Bowker's 1983 book *Beating Wife-Beating*, which included the standards of gratification theory. This was one of the best suggestions DeKeseredy ever received, and he and Martin Schwartz have consequently quoted Bowker's book countless times.

DeKeseredy's original theoretical perspective, published in 1988 and cited in chapter 1, was influenced by other scholars and other theoretical perspectives.[34] As pictured in figure 3.2, DeKeseredy argued that insecure young men stressed by dating or hurt by women who have rejected their advances commonly seek the support of male peers. These males might help in a variety of positive ways, but some peer groups instead encourage aggressive responses up to sexual, physical, and psychological assaults against women who pushed back against patriarchal domination.

With Martin Schwartz, whom DeKeseredy first met at the 1987 annual meeting of the American Society of Criminology in Montreal, the theoretical perspective behind DeKeseredy's original work was vastly expanded and enhanced. Shown earlier in this chapter in figure 3.1, our slightly modified version of the original perspective, published in 1993,[35] forms the theoretical backbone of this chapter.

The original DeKeseredy model was empirically supported, but it was based mainly on individual factors that did not recognize that men who abuse women do not operate in a social vacuum. On the other hand, the MPS theory offered here contends that male hockey players, like all men, learn a substantial number of actions, values, and beliefs from growing up in and being part of a larger culture – North American society, in this case. The values and beliefs they express are microsocial expressions of broader social forces, which in North America are too often patriarchal forces.

But what does it mean to say that our society is marked by patriarchal forces? It would be useful if there were a single definition of patriarchy that we could present here. Unfortunately, there is not, as that term is the subject of considerable debate. But if, for convenience, we were to choose a simple definition of patriarchy, it might be good to follow Claire Renzetti's conceptualization: "a gender structure in which men dominate women, and what is considered masculine is more highly valued than what is considered feminine."[36] Patriarchy, as stated in chapter 2, is certainly threaded throughout hockey, whether, as some close followers of the sport observe, it is

through the presence of ice girls or through the comments of the sports broadcasters, like Mike Milbury, who, in the context of the NHL's playoff bubble during COVID-19 in 2020, called women a distraction for hockey players. Women and non-binary people are judged by their clothes, how they speak, what they look like, how they act. Women in hockey are often harassed online in their direct messages and are often the recipients of sexist insults, questions about their hockey knowledge, or inappropriate comments. Those who are not cisgender men do not fit into this community.[37]

We could easily provide many more examples of how women are devalued in hockey and other male-dominated sports. One of the most important points to consider here, however, is that as a patriarchal institution, hockey, like other hypermasculine sports, separates men from women and heterosexual men from gay, bisexual, and other men who have sex with men. One of its most powerful means of doing so is through "its offering of ideal types and behaviors for men,"[38] which starts at an early age.

A central feature of our MPS theory is that adolescent and teenage boys suffer from stress and angst brought on by the pressure of developing interpersonal relationships, particularly with girls, combined with the pressures of puberty-driven body changes. MPS theory suggests that such young men in stress will turn to their male peers for advice, mainly in group settings. What is more, adolescent boys looking to cope with the various pressures involved in interpersonal relationships turn to sports as their main coping mechanism. The coping lesson that they often learn from teachers and peers is that they should develop sports aggression to be successful on the playing fields.[39] MPS theory includes an element suggesting that one central feature of an ideal masculinity is athletic success. The sports aggression fostered by most male youth sports teams is often produced by the promotion of anti-female, homophobic culture. By high school, male athletes may start to recognize the role that sport plays in this generation of hegemonic masculinity, but they still support a specifically anti-female, homophobic culture.[40]

Young hockey players' adoption of a masculinity based on misogyny and homophobia is facilitated by sex segregation. This separation into all-male groups cultivates in male team sports the dominant cultural discourse that promotes sexist, misogynist, and anti-feminine attitudes among these males. Their segregation limits their social contact with females, which makes it easier to adopt an oppositional masculinity that incorporates views supporting violence against women. Interestingly, one study found that these attitudes do not develop or that they disappear when men are involved in sex-integrated sports. This inquiry compared team sports such as cheerleading, track, and golf to physical contact sports like hockey and football.[41]

Sex segregation within the world of hockey, as Laura Robinson discovered, creates team subcultures that, to a large extent, have their own norms and schedules that function independently from the larger culture in which they exist.[42] Drawing upon the work of the late Canadian sociologist Erving Goffman, Robinson defines hockey team subcultures that perpetuate and legitimate sexual assault and other forms of woman abuse as *total institutions*. Goffman explains the concept here:

The central feature of total institutions can be described as a breakdown of the kinds of barriers ordinarily separating these three (where we sleep, where we work, and where we play) spheres of life. First, all aspects of life are conducted in the same place and under the same single authority. Second, each phase of the member's daily activity will be carried out in the immediate company of a large batch of others, all of whom are treated alike and required to do the same thing together. Third, all phases of the day's activities are tightly scheduled, with one activity leading at a prearranged time into the next, the whole circle of activities being imposed from above through a system of explicit formal rulings and a body of officials. Finally, the contents of the various enforced activities are brought together as parts of the single overall rational plan purportedly designed to fulfill the aim of the institution.[43]

Robinson and sports sociologist Steven Ortiz both point out that everything Goffman describes is found in professional male sports teams, which they define as *mobile total institutions*.[44] "What matters most to sports teams is not location, but rather the presence of the coach, a team that obeys the 'rules' and the psychological and physical power the team and coach command over any space they occupy."[45]

Highly competitive hockey teams resemble total institutions, but it would be hard to imagine their continued influence in a sexist, homophobic manner if they were not actively or at least tacitly supported by society at large or powerful elements of it. To again quote Laura Robinson, "It is difficult to write about hockey as a total institution in Canada because there is such a pro-hockey bias in the media and amongst many Canadians."[46] Similarly, Jack Levin and Jim Nolan, two of the world's leading sociological experts on hate and bias crimes, identify a variety of supporters such as hatemongers, dabblers, and sympathizers, and strongly argue that while a small number of people commit these crimes, the enabling support of ordinary and powerful members of mainstream society is essential for such criminal behavior to continue.[47]

Living proof of this are the events that occurred on January 6, 2021, in Washington, DC, as described by criminologist David Kauzlarich:

> A cacophonic spectacle of right-wing groups, Trumpists, hate groups, neo-Nazis, Republicans-proper, extreme conspiracy theorists, and lone wolves gathered to advance delusional rhetoric about the supposed rigging of the [2020] U.S. election in favor of Joseph Biden against Donald Trump. Several hundred of those people, at the suggestion of then-President Trump and his supporters, marched to and then breached the U.S. Capitol building, wandered the hallways, breaking into mostly Democratic political offices, and destroying and stealing state and personal property, only to retreat once more federal agents, police, and military reinforcements arrived.[48]

We wish we could say this was a rare event, but more support for our claim comes from the Unite the Right rally that occurred in Charlottesville, Virginia, August 11–12, 2017. *Washington Post* reporter Joe Helm vividly recounts how this rally of white nationalists and supremacists turned out to be "a horrific 24 hours in this usually quiet college town that would come to be seen by the nation and world as a day of racial rage, hate, violence, and death."[49] On August 12,

heavily armed rally participants were confronted by coun-
terprotesters and a violent brawl erupted. One of the most
horrific moments was when rallygoer James Alex Fields
Jr. intentionally drove his car into a crowd of pedestrians
peacefully protesting the rally. He killed Heather Heyer and
injured dozens of others.

Rather than aggressively condemn the rally, on August
13, 2017, then president Donald Trump enabled alternative
right (alt-right) groups led by people like Richard Bertrand
Spencer[50] by providing this widely televised response to the
violence that erupted in Charlottesville:

> You had some very bad people in that group, but you also
> had people that were very fine people, on both sides. You had
> people in that group ... There were people in that rally – and
> I looked the night before – if you look, there were people pro-
> testing very quietly the taking down of the statue of Robert
> E. Lee. I'm sure in that group there were some bad ones.
> The following day it looked like they had some rough, bad
> people – neo-Nazis, white nationalists, whatever you want
> to call them. But you had a lot of people in that group that
> were there to innocently protest, and very legally protest.[51]

What does this have to do with professional hockey? Our
point is that like racist groups, hockey subcultures that
promote a narrow conception of masculinity, homophobia,
and woman abuse under certain conditions are most widespread and effective when they resonate and coordinate
with a broader discourse found in society at large and across
different institutions like the mainstream media. Remember

that there was much support for the Montreal Canadiens drafting convicted sex offender Logan Mailloux, and Bobby Hull is still generally considered a hockey legend rather than an abusive man.

Included in our MPS theory is the fact that alcohol is a common feature of many young men's social networks, such as US college/university fraternities. It is, as well, often involved in sexual assaults committed by male athletic groups,[52] as proven by the case of the Boston University men's hockey team described in chapter 1. Once labeled by Pierre McGuire, former Ottawa Senators' senior vice president of hockey operations, as hockey's "dirty little secret,"[53] alcohol is also strongly associated with hockey players' physical assaults on women as illuminated by what Bobby Hull did to his second ex-wife. A more recent "eerily familiar story," especially considering what Patrick Roy did to his wife in October 2020 (recall that Roy then played goal for the Colorado Avalanche), is former Avalanche goalie Semyon Varlamov's behavior on October 30, 2013. Under the influence of alcohol, he threw his girlfriend Evgeniya Vavrinyuk into a wall, stomped on her, dragged her around the house, and threatened her. He allegedly told her, "If this were Russia, he would have beat her more."[54] Varlamov had been drinking for more than twelve hours before he beat Evgeniya, and she testified in court that "he was having fun, he was laughing" while he beat her. She added, "He has no concept of when to stop drinking and when he drinks, he turns into an animal."[55]

A year later, former Los Angeles Kings player Slava Voynov, also heavily intoxicated, brutally beat his wife,

Marta Varlamova. *Los Angeles Times* reporter Nathan Fenno describes what happened to her on the night of October 18, 2014:

> Blood seemed to be everywhere when Redondo Beach police officer Gregory Wiist toured the master bedroom of the multimillion-dollar home on Avenue C ...
>
> "My blood, all over bedroom and bathroom," Varlamova, said in a recording. "And it's not first time." ...
>
> While the couple argued during a Halloween party for Kings players, Voynov removed his wife's costume glasses, stomped on them and punched her in the left jaw, the police report said.
>
> The dispute resumed when they returned home. Varlamova told police Voynov choked her with both hands three times ...
>
> Voynov kicked her five to six times on the ground, Varlamova told police, while she screamed for him to stop. When she tried to get up, he pushed her into the corner of a flat-screen television mounted on the wall. That opened a 1.2-inch laceration above Varlamova's left eye that required eight stiches to close.[56]

Though many people see a direct relationship between alcohol and violent acts committed by men like Voynov and those who sexually assault women, leading experts in the field argue that the link is not real but more of an illusion. Men have a strong expectation of alcohol's effects, which fuels their misperceptions of women's sexual intentions and may serve as a justification for men's sexual violence. The real physiological effect may not be very important.[57]

The relationship may not be causal, but alcohol abuse is definitely strongly related to assaults on women. Sociological criminologists who specialize in MPS,[58] for instance, find that alcohol abuse plays a major role in peer group processes related to violence against women. Alcohol, in fact, is often used in all-male social contexts that support patriarchal conversations about women's sexuality and how to control it. Some men, including those who are professional hockey players, gather at bars or pubs to drink, have fun, and to avoid women. Women are not allowed to join them because female exclusion serves to validate and sustain masculine superiority, solidarity, and dominance.

Men often use bar events, especially "nights out with the boys," to prove to each other that they are not "under the thumbs" of their wives or girlfriends. Nevertheless, women remain a focal point of conversation. What's more, drinking with male peers helps some men explain away, rationalize, and excuse embarrassing, unsightly, and even violent behavior,[59] such as aggressive and violent behavior toward women. Group discussions in bars, too, often emphasize violence as a means of maintaining control and may even encourage some men to become sexually aggressive toward specific women.

Some sports bars are "safe havens" off the ice in numerous communities where hockey players are treated like gods. They are privileged, allowed to drink "on the house," and given permission to abuse women and engage in conversations that objectify them in these places. For example, one of the five former college/professional hockey players interviewed by Nick Pappas and his colleagues said the following:

I think that date rape is prevalent among the jock culture. There are things that are not violent but they just seem kind of wrong

that guys do in terms of how they relate to women – off the
ice. They treat women like objects – sexual objects. They talk
about them as if they aren't there, as if [the athletes] were in
the locker room talking ... and don't care what they say at all
because they think they're still going to have sex or whatever.
Things like that machismo group mentality, that locker room
mentality, comes out in off-ice behavior ... treating women really
bad ... like one-nighters or short-term girlfriends or someone
they didn't care very much, just as objects or sex partners.[60]

In sum, one cannot understand hockey players' violence
against women without factoring in the role of alcohol. Its
use and abuse among these athletes is "nearly universal,"
and hockey is a "culture that is defined, in part, by the use of
alcohol in leisure."[61] Perhaps this is best described by *Yahoo!
Sports* reporter Justin Bourne:

The culture of the game carries with it a few things that aren't
a ton of fun to talk about (you know, rampant homophobia,
casual misogyny, etc.), but it also proudly unites those who
like to have a good time, a pursuit in which The Sauce plays a
fairly significant role. From rec leaguers to the show, drinking
is just part of the lifestyle ...

It's simply woven into the fabric of our game – hell, the
NHL is sponsored by Molson. We're in this together, beer ...

I'm just explaining – it's part of our game at every level,
including junior.[62]

It is vital to examine how alcohol contributes to hockey players' abuse of women, but a richer understanding is obtained

by examining the off-ice all-male group contexts in which hockey players consume it. Throughout many years of study, Walter DeKeseredy and Martin Schwartz have discovered over and over again that men who admit to physically and sexually assaulting women are among the heaviest drinkers in their studies and they have heavy drinking buddies who perpetuate and legitimate their misogynistic behaviors.

On top of learning to sexually objectify women and adopting a heavy drinking lifestyle, a narrow type of masculinity, and homophobic attitudes and beliefs, men are taught other negative things in sexually segregated mobile total institutions such as professional hockey teams, but one of the most notable, according to MPS theory and the data that support it, is *group secrecy*. Group secrecy keeps men from revealing the deviant behavior of their teammates to "outsiders." It also tells violent men that their actions are not wrong. Still, the connection between male athletes' abuse of women and group secrecy is seldom, if ever, effectively addressed by sports journalists.[63]

On the other hand, criminal subcultures' concealment of their hidden transgressions and protection of their members continue to be "hot topics" in fictional and nonfictional media portrayals of crime. Consider the recent popularity of *Law & Order: Organized Crime*, an NBC crime-drama series that premiered on April 1, 2021. Frequent consumption of prime-time crime TV shows like this one explains, to a large degree, why the public views the relationship between group secrecy and crime as existing mainly in organized crime groups, such as drug cartels. The mass media have a major influence on this viewpoint. In fact, for many, if not most, people, the mass media are their major source of information on crime and its control.

According to the US Bureau of Labor Statistics' 2020 American Time Use Survey, outside of sleeping, US residents spent the bulk of their time watching TV, averaging about 3.1 hours per day, which is just slightly more time than they spent working for wages.[64] Furthermore, data presented in the *Hollywood Reporter* reveal that shows about law-enforcement officials (e.g., police officers and detectives) made up nearly one-fifth of the scripted shows broadcasted by television networks in the 2019–20 season. In fact, crime shows greatly outnumber (and have for a very long time) every other drama subgenre, and they are among the most-viewed TV series.[65] Perhaps, then, the words of British criminologist Eamonn Carrabine are most fitting here: "If, as is often said, we currently live in the golden age of television, then it is the crime drama that lies at the heart of this cultural renaissance."[66]

Regardless of the nature of the current state of popular knowledge about criminal group secrecy, it should not only be included in our MPS theory but must also be reckoned with in attempts to curb athletes' violence against women. Group secrecy is an integral part of patriarchal male athletes' *culture of protection*,[67] and it operates in ways described below.

Before presenting some real-life examples, it must be stressed that although it happens often enough, the usual case of group secrecy is not a conspiratorial plot. Senior team executives and male athletes who work for them usually do not sit around tables, like some terrible made-for-TV movie about the Mafia, discussing group secrecy and the penalties for those who violate "the code," but there is some evidence that this happens. Consider the reports, described in chapter 2, on how the Pittsburgh Penguins organization handled the allegations of sexual assault levied against former Wilkes-Barre/Scranton head coach Clark Donatelli. Penguins assistant general manager Bill Guerin, whose job involved overseeing this NHL team's farm club, told Jarrod Skalde to "keep quiet" about this traumatic incident. Skalde, also noted in chapter 2, alleged that the Penguins violated Pennsylvania's whistleblower laws and dismissed him on May 5, 2020, because he reported Donatelli's abuse of his wife Erin to the team.[68]

Codes of silence and the demand for team loyalty mean that few crimes committed by popular male athletes are punished. Even if perpetrators of sexual assault and other crimes against women do end up in conflict with the law, it is rarely because of investigations initiated by team owners or high-ranking executives. Group secrecy, *institutional betrayal*,[69] and bureaucratic indifference usually stand in the way of "doing the right thing."

While not an example derived from professional hockey, Baylor University's response to sexual assault claims against football players between 2010 and 2015 is another recent disturbing case in point. On August 11, 2021, the NCAA Division I Committee on Infractions (COI) publicly released a Public Infractions Decision that includes this condemnatory statement:

Make no mistake, the conduct that occurred on Baylor's campus between 2010 and 2015 was unacceptable. Young people were hurt. They were hurt because the campus leaders they trusted to provide a safe campus community failed. At times, these failures heavily intersected with Baylor's football program and Baylor football student-athletes. At other times, they did not. And that is perhaps the most disturbing aspect of this case – that a campus-wide culture of sexual violence went unaddressed due to ignorance and leadership failings across campus. Baylor itself acknowledged moral and ethical failings. Even Baylor's former president described the institution's handling of campus sexual violence during this time as a "colossal operational failure."[70]

ESPN investigative reporters Paula Lavigne and Mark Schlabach found that "many things stood in the way" of the women who reported their experiences to trusted Baylor officials, some of which are key indicators of group secrecy:

> They encountered a city police department that was inconsistent in its investigations and withheld police reports involving students and student-athletes. A campus police department operating in a veil of secrecy that was more interested in issuing parking tickets and liquor violations than in helping women who came to them for help after an assault. An honor code that made women afraid to report being raped lest they get in trouble with the university for being at a party and drinking. And administrators, employees, and coaches who received reports of domestic violence or sexual assault and never shared the information, keeping secret the heightened and growing risk to women as they stepped foot on the Waco campus.[71]

Corroborative evidence is provided by the results of an investigation conducted by the Philadelphia law firm Troutman

Pepper Hamilton. In May 2016, Baylor's Board of Regents released Troutman Pepper Hamilton's report. As Lavigne and Schlabach note:

> The findings were damning and worse than they could have imagined. They found not just ignorance, but willful intent in trying to silence women who reported being sexually assaulted by some Baylor football players. They found university officials retaliated against victims and ignored survivors' needs for counseling, academic support, and, most of all, justice. And they found a problem that went far beyond their beloved football program.[72]

Despite Baylor's insensitivity to survivors' trauma, the criminal justice system "stepped up to the plate." Multiple football players were ultimately convicted of sexual assault. Tevin Elliott, for example, was convicted and sentenced to the maximum of twenty years in prison and a USD$10,000 fine in January 2014. In August 2015, former defensive end Sam Ukwuachu was convicted of sexually assaulting a female Baylor soccer player and was sentenced to 180 days in jail, ten years' felony probation, and 400 hours of community service. In December 2018, a student who was not on the football team, former fraternity president Jacob Walter Anderson, pleaded guilty to unlawful restraint and received three years of deferred probation and a USD$400 fine.[73]

The NCAA, on the other hand, gave Baylor what many people would consider "a slap on the wrist." It cited the world's largest Baptist university for several violations of collegiate athletic rules and levied a highly questionable punishment that entailed four years of probation and a USD$5,000 fine. What was the COI's rationale for such a weak sanction? NCAA president Mark Emmert's answer was as follows:

> Schools have taken many steps to address sexual violence on campus, but as the COI points out, the authority of the NCAA in this area is very limited today ... This is a clear demonstration of why the Association needs transformational change to create alignment between authority and responsibility to address the most critical issues in college sports.[74]

The NHL, too, requires a transformational change. It currently does not have any policies on sexual assault and domestic violence. What it does have is this clause (Section 18-A.5) in its collective bargaining agreement related to criminal investigations in general:

> The League may suspend the Player pending the League's formal review and disposition of the matter where the failure to suspend the Player during this period would create a substantial risk of material harm to the legitimate interests and/or reputation of the League.[75]

But what about the legitimate interests, health, and well-being of female survivors' of players' violence? Several NHL players (e.g., Patrick Roy) have been publicly identified as being involved in alleged domestic violence and sexual assault events, but in almost all of these cases, the NHL leadership took "a wait-and-see approach, opting in most cases not to suspend or terminate players."[76]

Many times, the culture of protection, which as noted above prioritizes group secrecy, also enables some perpetrators to "bounce back without serious ramification" shortly after they are convicted of some type of assault or sexual harassment.[77] Slava Voynov exemplifies such a life course trajectory. After he was arrested for domestic violence in 2014, the NHL, citing Section 18-A.5, suspended him indefinitely, and the Los Angeles Kings terminated his six-year, USD$25-million contract shortly after that. He also spent two months in jail and decided to return to Russia instead of facing deportation proceedings. He eventually "landed on his feet" and currently plays for the Kontinental Hockey League (KHL) team Ak Bars Kazan, and he played for the 2018 Russian Olympic hockey team.

Bouncing back or "moving on" in ways similar to those experienced by hockey players Patrick Kane, Auston Matthews, and Slava Voynov is what investigative journalist Jessica Luther refers to as one of the most common "go-to plays" in the media's section of the male combative sports' sexual and domestic violence playbook. Luther's extensive work on sport and patriarchal culture sensitizes us to the fact that

> there is nothing sports media love more than when a high-profile case about off-field violence seemingly comes to an end and we can all just move on. They practically beg us all to get back to the truly important stuff: talking about the minutiae of the sport that happens on the field.[78]

Recall from chapter 1 that Jim Hughson drew from the "moving on" playbook when he simultaneously minimized Matthews's transgression and praised Patrick Kane for getting into "a little trouble." Even so, all the blame for the use of this type of playbook cannot be placed entirely on sports journalists like Hughson. Many of them, under pressure from their superiors (e.g., newspaper editors and owners), are responding to a large readership that calls for this approach. Below, as an example posted by the *Montreal Gazette* on September 19, 2021, is one person's angry response to some *Gazette* reporters' critical perspectives on the Montreal Canadiens drafting Logan Mailloux (LM):

> This article ... [is] about EGO. Writers who continue to try and convince the posters and readers that as the voice of social reform these writers know best. The overwhelming comments by readers are in direct opposition to their continuing batters against LM (check the archives and add it up). Okay writers you prove your point ... GET BACK TO HOCKEY ... Let social reform and issues be handled by in the area they are destined to be in the paper. 3 articles in the last 10 days headlining LM in this the sports section by different writers proves this is an organized campaign of social reform not hockey by people who shouldn't point fingers.[79]

Protecting their livelihoods and the financial interests of the teams they work for are obviously two of the most important motives for the contributions to group secrecy made by hockey players and other male athletes. Yet, there are other reasons for remaining silent. Why would a player or other employee of an NHL team cover up for another player, coach, trainer, or higher-ranking team employee, who might not even be a friend, when to do so might mean engaging in serious criminal behavior? It cannot only be because members are afraid of reprisal. The source of the problem goes deeper than that. In the case of the players themselves, one reason is the development of a new self after joining an elite junior or college/university hockey team prior to entering the NHL or another professional hockey league (e.g., the KHL). "Bonds of brotherhood," created through hazing and other social interactions, encourage players to protect their teammates from public stigmatization and punishment, even if they must lie to investigators to achieve this end. Hazing in athletics, especially at US colleges, is hardly "good clean fun" and is shrouded in group secrecy. Perhaps it is best explained in this statement by the United States College Hockey Organization (USCHO):

Hazing in athletics happens mostly as a form of initiation or a rite of passage onto a team. Student athletes frequently give in to hazing because they are willing "to do anything" to gain acceptance. Hazing is believed to act as a bonding or unifying experience for athletes, particularly when it is practiced as a form of initiation to welcome, for example, new freshman to the team. But research shows that it can have the opposite effect. It can be more destructive to human relationships than constructive when it relies on substance abuse and/or the performance of acts that are self-destructive, isolating, socially offensive, hurtful, aggressive, uncooperative, or disruptive. The hazing comes at the expense of integrity, respect, civility, and responsibility within the team itself.[80]

Supporting USCHO's statement about the destructive nature of hazing is information included in chapter 1 about the London

School of Economics rugby club and the lawsuit filed in late
June 2020 against the CHL, the WHL, the OHL, and the QMJHL.
Furthermore, in the wake of the revelations of the 2003 and 2018
gang rape cases also discussed in chapter 1, a Toronto family
spoke out in early August 2022 about a physically and sexually
abusive "initiation" incident involving a twelve-year-old boy
that took place several years ago while he attended a week-long
overnight hockey summer camp. The then twelve-year-old boy
went into a cabin and was grabbed, thrown to the ground, and
held there against his will while four boys attempted to shove
a broomstick up his anus through his clothing, according to a
statement of claim filed in the Ontario Supreme Court in 2021.
The victim's family launched a CAD$1.45-million lawsuit
against the camp's owner and management for "intentional
and/or negligent conduct," and the family is suing the four
former campers for alleged physical and sexual assault. Three
of them were eleven years old at the time and one was twelve.
The camp is located in Sundridge, Ontario, north of Toronto.
On its website, the camp declares that it offers "the ultimate
summer hockey experience."[81]

Now mull over what happened to D'Arcy McKeown, son
of investigative TV journalist Bob McKeown. On August 27,
2005, as an eighteen-year-old freshman on McGill University's
football team, he was sexually assaulted with a broom handle
in a terrifying hazing ritual organized by a group of veteran
teammates. He shared his horrific experiences in a September
2013 interview with the QMI News Agency:

> They made us strip down to our shorts, hold hands, and walk
> double-file down to the athletics area of campus – calling us
> names along the way.

They stuck us in the squash courts and told us to kneel, each of us holding a penny to the wall with our nose. And they said for every time it slips, that's an extra inch from Dr. Broom.

Lights went off. Then veterans led the frosh, one by one, to a second squash court. The rest of the team watched from the stands, above.

Only the captains were down in the squash court, and they told you to strip down naked ... I refused to get naked.

I was actually forced down on all fours, had a dog's chew-toy shoved in my mouth ... [Then he was sexually assaulted with the broom handle.]

I got so angry that I stormed out. I threw the chew-toy up at the guys in the stands, just pissed off. A couple of players tried to prevent me from leaving, told me to just calm down ...

I got a very insincere phone call from one of the captains asking me to come back, to let's put this all behind us ... Basically the coach said he would figure it out, and never did ...

My thought was that this hazing has got to stop. This can't happen to anyone ever again, at least here. I can make some sort of impact.[82]

McKeown's revelations were corroborated by McGill's official investigation. McGill also passed a campus-wide ban on hazing and Canadian Interuniversity Sport (CIS), the national governing body of Canadian university sports (rebranded as U Sports in 2018), strengthened its anti-hazing policy and has since handed out severe punishments for offenders. As for McKeown, he had a successful four-year playing career with the University of Toronto from 2006–9 and is now a senior manager with the Toronto International Film Festival.[83] Unfortunately, many other targets of hazing continue to suffer long after their victimization.

One such case is Akim Aliu, who experienced what some label "the most famous hockey hazing incident of the past few decades." In 2005, Aliu was a sixth overall pick in the OHL draft, and during his first years with the Windsor Spitfires, a group of older players forced four rookies to strip naked and locked them inside a cramped bathroom at the back of the team bus on the drive home from a preseason road trip. Aliu refused to keep quiet and suffered from considerable fallout. Three weeks after the hazing incident, a video appeared on the local news in Windsor, then nationally, and a bit later on YouTube, showing Aliu fighting teammate Steve Downie, a first-round draft pick of the Philadelphia Flyers. Shortly after, Aliu revealed most of the hazing incident to the media. It is beyond the scope of this chapter to report all the negative things that subsequently happened to Aliu, but he paid dearly for, in his words, "standing up for what is right" and for not keeping "the worst aspect of hockey culture a secret."[84] Though he eventually played professional hockey, he did not get the permanent NHL job he wished for and concluded his precarious career playing overseas with HC Litvinov in the Czech Extraliga (ELH). Recall, too, from chapter 1, that former Calgary Flames coach Bill Peters directed racist slurs at him. In a recent interview with *Sportsnet* journalist Gare Joyce, Aliu revealed:

After the incident in Windsor, the people in the game looked at me differently. My reputation took a significant hit and for no good reason. I've always been in great shape, never a drinker or smoker. I've always tried to be a good teammate and to work with coaches. I continue to work on my game and stay dedicated. I still believe that my best hockey is ahead of me. I strongly believe the publicity around the hazing incident in Windsor turned my career sideways and to this day I've never been able to reclaim my reputation. I was humiliated as a target of hazing and then physically assaulted and yet somehow people looked at me as a villain and troublemaker.[85]

Many more examples of hazing in male athletics are readily available. The most important point to think about here is that the group solidarity that it and other initiation rituals promote makes men remain publicly silent about their peers' transgressions. Likewise, players know that their teammates will always "have their backs" and not cooperate with investigations into their own deviant behavior that may be conducted by the police and senior NHL officials like commissioner Gary Bettman. What is also so important in all this discussion is that group secrecy tells all violent men that their actions are not wrong. It is a lesson that many have learned very well and have subsequently put into action.

Many of the arguments in this book have so far centered on the presence of one or more factors that make it more likely that elite hockey players will abuse women. We argue that in a culture marked by male dominance, and in a group that provides male peer support for violence, ice men are more likely to assault women. Still, there are other things we should examine. One is deterrence. Are there factors that, if present, would tend to stop the behaviors in question? For example, in a town where jaywalking is a serious problem, will placing a couple of police officers handing out tickets for jaywalking put a dent in the number of people who violate that law? That is at least a research question.

The question asks about the presence of deterrence. One can also look at the absence of deterrence, which is the last factor in our MPS theory. It is not only connections and interactions with teammates that encourage and justify the criminal actions of athletes like Logan Mailloux. It is not a surprise that broader organizational forces, such as the NHL's insatiable hunger for profits, grants players permission to abuse women because they help achieve corporate goals on the ice.[86] The lack of meaningful punishments or negative sanctions are powerful institutional mechanisms that facilitate the harms covered in this book.

Criminologists generally make a distinction between two types of deterrence: *specific* and *general*. Specific deterrence refers to the effects of punishments on people to whom they are applied. If you are, like Logan Mailloux, suspended from playing hockey for the London Knights for the first half of the 2021–2 season, the assumption is that the pains of this punishment will be sufficiently high to make you want to avoid ever being suspended again; you will stop engaging in image-based sexual abuse.

General deterrence refers to the effects of the punishment of specific individuals on a wider audience. In this example, if hockey players hear about Mailloux's punishment, general deterrence predicts that they will be unlikely to commit similar crimes for fear of being suspended themselves. In Canada, driving under the influence of alcohol (DUI) laws are seen by the population at large as paragons of general deterrence. A DUI is a federal offense in Canada and results in a criminal record. The consequences of being convicted may include:

- a fine of CAD$1,000 or more for a first-time offense;
- two distinct driver's license suspensions: a criminal one imposed by the federal government and an administrative one imposed by the government of the province in which the driver resides;
- a thirty-day jail term for a second offense within a ten-year period; and
- a criminal record.

DUI penalties depend on several factors including the driver's status as a novice driver, commercial driver, or fully licensed driver; the driver's home province; and whether an injury or death occurred because of the driver's behavior. Most Canadians loudly proclaim their agreement with DUI penalties, but the reality is that they do little, if anything, to deter thousands of people from drinking and driving. In Canada, every hour, an average of ten federal criminal charges and provincial short-term license suspensions are handed out for DUI or drug-impaired driving.[87] Possibly more alarming is that Canada has the highest rate of drunk-driving deaths in the advanced industrial world, with an estimated 1,500 fatalities each year. In fact, driving under the influence is Canada's leading cause of criminal death, markedly higher than the 600 to 700 Canadians who annually die from homicide.[88]

What accounts for these disturbing statistics? The most common answer is: "The system is not tough enough." At first glance, there is merit to this claim. Reflect on what happened to this DUI offender in early February 2021:

> The Parole Board of Canada granted full parole to Marco Muzzo, a Toronto man responsible for one of the country's most horrific drunk driving crashes. A member of one of Canada's wealthiest families, Muzzo had just arrived on a private jet from a Miami bachelor party when, despite being so drunk he had peed himself, he decided to drive home from the airport in his Jeep Cherokee. Within minutes, after blowing through a stop-sign and striking a minivan, he had killed three young children and their grandfather.
>
> Although given a 10-year prison sentence in 2016, he's been on day parole since April 2020. And, in another eight years, Muzzo will be able to drive again.[89]

After reading or hearing about cases like this, how could anyone disagree with the assertion that the system is not harsh enough? Truth be told, increasing the costs of crimes committed by drunk drivers and others who cause much harm by breaking the law does not work very well. Generally, although many criminologists believe that some punishments are effective, the bulk of the most sophisticated research in the field done over a long period of time shows that punishment does not tend to stop, deter, or control crime. It may exact retribution or get people off the streets, which are different issues, but it does not particularly stop, deter, or control crime.

Even the death penalty is an ineffective means of deterring people from murdering others in the United States. Homicide remains the leading cause of death for young Black males, and some cities like Chicago, Baltimore, and St. Louis rank among the most violent urban areas in the world. And, in October 2021, the Centers for Disease Control and Prevention's National Center for Health Statistics reported that the US recorded its highest homicide increase in modern history. It rose 30 percent between 2019 and 2020.[90] All the same, these data should not be an excuse for the trauma caused by Muzzo and other drunk drivers.

What does seem to have some effect are informal sanctions. When people you really care about are very unhappy or even angry with you, you are more likely to reassess your behavior. Furthermore, when you have something serious to lose, such as an excellent job or a good set of human relationships, your chances of being deterred are much stronger than with formal punishments. Thus, what we learn from criminological research is that the best way to stop hockey players' assaults on women would be to develop a workplace culture where such behavior is not tolerated, where the men involved would be ashamed of themselves, and where they would stand to be shunned by people who were their teammates and friends.

This does not have to be a situation where such men are automatically banished, to become bitter and angry and even more abusive to other potential victims. There are mechanisms that can shame men into stopping their violence against women but at the same time provide an avenue for them to be accepted back into the community if they do so. The problem is that it is simply not true in the world of elite hockey that men who abuse women will be given the message that this behavior is not tolerated. Quite the opposite, in fact.

For example, in 2018, Nashville Predators player Austin Watson was arrested and charged with domestic assault and was supposed to be suspended for twenty-seven games after a league investigation. NHL commissioner Gary Bettman announced, "Today's ruling, while tailored to the specific facts of this case and the individuals involved, is necessary and consistent with the NHL's strongly held view that it cannot and will not tolerate this and similar types of conduct."[91] The league may claim that it has a "strongly held policy," but as documented earlier in this chapter, it doesn't. Rather, it reviews violence against women incidents on a case-by-case basis. This allows the league to hand out punishments that can easily be struck down by an arbitrator who disputes the decision. Note that the NHLPA appealed Watson's suspension and an arbitrator reduced it to eighteen games.[92]

There is evidence that formal sanctions can have *some* effect on behavior. The problem is that the NHL's approach is toothless. What is also problematic is the consistent pattern of players punished by the criminal justice system for their assaults on women being warmly welcomed back on the ice. Logan Mailloux is a recent good example, but there are other cases that occurred well before his. The decision to sign or draft someone like Mailloux is often publicly announced as one that "was not taken lightly," and the players in question are frequently depicted by the teams that exonerate them as being on "the road to recovery."

At the risk of belaboring the Mailloux image-based sexual abuse case, the Canadiens' narrative about drafting him as well as the narratives offered by other teams that give players well-known for assaulting women a "second chance" always center on "the alleged perpetrators and their redemption while giving little or no consideration to the survivors ... It sends a very clear message that two things – on-ice performance and the player's redemption – are more important than anyone harmed by off-ice conduct."[93]

The Edmonton Oilers is another team to use the second chance narrative. On January 13, 2022, in grave danger of not making the playoffs and desperate to avoid this costly fate, the Oilers spoke to Evander Kane about the possibility of him joining their team, which he did at the end of January. He was available because the San Jose Sharks put him on waivers at the end of November 2021 and demoted him to the American Hockey League (AHL) when he went unclaimed. Kane was placed on unconditional waivers on January 8, 2022, which then enabled the Sharks to terminate his lucrative contract, making him a free agent. To put it bluntly, the Sharks were fed up with Kane. He not only faced allegations of abusing his wife but also of gambling on hockey and purposely losing games he bet on. Additionally, on October 18, 2021, the NHL suspended Kane for twenty-one games for submitting a fake COVID-19 vaccination card. When the suspension was lifted in late November 2021, Kane's tenure with the Sharks essentially expired.

Oilers general manager Ken Holland's public rationale for talking with Kane was as follows:

I believe in second chances ... It's hard to be perfect ... we're all people. We all make mistakes. Some make big mistakes, some make little mistakes, but it's hard to be perfect ...

If somebody makes a decision or does something in their
life, and they make a mistake, I think they have to try to
learn from it and try to change ... And then they should be
entitled to a second opportunity once they do some of those
things.[94]

Sound familiar? Holland's words and actions are old. We
have heard them for decades.[95] This is, as *Yahoo! Sports* reporter Justin Cuthbert observes, just "another example, laid
bare, of the bigger issues in hockey and the idea of winning
superseding morality. It's the same line of thinking which
enabled the cover-up of sexual abuse inside the Chicago
Blackhawks organization."[96] But please don't put the entire
blame on Holland and other senior Oilers executives. They
had lower-level male peer support, which Oilers captain
Connor McDavid embodies. Despite public opinion tilting
heavily against signing Kane, this didn't matter to McDavid.
The same day that Holland spoke to the press, McDavid told
journalists that he supports his general manager and indi-
cated that he and his colleagues are willing to do whatever
is necessary to win no matter what the cost:

Obviously, Evander is an amazing player and he's had lots of
success over the last couple of years. Whatever else is going
on, it's not something I look into much.

I'm not really here to discuss optic issues. If fans don't like
it, or the media doesn't like it, or whatever. It is what it is ...

I'm sure there's lots of things that go on, on the ice and
what not that fans don't like. We don't necessarily have to
discuss those with you guys ...

The public opinion is obviously something that matters a lot but we're here to try to win games.[97]

The narratives examined here, and the lack of clear-cut violence against women policies, partially explain why there are so many male athletes in the upper- and lower-ranks of combative sports like hockey who are pro-abuse and who engage in pro-abuse activities. If the key issue is to get men to worry about what might happen to their careers if they were discovered as woman abusers, then it should be obvious why there is so much woman abuse in sports that are the most profitable and popular. As a broad and general statement, most men in these sports will not lose much if conduct abusive to women comes to the attention of team owners, coaches, and league administrators. The reason, simply, is that men like Logan Mailloux, Patrick Roy, and Kobe Bryant are not likely to receive major punishments for assaulting women.

One explanation for the failure to sanction male athletes who abuse women is that the bulk of contact sports teams' executive departments are dominated by male decision makers who lack a sensitivity to women's concerns. Some top executives in the NHL and the teams that are affiliated with it are either uncomfortable with or are uninterested in formulating policies designed to reduce the number of women who are victimized by players, coaches, and other personnel off the ice. Some teams, such as the Montreal Canadiens, assert that they now take complaints of woman abuse seriously, but there is still ample evidence provided in this book and elsewhere that professional hockey teams and the NHL's head office still provide institutional support for the male peer group dynamics that perpetuate and legitimate female victimization and for the abusive behaviors of individual and group perpetrators.

Professional hockey life is where "connections" are made on the way to career achievements that not only involve scoring goals, getting assists, or stopping pucks. As former Montreal Canadiens goaltender Ken Dryden points out in his biography of Scotty Bowman (who is widely recognized as the best NHL coach in hockey history), upward mobility isn't

> really a coincidence, but is instead part of the game's web – which begins with street hockey games and neighborhood parks, extends to local rinks, and spreads to who knows where through stories and memories, especially if, like Scotty, you remember everything. And especially if, like Scotty, you were brought up to understand that no little moment or seemingly small encounter in your past is less important than any seemingly big moment or person in your present.[98]

Lessons learned from one's teammates can spill over into a boardroom later. Most NHL general managers and a sizeable portion of higher-level executives, for instance, were former players, with Marc Bergevin being a prime example. But, in the context of this chapter, what is most important is that the attitudes men develop and learn through playing hockey can result in some men, under strong peer influence, attacking women physically, sexually, and electronically. Senior team and league officials are fully aware that these assaults are taking place, and their silence and other insensitive responses must be considered when developing sound theories or explanations for why athletes who participate in hypermasculine, high-revenue generating sports like hockey and football have higher rates of violence against women than do other male athletes like professional cyclists.

On the question of changes being made, some researchers argue that a "soft masculinity" is now found in such places as Australian rules football, which is experiencing a growth in male players' peer group efforts to prevent sexual violence and is aligned with the establishment of a professional women's Australian rules football league.[99] As well, homophobic masculinity is seen as on the decline in this sport, and with it the need for men to forcefully and vocally act hypermasculine to prove to themselves and others that they are not homosexual.[100] There are similar findings of reduced homophobia in other places, but the question remains as to whether these behaviors are real behavioral and attitudinal changes that must be accounted for or simply superficial changes that allow men to look progressive while at the same time enabling these same men to both reap and promote the advantages of gender privilege.

Others argue that major changes are occurring at the organizational level in professional contact sports. In 1997, for instance, the NFL began a program to suspend players arrested for domestic violence or sexual assault – or at least those caught committing such acts on videos that were so widely spread on social media that the NFL could not ignore them. Nonetheless, local prosecutors, more often than not, drop charges against professional football players, and the NFL typically does not impose any punishment unless the player is found guilty of a serious crime. In some cases involving players who abused women (e.g., Johnny Manziel and Antonio Brown), the league took no action at all because the players were fired and not affiliated with a team. Additionally, NFL teams continue to give some players who assault women a "second chance" based, arguably, on how valuable these players are on the field. What's more, second chances are normally decided by teams, not the NFL head office, and team tolerance for woman abuse varies.[101]

Major institutional transformations are not evident in the NHL, and second chances are still the norm, as the case of Logan Mailloux and his supporters demonstrates. Mailloux rejoined the London Knights, and Marc Bergevin was hired as senior advisor to Los Angeles Kings general manager Rob Blake on January 9, 2022. In a team-released public statement, Blake said, "Marc brings a wealth of knowledge and experience to our hockey operations staff and will be a valuable addition to our group ... We look forward to his contributions."[102]

Lisa Dillman of *The Athletic*, like many other people (including us), is not impressed with the Kings' decision to hire Bergevin and then not make him available to the media. "What are the Kings thinking?" she asked. "It's difficult to figure out the reasons behind the decision made by an organization often fixated on optics and perception, yet unwilling to answer questions about the addition of a consultant."[103] Actually, the Kings' reasoning, based on information provided throughout this book, is not hard to discern. It is a symptom of a capitalist terrain that excuses abusive hockey players and those who employ them if they help bring in large chunks of money. It is also an integral part a particular type of playbook, one that is routinely followed by profitable NCAA contact sports teams. All playbooks need fields or arenas on which to run plays. The arena for the Kings' playbook, like the fields for the playbooks used by NCAA and NFL football teams, is a "culture saturated with masculinity which can manifest in horrible ways."[104]

In summary, male peer support for the abuse, objectification, domination, and dehumanization of women is part and parcel of contemporary profitable, combative, all-male sports like professional hockey. This does not surprise violence against women researchers for reasons described in chapter 1. To repeat Lee Bowker, "It is spread throughout all parts of society."[105] The new theoretical perspective offered here helps us make sense of the connection between MPS and ice men's violence against women.

It may seem painfully obvious but is worth saying anyway: it is not only MPS that contributes to woman abuse. Of course, it is, for any responsible expert on the topic, impossible to simply pick out one "reason" and announce that it always covers all cases. Undoubtedly, hockey players' victimization of women is behavior that is socially learned in interaction with specifiable or *reference others*. These are, according to hockey violence expert Mike Smith, "persons or groups who provide some sort of orientation for the individual in the development of a course of action or attitude."[106] Yet, other factors missing from our MPS theory also influence hockey players and other male athletes to abuse women. These determinants, including some elements of the mass media (e.g., pornography), are examined in the next chapter.

4

Other Key Elements of a Rape-Supportive Culture in Professional Hockey

Rape culture is around us all the time. It is a culture where people, mainly women, come to expect a form of sexual harassment, assault, or rape at some point, perhaps daily, because we minimize, ignore, or make excuses for the reality of sexual violence in many people's lives. It blames the victim when violence does happen and it rarely punishes the perpetrator for inflicting it. It is a culture where, no matter what the statistics tell us about the rarity of people lying about being sexually assaulted but also the prevalence of sexual violence, it is nonetheless easy to believe the victim is lying.

– Jessica Luther[1]

In the last chapter, we introduced our MPS theory to explain how certain factors motivate professional hockey players to abuse women. In this chapter, we cover some important influences absent from this explanation and devote more attention to the first determinant of MPS – patriarchal society. This task is essential because no useful account of the deviant behaviors covered in this book is complete without focusing on larger patriarchal social structures that affect the socialization patterns of men and how they learn to do masculinity. Many men are taught that there is nothing wrong with forcing women to have sex with them or with engaging in a myriad of other types of online and offline violence against women. This sometimes flows naturally from the objectification of women, the acceptance of rape myths, and the lessons learned from contemporary pornography.

One key element of contemporary rape culture – the *continuum of sexual violence* – first calls for attention because it is an extremely traumatic outcome of the other factors to be discussed here and that were examined in chapter 3. Although she doesn't describe it exactly this way, Jessica Luther, quoted above, explains how most women's lives exist today on a continuum ranging from nonphysical assaults, like the one committed by Logan Mailloux, to physical acts such as rapes or beatings. Although the idea of a continuum is often used to portray moving from the least serious to the most serious, to scholars like Liz Kelly, who developed this concept, all these behaviors have a "basic common character." They are all means of "abuse, intimidation, coercion, intrusion, threat and force" used mainly to control women.[2] No behavior on the continuum is automatically considered more hurtful than another, and, as Kelly states, women's experiences "shade into and out of a given category such as sexual harassment, which includes looks, gestures and remarks as well as acts which may be legally defined as assault or rape."[3]

Viewing all forms of physical abuse and touching as more serious than non-physical types of victimization obscures the reality that behaviors like in-person stalking, cyberstalking, verbal sexual harassment, and some social media attacks are perceived by many women as more terrifying than what the criminal law defines as assaults. For example, we have been told by many women that bruises heal – even broken bones heal – but the psychological damage from harming pets, destroying creative work or favorite possessions, or public humiliation can last for a lifetime.

Worse yet, non-physical forms of woman abuse, especially sexual harassment, are much more common in women's lives than are physically violent acts committed by current or former male partners, and these behaviors can influence women to avoid going into public places, quit an otherwise great job, or leave school and a degree unfinished.[4] It can be terrifying to the point of psychological harm to experience such things as a car of teens following you down the street yelling obscenities at you. What Liz Kelly and Jill Radford stated decades ago still holds true today: "At the time women are being followed/flashed at/harassed they do not know how the event will end. It is only in retrospect that such events can be defined as 'minor.'"[5]

In sum, the continuum of sexual violence focuses on the cumulative effect of a broad range of highly injurious inter-related behaviors that women experience, many of which are both exempt from the coverage or scope of criminal law and simultaneously trivialized or minimized by the mainstream media and society in general. Researchers like Walter DeKeseredy and Martin Schwartz devote extensive energy to analyzing the long-term effects of specific instances of sexual harassment, sexual violence, stalking, beatings, and other harms, or they analyze repeated patterns of one of these, such as physical assaults on a current or former intimate female partner. However, for thousands of women around the world, these forms of abuse "seep into one another."[6]

The continuum of sexual violence also makes us aware that, as uncovered by F. Vera-Gray's research, every day in a rape-supportive culture, "women trade freedom for safety." Vera-Gray asks, "Have you ever considered how much energy goes into avoiding sexual violence?" She then presents data showing that, as she puts it, "the work that goes into feeling safe is largely unnoticed by the women doing it and by the wider world, yet women and girls are the first to be blamed for the inevitable times when it fails."[7]

Many men don't understand how women manage or negotiate physical and sexual danger in everyday life, a problem feminist scholars and activists have been pointing out for decades.[8] To help their students, especially the males in their courses, understand how violence is an ongoing concern for most women, Walter DeKeseredy and Martin Schwartz (among many other professors in their field) first present statistics on the extent and distribution of woman abuse in North America. They fully recognize, though, that numbers are, for many people, little more than abstract clusters of symbols that students often use to distance themselves from a social problem. Further, researchers and instructors often deal with those who assert that "you can't believe statistics," especially if the data supplied to them do not support their opinions. Thus, Walter and Martin always try to encourage students to think about what it is like for women to constantly live with the fear of male violence.

To achieve this goal, following Jackson Katz,[9] they draw a line down the middle of a chalkboard, sketching a male symbol on one side and a female symbol on the other. They then ask the men in the class to describe the steps they take to prevent becoming a rape victim. At first, none respond. Eventually, one or two will say something like, "Avoid going to prison." They might say they stay out of bad areas of town at night. This is written down under the male symbol. Next, the women are asked to describe their rape avoidance strategies. A completely different picture appears. Under the female symbol, a long list of responses is written, including avoiding night classes, not walking alone at night, carrying pepper spray and whistles, calling the campus foot patrol for escorts to the bus or a car, carrying keys as a weapon, avoiding laundromats after dark, and a host of other preventative measures. The women's responses during this exercise generally go on for almost forty minutes. And, as Katz routinely discovers during his own exercises, very few of the female students think about how their avoidance strategies are functions of living in a patriarchal society. Rather, they say, "It is what it is" and suggest that men's hurtful behaviors and sexist attitudes are routine and regularized parts of campus life.

Karen Weiss, who works in West Virginia University's Department of Sociology and Anthropology, uncovered similar female reactions to male everyday violence in her campus social climate study. Consider the responses to unwanted sexual touching uncovered by her interviews with female undergraduates. Of all the student's statements, this one by a twenty-one-year-old sophomore (second-year student) is the most illustrative of women's common reactions to sexual grabbing or touching at their school:

> Everyone at the club grabs someone at least once, and it is almost impossible to catch everyone. So, you just have to accept it. It can be annoying at times, but it really isn't so bad. Actually, it can be pretty funny just how pathetic some of these guys are.[10]

Weiss also found that some types of unwanted sexual contact constitute a "rather ordinary occurrence." As she puts it, "Students get used to it, minimize it, and excuse the behavior. They know the risks going in, and apparently the risks are worth taking."[11]

This, to quote Katz, is "a sad situation," and one that is addressed further in chapter 5. But precious time is rapidly ticking away. So, if possible, before reading the next chapter, try to raise awareness about the destructive nature of contemporary rape-supportive culture by getting your friends, family members, and others to participate in, or to use, Katz's interactive exercise, because it serves three important functions. First, it shows men that many women worry about their safety and that their routine activities are regulated by a well-founded fear of violent men. Second, women who thought they were the only ones who worry about being victimized will discover that they are not alone. Third, it enables you to ask this question: "Why do so few women commit murder, given the alarming amount of male violence against them in private places?"[12] Then, share female homicide statistics showing that the bulk of domestic murders committed by women are in self-defense; that is, women killing the men who sexually and physically assault them. Whoever you talk to will quickly learn that most women who kill are like Melzena Moore (see chapter 2) and not like popular portrayals of Aileen Wuornos, who in 1989–90, while engaging in street sex work in the US, shot and robbed seven male clients.

Women's fear of crime is endemic to patriarchal societies and so are stereotypes of women who kill. If people's knowledge of female homicide offenders is based only on watching Hollywood movies, they don't think of cases like Moore's. They probably see women who kill men as masculinized monsters, lesbian villains, or pathological killer beauties. *Monster*, by the way, is the title of the 2003 biographical crime drama about Wuornos, for which Charlize Theron won the Academy Award for Best Actress. Professors Meda Chesney-Lind and Michele Eliason observe:

The film used several strategies to masculinize the character of Lee Wuornos. She is dressed in men's clothing, she is depicted as physically larger and dominates her petite, more feminine partner ... [played by] Christina Ricci, who in no way physically resembles her real-life partner, Tyria Moore. Wuornos is depicted as the sole provider and the one who controls physical contact in the relationship. Placing the film's killing spree entirely within a nine-month period beginning with the initiation of her intimate relationship with a woman implies that her lesbian relationship, rather than her appalling life circumstances up to that point in her life, [was] to blame for her murders. Even the title suggests that to be lesbian and to be violent casts one into a non-human role. For a movie that is supposedly sympathetic to the horribly abused Wuornos, to name the film *Monster* is to perpetuate myths about the woman.[13]

Wuornos had a history of abuse akin to Ms. Moore's, but the media sidelines it. She was sexually assaulted when she was a little girl and gang raped by high school "friends." As well, while doing sex work to support herself, she was physically and sexually assaulted countless times. She claims that the seven men she murdered had raped her or tried to rape her, and that she killed them in self-defense.[14]

A question raised in chapter 3 needs to be repeated here: What does this have to do with hockey? Societal reactions to Aileen Wuornos's deadly acts are, in fact, highly relevant in at least two ways. First, stories of heinous crimes committed by members (or perceived members) of the LGBTQ+ community, such as Wuornos, normally receive bigger headlines and far more moral indignation than those committed by heterosexual or cisgender offenders, and this is certainly the case with offenses committed by male adult perpetrators affiliated with male youth hockey teams.[15] Sheldon Kennedy's experiences (see chapter 1) are a poignant example. So are the events entailing seven former employees of Maple Leaf Gardens (former home to the Toronto Maple Leafs) who sexually abused dozens of young boys in the 1960s, 1970s, and 1980s.[16] Cases like these, nonetheless, are highly atypical. Most child sex offenders are adult men, but almost all of them are heterosexual, and the bulk of the victims are girls.[17]

Rare female violent acts like those committed by Wuornos and deviant practices in the world of male hockey have another thing in common: they occur in patriarchal societies. Patriarchy is an age-old structure, and men have abused women within this structure for centuries. Pavla Miller, professor of historical sociology, reminds us that "patriarchy ... particularly as embedded in the Old and New Testaments in the Bible and in Roman legal precepts, has been a powerful organizing concept with which social order has been understood, maintained, enforced, contested, adjudicated and dreamt about over two millennia in Western history."[18] Women throughout time have endured a lower position not only in hockey but also in society as a whole. That position has shifted and taken various forms over the decades, but women are constantly reminded that their worth is considered less than a man's. This is evident in the unequal distribution of labor, in lower pay for the same work, in the types of interpersonal violence that take place in public and private places, and in the violence and objectification that appears in advertisements and media. Add differences of color or sexual orientation, and we see even greater levels of discrimination and victimization.[19]

Misogyny is an ideology or belief system that has been connected to patriarchy for thousands of years. It is a word of Greek origin and is defined as hatred of, or hostility toward, women. This term is the philosophical underpinning of many subtle and overt acts of violence against women. These acts can be criminal or also coercive and subliminal in politics, the work environment, and advertising, which can perpetuate a cycle of violence against women.[20]

Misogyny exists in Canadian recreational and amateur youth hockey. A 2021 Angus Reid Institute online survey of 1,601 Canadian adults, 400 of whom were former hockey players, coaches, managers, or referees, supports this claim.[21] Of team alumni, 56 percent revealed that they perceive young male hockey players' treatment of women and girls as misogynistic or disrespectful. This figure increases to 63 percent when including survey respondents who did not play hockey but who identified as being part of the game by cheering on a family member, friend, or partner. In an interview with CBC reporter Jon Hernandez, Shachi Kurl, president of the Angus Reid Institute, said, "What is very noticeable is that those who have lived experience on the ice or around the rink ... are much more likely to say that racism is a significant problem, or misogyny or disrespect to women or girls is a problem."[22] These troubles, as demonstrated by evidence spread throughout this book, also exist in the CHL, the NHL, and in other professional hockey leagues.

Further recent support for this scientifically based claim is found in a report prepared by the Independent Review Panel (IRP) appointed in July 2020 by the CHL, which is the umbrella organization that represents the WHL, OHL, and the QMJHL.[23] Chaired by former New Brunswick premier Camille Thériault and including former NHL player Sheldon Kennedy and former Canadian women's hockey team coach Danièle Sauvageau, the IRP submitted its report to the CHL in December 2020, but the league did not make it public until January 21, 2022.

The IRP's mandate was to examine CHL policies and practices related to hazing, abuse, harassment, and bullying, as well as the allegation that players feel uncomfortable reporting behaviors that violate CHL policies. The IRP's report is based on examinations of these sources of information:

- QMJHL, OHL, and WHL policies;
- maltreatment complaints made from 2017 to 2019 in the QMJHL, OHL, and WHL;
- presentations from senior CHL leaders;
- presentations and interviews with subject matter experts;
- confidential interviews with agents, players, former players, general managers, coaches, owners, senior leaders of other Canadian sports organizations, representatives of other leagues within and outside of Canada, and Hockey Canada leaders;
- research papers; and
- results of a web survey of 655 members of the CHL conducted by Leger, a Canadian-owned market research and analytics company.

Described in greater detail in its report, the IRP discovered that

off-ice misconduct does exist in the CHL, and that the systemic culture in the league has enabled this to become a cultural norm. Maltreatment that, outside of hockey, would not be acceptable, has become an embedded behavior in this hierarchical organization and the level of acceptance is too high ... As a result of the systemic nature of the issue, a perpetuated behavior and lack of change occurs. Reasons for accepting the behavior include modeling by more senior members (owners,

GMs, coaches, older players), stressors experienced by players, desensitization over time to the perpetuated behaviors, and general acceptance of the behavior by others. In addition, there is an unspoken code of silence around maltreatment that enables off-ice misconduct to continue. The code of silence also prevents athletes from disclosing their experiences. Reasons for this may include fear of retaliation or punishment, power imbalances, and loyalty.[24]

While the IRP does not explicitly refer to empirical and theoretical work on male peer support, its findings lend more credence to our MPS theory. Also worth mentioning here, is that days before the IRP was formed, a class-action lawsuit, briefly discussed in chapter 1, was filed by former NHL player Daniel Carcillo and ex-WHL player Garrett Taylor against the CHL. Koskie Minsky LLP, the law firm representing them, stated that the lawsuit "is on behalf of children aged 15–17 who were sexually and physically assaulted, hazed and otherwise abused while away from home and playing for CHL teams."[25]

The misogyny and rape culture narratives that exist within elite hockey leagues not only influence players to engage in harmful patriarchal behaviors, but they also encourage rape myth acceptance in the general population, especially among those who are frequent viewers of televised games. Of course, on-air sports are not solely responsible for creating a disrespectful environment for women, but they are, nonetheless, highly influential. Readers who regularly watch NBA and NFL games are all too familiar with close-ups of scantily dressed cheerleaders, and such sexism and sexual objectification lead to problems, as uncovered by communications studies scholars

Kathleen Custers and Jenna McNallie. They conducted an online survey of 465 undergraduate students enrolled at a large, Midwestern university and found that increased televised sports viewership is strongly related to hostile sexism, benevolent sexism, and sexual objectification. These factors, in turn, were strongly associated with rape myth acceptance.[26] Other researchers uncovered data showing that these four elements are major components of a rape-supportive culture that is also made up of masculine gender roles, feminine gender roles, and adversarial sexual beliefs.[27]

Misogyny's tentacles are knitted into other types of mass media, too, including the pornography industry, and those involved in this business are aware of the NHL's popularity and large viewership. In August 2020, porn star Phoenix Marie took to Twitter to celebrate the return of the NHL after COVID-19 forced the pause of the 2019–20 regular season. She posted, "All my hockey lovers and players slide in my DMs." She also promoted her OnlyFans account on Twitter and gave away free thirty-day access.[28]

Traces of porn appear in televised hockey games, and you may periodically hear announcers make statements like these:

- "The goalie is weak between the legs."
- "He managed to barely slip it in there."
- "He got nailed from behind."
- "He just gave him a reach around."
- "He stuck his stick between the opposing player's legs."
- "He took that shot from the opposing player right in the face."
- "He was looking backdoor and he snuck it in there."[29]

These examples, many would argue, hardly prove that pornography is closely connected to hockey players' sexual objectification and abuse of women. Fair enough. But sociological research shows that male peer support is a major part of the equation. In fact, male bonding through drinking while viewing pornography is much more common among hockey players than one might think, and it can be a "gateway to sexual deviancy," as uncovered by Nick Pappas's interviews with collegiate hockey players. One interviewee told him that

> two thirds of his team would show up late night to participate in a competitive drinking event that involved pornography, team bonding, camaraderie, and perhaps some peer pressure as well. Furthermore, it is apparent that these activities were normalized within this team's culture because the players knew exactly how much time they had to finish their "30 pack" since they were all too familiar with the pornography scenes and its accompanying binge drinking.[30]

Two other players told Pappas they were convinced that porn caused violent sexual behaviors since frequently viewing demeaning acts made them "more acceptable" and provided "a lot of ideas." One of them said:

> I don't want to be a porn star you know, but ... when you see something on a porn [video], maybe I'm going to try that tomorrow or tonight when I bring a girl home. I think a lot of ideas come, where we get these ideas, comes from that. They're not natural, some of the things we tried to do. Like

the two-on-ones, the three-on-ones, whatever. I think it has a big influence [on sexual deviancy] ... I think it's the stuff you've heard about, stuff you've seen – the porno stuff, or guys' older brothers have done and told them about it.[31]

All-male group viewings of degrading porn are common today. This is what sociologist Michael Kimmel saw in his study of "guys" (men between the ages of sixteen and twenty-six): "Guys tend to like the extreme stuff, the double penetration and humiliating scenes; they watch it together, in groups of guys, and they make much fun of the women in the scene."[32] Kimmel also observed these group activities:

They get angry. Each time I happened on a group of guys engaged in group pornography consumption, they spent a good deal of time jiving each other about what they'd like to do to the girl on the screen, calling her a whore and a bitch and cheering on the several men who will proceed to penetrate her simultaneously.[33]

Using porn videos to strengthen male misogynist bonds is nothing new – it dates to the 1890s.[34] Cinematic pornography originated in 16 mm silent films

usually shown in private all-male "smokers" in such contexts as bachelor parties and the like. Within such a context, the men laughed and joked and talked among themselves while watching the sexually explicit films about women, who though were absent from the audience, were the likely butt of the jokes, laughing, and rude remarks.[35]

Porn has also infiltrated some elements of women's hockey. In 2017, Pornhub, the world's largest internet porn site, sponsored an adult women's street roller hockey team from Perth, Ontario. The team was called "PerthHub: Two Girls One Puck," and it got "a bunch of cash" for uniforms and equipment after the team sent off a "really average email" to the company. In exchange, Pornhub only asked for a photo of the women in their new jerseys. Maddy, a player and team marketing manager, justified the sponsorship by claiming, "Porn is definitely not going anywhere any time soon, and we think it's just one of those things it's best to accept."[36]

Like Rachel Nichols discussed in chapter 2, Maddy and her teammates are exonerators. Exonerators do not only turn women against each other, like Nichols tried to do. They also apologize for the patriarchal status quo and absolve men who oppress them and other women. Additionally, they find value in pornography.[37] Years of research conducted by Gail Dines, one of the world's leading anti-pornography activists and founder and president of Culture Reframed,[38] confirms that this is due, in large part, to their "internalizing porn ideology, an ideology that often masquerades as advice on how to be hot, rebellious and cool in order to attract (and hopefully keep) a man." Dines further points out that thousands of young women today accuse anti-porn activists like her of "denying them the free choice to embrace our hypersexualized porn culture" since, as "rising numbers of the next generation's elite," they see "no limits or constraints on them as women."[39]

Pornhub's sponsorship of Maddy's team is yet another one of its attempts to portray itself as socially responsible. Ten years ago, it tried to paint itself as environmentally friendly by planting trees during the week following Arbor Day (April 25, 2014). The Pornhub event site, still active today, features this message:

> This Arbor Day Pornhub will do what it does best and give America some serious wood by donating 1 tree for every 100 videos viewed in our Big Dick category. The more videos that are viewed, the more trees we will plant!
> How can you help? Click below to see the best Big Dick videos on Pornhub. While you're watching some nice pieces of ash, you'll also be helping to spruce America up! (Bushes are optional).[40]

For criminologists, this recalls the concept of *techniques of neutralization*.[41] These are easy and acceptable rationales for committing crimes or violating social norms. One technique that is directly pertinent to this discussion of Pornhub is *appealing to a higher loyalty*. Porn producers and consumers assert that while they may have offended or hurt many people, they are adhering to progressive legitimate norms, which are higher principles that justify their actions. Consider this statement made by Scharon Harding in her 2014 report on Pornhub's tree planting: "So if you're still in the Arbor Day spirit – and perhaps in the mood for something else – check out Pornhub this week. You'll feel good in more ways than one."[42]

To the best of our knowledge, there was no public response from environmental groups to this marketing strategy. Plus, this isn't Pornhub's only attempt to link itself to environmentalism. Harding found that Pornhub was also involved with Green Is Universal and posted Go Fossil Free ads before letting people view its collection of sexual videos.[43] What's more, Pornhub prides itself on providing snowplows to clear Boston streets and donating to organizations that struggle for racial equality.

This ostensibly "moral" company receives over 3.5 billion visits a month, which is much more than what Netflix, Yahoo!, or Amazon gets. It also gleans roughly 3 billion ad impressions a day. One ranking lists Pornhub as the world's tenth-most-visited website.[44] One must wonder, however, if Maddy and her teammates, as well as millions of other people familiar with Pornhub, are aware of this disturbing information uncovered by *New York Times* investigative journalist Nicholas Kristof:

> There's another side of the company: Its site is infested with rape videos. It monetizes child rapes, revenge pornography, spy cam videos of women showering, racist and misogynist content, and footage of women being asphyxiated in plastic bags. A search for "girls under18" (no space) or "14yo" leads in each case to more than 100,000 videos. Most aren't of children being assaulted, but too many are.
>
> After a 15-year-old girl went missing in Florida, her mother found her on Pornhub – in 58 sex videos. Sexual assaults on a 14-year-old California girl were posted on Pornhub and were reported to the authorities not by the company but by a classmate who saw the videos. In each case, offenders were arrested for the assaults, but Pornhub escaped responsibility for sharing the videos and profiting from them.[45]

Pamela Paul, author of the 2005 best-selling book *Pornified*, is, like Gail Dines, among the first to show us that pornography is now "seamlessly integrated" into mainstream society.[46] They belong to a rapidly growing cadre of scholars, journalists, and activists that supplies piles of evidence for the *pornification* of popular culture, of which hockey is a major part. This is a summary of examples offered by Dr. Bernadette Barton, and you will certainly be able to think of many more:

Welcome to the raunch culture in the 2020s – when the United States has devolved into a *Hustler* fantasy. Naked and half-naked pictures of girls and women litter every screen, billboard, and bus. Pole dancing studios keep women fit while men airdrop their dick pics to female passengers on buses, planes, and trains. Christian pastors compliment their "hot" wives from the pulpit, and we have whole television programs devoted to "the girlfriend experience" – a specialized form of prostitution. People are having sex *before* they date, and women make their own personal porn to share on social media. Rape and pedophile jokes are commonplace, and those who don't like them are considered prudish … Internet porn drives trends in programming, advertising, and social media, not to mention the technological development of the web. The first lady modeled nude[47] and the "leader of the free world"[48] bragged about grabbing women "by the pussy."[49]

Raunch culture is, to no one's surprise, not restricted to the US. Routinely visited by millions of people around the world, Pornhub, owned by MindGeek (formerly Manwin), is a Canadian company that was born in Montreal in 2007.

And Pornhub is not the only business contributing to the pornification of women's hockey. Calendars, for example, featuring semi-clad female hockey players are easily available online, one of which was recently produced by the Russian Women's Hockey League (RWHL). It features twelve players half-naked with flowers and fruits barely covering their bodies. According to a RWHL marketing statement, this 2020 calendar reveals that "along with tough hockey qualities, [each] player has tenderness, sincerity and delicacy."[50]

Other types of female hockey players take it to a higher level. In 2015, members of the Lytham St Annes [Field] Hockey Club, based in Lancashire, UK, posed naked to raise money for the Lytham Sports Foundation. David Perkins, chairman of the club, said, "I am so proud of all the girls that have taken part in the hockey calendar ... Lytham Cricket and Sports Club has always felt like a family and to see the girls supporting our charity to ensure the future of our club continues for generations is brilliant to see."[51] Doesn't this sound like appealing to a higher loyalty to justify the objectification of women? Surely, there must be alternative successful ways to raise money for community organizations.

There are, of course, but some of these methods are also degrading. A recent example is the Sioux Falls Stampede hockey team's "Dash for Cash" event that took place on December 11, 2021. Ten local teachers crawled on the ice to collect dollar bills to help pay for their classroom supplies in front of a live audience. The Stampede is a United States Hockey League (USHL) team based in South Dakota, a state that in 2023 ranks second last in the country for average teacher salary.[52] Reynold Nesiba, a state senator representing a portion of Sioux Falls, pronounced, "Teachers should never have to go through something like this to be able to get the resources they need to meet the basic educational needs of our students – whether it's here in Sioux Falls or anywhere in the United States."[53] Likewise, be it in Russia, the UK, or any other place for that matter, female hockey players should not have to go through a pornification ritual to generate money for their teams' survival. Naked calendars are not simply fun ways to raise money. Similarly, the equipment and uniforms provided by Pornhub to the PerthHub women's street roller hockey team portray women as sexual objects, damage their self-esteem, minimize their athletic talents, and make them feel undervalued.[54] Female hockey players should be treated with as much respect and dignity as their male counterparts – not as "something to be bought, sold and then tossed away."[55]

It is not surprising that pornography poisons hockey. Pornography affects millions of people's relationships, attitudes, values, beliefs, and behaviors because it is widely used and distributed around the world. Porn consumption is not a rare act committed by a small group of pathological people, and there is much cultural and health-related damage associated with porn use.

This current era features the degradation, abuse, and humiliation of women never before seen in the mass media. We are not talking about *erotica*, which is "sexually suggestive or arousing material that is free of sexism, racism, and homophobia and is respectful of all human beings and animals portrayed."[56] Rather, our conceptualization of porn focuses squarely on what Linette Etheredge and Janine Lemon refer to as sexual media that are "violent and regularly depict participants (mainly young women) in distressed situations or scenarios where they are being violently and inhumanely treated."[57] Such images and writings are the most profitable in the industry and have two primary things in common. First, females are characterized as subordinate to men, and the main role of actresses and models is the provision of sex to men. Second, in the words of Gail Dines, most of today's porn "depicts hardcore, body-punishing sex in which women are demeaned and debased."[58] A routine feature of contemporary internet porn is painful anal penetration, as well as brutal gang rape and men slapping or choking women or pulling their hair while they penetrate them orally, vaginally, and anally.[59]

One of Walter DeKeseredy's friends and colleagues, Dr. John Foubert, recently interviewed Dr. Robert Jensen, an emeritus professor of journalism at the University of Texas at Austin and author of *Getting Off: Pornography and the End of Masculinity*. Jensen has devoted the bulk of his academic life to studying the harmful effects of violent and racist sexual imagery, and he told Foubert what he sees today:

> In the last twenty-five years we know that porn got more aggressive, porn got more extreme. The sexualization of male dominance over females intensified. That is unquestionably true. Nobody in the industry would argue that ... We also know that porn got more culturally acceptable, not that everybody likes it, but it is part of mainstream culture in a way it wasn't before. That is the paradox of porn. You would think that something that got more cruel, more callous, more aggressive and more racist at the same time would not become more

acceptable in the culture. That tells you something important. It tells you that pornographic values are in fact mainstream. In some sense a lot of that was predictable. What wasn't predictable I think, although in retrospect it should have been, is the degree to which younger women would embrace porn as a sign of liberation. That caught me by surprise.[60]

Jensen says that we now live in a "post-*Playboy* world."[61] Yes, today's porn depicts much more than only women's exposed breasts and buttocks, as was the case with *Playboy* magazine. Nonetheless, the cable television network A&E's 2022 documentary *Secrets of Playboy* brings to light the fact that Hugh Hefner and his friends' violent traumatization of porn models was not a new phenomenon but, until recently, stayed a secret. Hefner was *Playboy* magazine's founder and editor-in-chief. Although Hefner has been deemed progressive by a legion of followers because of his perceived strong support for women's rights, civil rights, and free speech, the documentary features former employees of his disclosing that some of the women who lived at Hefner's mansion and who worked at his Playboy Clubs were raped by guests. As well, some of Hefner's former sexual partners reveal that he drugged them so that they would give in to his desires.

One of Hefner's former girlfriends, Holly Madison, called *Playboy* "cult-like" and said her first sexual encounter with Hefner was traumatic. Sondra Theodore, another former girlfriend, has accused Hefner of "grooming her at 19, manipulating her into participating in orgies and filming sexual partners without their consent."[62] But for reasons such as convincing eminent left-wing writers like James Baldwin and Margaret Atwood to contribute their writings to *Playboy*, Hefner was able to occupy a "Trojan Horse of respectability" and escape public stigmatization and criminal prosecution.

In a January 25, 2022, Facebook posting, Gail Dines described Hefner and his entourage's patterns of sexual deviance management as a "mass cover-up by the media, and eco-system of patriarchy, for almost 70 years!" She adds:

> Last night's documentary on *Playboy* showed that Hefner used the same playbook as Epstein.[63] Pimping, drugging and raping women, employing the techniques of a batterer to break down the women, and keeping them almost prisoner in the mansion. All his "girlfriends" had the same story, and Hefner's vile friends defended him as an intelligent, sensitive romantic.[64]

Thousands, if not millions, of people didn't know, and still don't know, what, as Rowan Pelling puts it, "*Playboy* is all about,"[65] and that large group probably includes some wives and girlfriends of hockey players. For example, Noureen DeWulf posed (though not naked) while pregnant for *Playboy* in 2015. Flash forward to 2020, when Dasha Mart, wife of Belarusian hockey player Alyaksandr Baradulya, appeared on the cover of Mexican *Playboy*. Lindsey Vecchione, the girlfriend of Chicago Blackhawks star Jonathan Toews, also modeled for *Playboy* and played in the Lingerie Football League for the Chicago Bliss.

In light of the information about the terrifying treatment of women graphically reported in the A&E documentary, Pelling rightly asks, "What Did *Playboy* Ever Do for Women?"

For sure, the three women mentioned above garnered considerable attention, but they also taught young girls that it is easier to get noticed with their appearance than with their intellectual skills. Given the popularity of magazines like *Playboy*, it is not surprising, then, that many women learn to objectify themselves.[66]

Many young women featured in *Playboy* or who want to pose in it are not imprisoned and abused in ways like what Hefner and his famous friends did to some Playboy Bunnies (waitresses at Playboy Clubs). One horrific case that went viral in early February 2022 is what the late *Soul Train*[67] creator Don Cornelius did to two Bunnies. P.J. Masten, an ex-"Bunny Mother," told A&E producers the following:

> It was probably the most horrific story I've ever heard at *Playboy*. This story is the story of a massive cleanup that never hit the press. These two young girls got in his Rolls-Royce, went up to his house and we didn't hear from them for three days. We couldn't figure out where they were.

Masten also revealed that the two women were

> bloodied, battered [and] drugged. They were tied up and bound. There were wooden objects that they were sodomized with and [one sister] could hear [the] other sister being brutalized. It was horrible, horrible.
>
> The thing that was so outrageous to me, that made me so angry, was that no charges were filed and Don Cornelius' privileges as a number one VIP were never suspended. He was back in the club the following week.[68]

An unknown number of women aspiring to become "hot" women like those in pornographic media are not physically abused, but they are bound up in invisible chains. They are, as Gail Dines observes,

> held captive by images that ultimately tell lies about women. The biggest lie is that conforming to this hypersexualized image will give women real power in the world, since in a porn culture, our power rests, we are told, not in our ability to shape the institutions that determine our life chances but in having a hot body that men desire and women envy.[69]

Porn today transcends videos, pictures, and adult novels. The sexual objectification and degradation of women occurs in a wide range of contexts, including calendars featuring pictures of naked and half-naked female hockey players. In response to the common question, "What's next?," some researchers direct us to the rapid emergence of the *gorno* or *gore porn* genre of movies like the *Hostel* and *Saw* film series.[70] These films combine sadism, torture, and porn, and they generate huge revenues for their producers and distributors. That there are often sequels (or multiple sequels) to some popular gorno movies is a powerful commentary on how violent pornography has seeped into mainstream popular culture.

Incidentally, Jason Voorhees, the main antagonist of the grisly *Friday the 13th* film series, wears a goalie mask that is a replica of a 1970s-era Detroit Red Wings fiberglass version.[71] An unspecified number of people who masquerade as Jason on Halloween typically buy Jason hockey masks online from eBay, Amazon, and other digital retail outlets. Reflect on the banal way Amazon advertises the Wen XinRong model. Instead of saying it is a symbol of horrific violence, the Amazon ad lists these features (typos/mistakes and all):

- This Jason hockey mask is made of Environmentally Friendly PVC and is non-toxic.
- Perfect for Halloween, Masquerade Parties, mardi gras celebration, theme parties, Costume Parties, Christmas, Easter, etc.
- Adjustable Elastic Band: Elastic straps with adjustment keep the mask in position. Easy to wear and remove. One size fits everything.
- The mask is comfortable and breathable, you can see the outside through the two holes in the mask's eyes, without worry about shifting or falling off have fun all night long.
- SATISFACTION CUSTOMER SERVICE: If you have any questions, please contact us so we can make it right. We are always engaged in providing high quality products and best service for you.[72]

Those who buy Jason masks and who are fans of the *Friday the 13th* movies tend to be oblivious to the fact that most of the women Jason kills are sexually active and those who escape his wrath abstain from sex. Additionally, female characters in a sizeable portion of slasher films are much more likely than men to be targeted by a broad range of violent behaviors, including various types of psychological terror and confinement. The gruesome "punishment of immoral women" who violate patriarchal gender norms by having pre-marital sex is

186 | Skating on Thin Ice

a routine major theme in slasher films. *Friday the 13th* movies and similar ones, some argue, therefore contribute to keeping women "in their place." Moreover, stigmatizing women who violate gender norms helps groups of men rationalize their own deviant or criminal assaults on women.[73]

Torture and porn are combined in a new subgenre of heavy metal rock music – *pornogrind*. It includes themes of sexual violence against women and necrophilia and gained much international attention a few years ago because Connor Betts, the mass shooter who killed nine people and injured twenty-seven others in Dayton, Ohio, on August 4, 2019, was a member of the Menstrual Munchies, a three-person pornogrind band. One of the band's song titles is "Cunt Stuffed with Medical Waste – Sexual Abuse of a Teenage Corpse." To make matters worse, one of the band's album covers shows a woman consuming feces.[74]

Racism is another main element of today's pornography. Black men and women are routinely exploited and stereotyped as being hypersexual, and there is much demand for videos featuring "hot-blooded" Latinas and "submissive" Asian women. Most, if not all, anti-pornography researchers, activists, and practitioners would agree with Dines's claim that "irrespective of the ethnic group, the framing of the narrative is the same – the women's race makes them that bit sluttier than 'regular' white porn women."[75]

Other variants of violent porn are being developed while you read this chapter. The rapid growth of the internet has globalized lightning-fast access to violent and degrading depictions of women and other potentially vulnerable groups (e.g., children) in online and offline environments. Such media are diffused to millions of people in only seconds, and what used to be hard to obtain and a secret phenomenon is now accessible to virtually anyone and is a huge business with operations around the world. The internet not only eases accessing previously inaccessible materials, but it also buttresses gender and racial inequality and helps create an environment that normalizes hurtful sexuality, racism, and even seeking revenge on female ex-partners. What Dines declared nearly fifteen years ago still holds true today: violent and racist porn have "come to dominate the internet."[76]

Pornography is the most lucrative business in the world, and pornographers are pioneers of new electronic technologies. They are closely associated with the development and success of video streaming, "tweeting," DVDs, smartphones, and broadband.[77] Moreover, many people watch sexual videos at home by themselves, and this market has driven the home entertainment industry. It is impossible to answer just how far technology would have gone without pornography, but it is certain that many advances, including the availability of video in the home rather than in theaters, were driven and sped up by the pornography industry. In other words, porn drives the technology and sex plays a key role in shaping the internet.

Estimated worldwide, pornography revenues from a variety of sources (e.g., internet, sex shops, etc.) recently topped USD$100 billion. This is more than the combined revenues of Microsoft, Google, Amazon, eBay, Yahoo!, Apple, and Netflix. The money that porn makes in the US every year, nearly USD$13 billion, exceeds the combined revenues of the NFL, Major League Baseball, and the NBA.[78]

Pornography use, production, and distribution will only get worse due to easy access offered by the internet. Recall the Pornhub visits data presented previously in this chapter. What is more, traffic on Pornhub increased nearly 10 percent in both Canada and the US during the early stages of the COVID-19 pandemic in March 2020.[79] Here are some more disconcerting statistics:

- A third of young people have seen porn by age twelve.
- 88 percent of scenes in top rented and downloaded porn contain violence against women.
- 35 percent of all internet downloads are porn.
- 20 percent of sexts[80] are photos of children, mostly girls, fifteen years old or younger.[81]

Any group of people or any subject is "ripe for the picking" in the porn industry, and the coronavirus is no exception. On February 2, 2022, Walter DeKeseredy visited Pornhub's site and 1,335 "Coronavirus Quarantine Porn Videos" were then available. Examples of the titles he found are "Tied, Teased & Tormented! Coronavirus Quarantine Boredom Cure," "I Am Stuck Home During Lockdown with My Black Ex-Girlfriend and She Is Horny So I Deliver," and "Taboo Coronavirus Quarantine – Stepmom & Stepson Try to Escape COVID-19." Not surprising, as well, are the hockey porn videos offered by Pornhub. Among the eighty-four listed on February 2, 2022, are "Getting Her Goalie Off," "Hockey Wife Cheats on Husband," and "Hockey Night Booty Call." How does the Toronto Maple Leafs organization feel about people viewing the video titled "Hockey's Back!!!!," which features a woman in a Leafs jersey masturbating?

Again, porn consumers can find anything that suits their fancy on the internet. It is not our intent to engage in "shock theater," but Natasha Vargas-Cooper's observation is worth repeating here since much of what she describes is now "typical":

Groups of men have sex with women who are seven months pregnant; the ho-hum of husbands filming their scrawny white wives having sex with paunchy Black men in budget hotels; simulations of father-daughter (or mother-daughter) incest; and of course, a fixture on any well-trafficked site: double anal.[82]

What men and boys consume online, often in groups, are not simply "dirty pictures that have little impact on anyone." Rather, the images typically endorse "women as second-class citizens" and "require that women be seen as second-class citizens."[83] Also challenging the assertion that "pornography is just fantasy" are studies done around the world showing that degrading sexual images featured on the internet and elsewhere are strongly associated with violence against women. Of major importance to this book is this fact uncovered by Nick Pappas: athletes' (including hockey players) pornography consumption "can be rampant" and serves "as a 'how to guide' for sexual deviancy/aggression."[84]

Walter DeKeseredy and Martin Schwartz have given an immeasurable number of presentations on the relationship between the injurious symptoms of patriarchy and male athletes' violence against women to students, academic organizations, and practitioners. Each time they inevitably hear some members of the audience, particularly those who are hostile to feminism, mutter under their breath, "I don't want to hear this stuff." Then there are those who are not averse to a gendered understanding of the technological "dark side of male sports," but they claim that DeKeseredy and Schwartz overlook a fundamentally important determinant of hockey players' violence against women. As some have told them, "Follow the money." They are right – gender inequality often intersects with other forms of oppression such as racism and social class inequality. In fact, you cannot fully understand the absence of deterrence, covered in chapter 3 and other parts of this book, without taking another broader structural variable – corporate capitalism – into account.

How does corporate capitalism fit into the equation? What, exactly, is going on? The answer to these questions is, quite simply, money. More specifically, your money. John R. Gerdy, author of *Sports: The All-American Addiction*, states what many of us already know:

Team owners want more of it. Television networks want more of our money as do sneaker and apparel companies.

Perhaps we have simply become numb to the business of sports. The numbers have become so outlandish, almost surreal, so large that they no longer mean anything, as if it were Monopoly money. The reporting of the signing of a $100-million-per-year player will likely be greeted with not much more than a yawn at most breakfast tables across the country. The fact is professional sports has always been about business.[85]

Television is an especially important part of this business, as demonstrated in Figure 4.1. Developed by independent writer

FIGURE 4.1. *How the money flows*

Source: Adapted from Varda Burstyn, *The Rites of Men: Manhood, Politics, and the Culture of Sport* (Toronto: University of Toronto Press, 1999), 117. Used with permission.

and scholar Varda Burstyn for her book *The Rites of Men: Manhood, Politics, and the Culture of Sport*,[86] it helps you follow the money, and there is a lot to follow. Evidence of television being a "cash cow" is provided by ESPN and the NHL recently striking a seven-year deal worth USD$2.8 billion, with ESPN now being the main rights holder for NHL games. The league also signed a seven-year deal with Turner Broadcasting, which lets Turner Sports broadcast up to seventy-two regular-season games and half of the first three rounds of the Stanley Cup playoffs each season. This deal adds USD$225 million yearly to the NHL's revenue, and thus the NHL will earn close to USD$625 million annually over seven seasons from its television deals. Its earlier ten-year contract with NBC brought in USD$200 million per season. Adding the new television revenues to the NHL's advertising profits means that it will recoup the money lost from hosting empty arena games during the COVID-19 pandemic and surpass its fiscal profits like never before.[87]

Most consumers of televised sports and other types of television shows despise being bombarded by advertising, but the NHL and other major professional sports leagues don't care. News broke in August 2021 that, following the NBA, the NHL will put a 3 x 3.5-inch rectangular advertisement on the front of teams' jerseys starting in 2022–3. Since the 2016–17 season, the NBA has included advertising on its jerseys in the form of a 3 x 3-inch square, which resulted in an added USD$9.3 million in revenue annually, per team. The NHL now has a helmet ad campaign, launched in the 2020–1 season, which has so far generated a reported USD$15 million.

Much money is made from what Burstyn coins the "media sectors of the sports nexus." Some other key components of this nexus are not examined here, but the money generated by all parts of it combined is, as uncovered by Burstyn,

> equivalent to the gross national products of small nations, or the budgets of large states, provinces, and cities. The public pays heavily through "leisure" dollars, through taxes for sports training and infrastructure, and through sports-related consumption that benefits a small number of owners, sponsors, and star athletes far more than the public itself.[88]

Made explicit in other parts of this book is that players' performance on the ice and the revenue they produce can trump their criminal and deviant behaviors, but the above financial data add an exclamation point to what we said earlier. Much money is lost if a marquee, albeit deviant, male athlete is not televised, as is what happened when champion golfer Tiger Woods took a hiatus from PGA Tour play after the maelstrom that followed his wife uncovering his infidelities in November 2009. Woods announced his indefinite leave a month later, which, as former CBS Sports executive producer Rick Gentile said, caused "not so much a ripple effect, but a tsunami."[89] Ponder these financial effects:

- Tournament crowds dropped by 20 percent.
- Television audiences shrunk by 50 percent.
- Television advertising dropped by nearly 40 percent, and some experts estimated that ad losses would be at least USD$192 million if Woods was out all year.
- Nike, which sponsored Woods, lost nearly USD$30 million in sales.

So far, conspicuously absent from our examination of the billions of dollars in revenue made by the NHL is a focus on the economic impact of sports betting since the US Supreme Court's 2018 landmark decision to strike down the federal ban on sports gambling in all states except Delaware, Montana, Nevada, and Oregon. Only Nevada had a major gambling infrastructure and thus, effectively, it was the only state that allowed sports betting. Many states have now legalized sports betting and others will shortly follow suit.[90]

According to an Oxford Economics study commissioned by the American Gaming Association, because of a legal, regulated sports betting market, the four major US professional leagues will generate combined revenues of over USD$4.2 billion per year through TV advertising, sponsorship, data/product revenue, media rights, merchandise, and ticket sales. The total projected revenue for the NHL is USD$216 million per year. Here are some of the study's other key findings:

- Legal sports betting operations, including wages, salaries, benefits, and tips, are estimated to support USD$11 billion of total labor income.
- Total jobs supported in the US, both direct and induced, are predicted to be 216,671.
- Legal sports betting is expected to contribute USD$22.4 billion to the US gross domestic product.
- Fiscal impacts, consisting of state, local, and federal taxes, are estimated to total USD$84 billion.[91]

Since 2019, the NHL has created betting partnerships with MGM Resorts, DraftKings, FanDuel, William Hill, PointsBet, Ballys, and other sportsbooks. The NHL's next step is puck and player tracking. Licensed to bookmakers like MGM, this enables betting on the distances skated by players, the velocity of shots, and the location on the ice from where the next goal is scored. In August 2021, NHL commissioner Gary Bettman proudly told ESPN reporters Greg Wyshynski and David Purdum the following:

Our original goal in creating this technology was to create a broadcast enhancement that can be used in real time, which no other sport has. While not developed with this in mind, the application to sports gaming could create even more fans.[92]

Some individual NHL teams have also developed relationships with gambling organizations. The Washington Capitals, for instance, transformed a sports bar chain restaurant into a William Hill Sportsbook, which was the first one inside a US sports arena.[93] Welcome to the new world of professional hockey, and expect even more changes of this sort in the future, including a major increase in online sites offering hockey betting tips. DraftKings is already in on the act. This is an excerpt from its hockey betting guide:

> The winter is all about hockey, and betting on hockey can make the season much more exciting. With 1,271 regular games to bet on, hockey offers lots of opportunities to win. Learn the ins and outs of hockey betting, from NHL puck line to common hockey mistakes, so you can successfully bet on NHL games with DraftKings Sportsbook.[94]

Sociologist Erving Goffman, who developed the concept of the total institution mentioned in chapter 3, observed that spectator sports like hockey provide one of many contexts "where the action is."[95] Sports fans, however, are unable to experience the action directly encountered by players on the ice or on the football field, so they seek action by watching them "taking chances" and "putting it on the line."[96] Their desire for action entails not only watching, but also betting, which is something major league sports teams warmly embrace. Still, as noted by the late Michael D. Smith, many sports bettors do not wager "seemingly irrational sums of money" purely for material gain but also for things that are sometimes of much greater significance to them such as honor, dignity, respect, esteem, and status among their peers.[97]

Former Montreal Canadiens stars John Ferguson and Serge Savard (also former GM of the Canadiens) are examples of such bettors. Both were teammates and good friends in the 1960s and 1970s, and they loved horse racing. They cherished this sport so much, in fact, that the day before a road game, they would rush to Montreal's Blue Bonnets racetrack immediately after practice.[98] Horse racing was also a routine part of their road trips. In an interview with *Trot* reporter Chris Lemon, Savard fondly recollects some of his fun times at the track with Ferguson:

> Whenever we were on the road when we played together on the Canadiens, he would wake me up and start looking at the racing form. We would have our team lunch at 12:30 and then we were off to the track for an hour or so. Whenever we were in Los Angeles, we'd go and visit the backstretch and they treated us so well. That's what we did the very first time I was with the team and we did it a lot more times whenever we were there.[99]

Savard also revealed to Lemon that his close friendship with Ferguson was temporarily put on hold once a race started. "Bragging rights were on the line. Win and you got to rub it in their noses. Finish last and you'd never hear the end of it." He and Ferguson always wanted to "one-up" each other at the racetrack, and, especially for Ferguson, that place was where the action was. "I clearly remember being at the track together," said Savard. "He just loved being there, watching the races and enjoying himself. It didn't matter what track it was. You could see how happy he was every time we'd go." He recalls, "I can still remember his voice: 'Serge, come on, we're going to the track.' I miss those days. They were great times."[100]

Regardless of why they bet on sports, all sports bettors seek drama, no matter which events they watch. Most people don't tune in to TV broadcasts of horse racing because it is a fantastic sport. They, like Savard and Ferguson did, bet on it, which can make any sport or game exciting. And this excitement translates into bundles of money flowing into team owners' pockets.

Will gambling worsen the NHL's neglect to sanction players who abuse women? At this point in time, there are no data that supply reliable answers to this question. Some critics of sports betting nevertheless stress that "game-fixing" will become rampant, while supporters of legalization assert that it leads to more transparency. University of Paris economist Wladimir Andreff opposes legitimate sports betting and told ESPN reporter Chris Eden: "All economic analyses conclude that the more money there is inflowing to sport, the greater the sport corruption."[101]

Andreff did not offer Eden sound evidence to back up his prediction, but this is not to say that game-fixing is a rarity or a thing of the past. Recently, Sportradar Integrity Services, a partner to more than 100 sporting federations and leagues, used its betting monitoring method, the Universal Fraud Detection System (UFDS), to find suspicious activities across twelve sports in over seventy countries. The results of its study date back to the beginning of the COVID-19 pandemic and show that soccer is the sport most at risk of game-fixing linked to betting.

In 2021, the UFDS detected suspicious activity in 500 soccer games, 37 tennis matches, 19 basketball games, 9 hockey games, and 6 cricket matches. Europe was identified as the worst region, with 382 suspicious matches. Latin America had 115, Asia Pacific 74, the Middle East 10, and North America 9. Andrea Krannich, managing director of Sportradar's Integrity Services, told *Guardian* reporter Jacob Steinberg: "As our analysis shows, match-fixing is evolving, and those behind it are diversifying their approach, both in the sports and competitions they target, and the way they make approaches to athletes, such as the rise in digital approaches."[102]

The NHL's investigation into Evander Kane's gambling activities found no evidence that he bet against his own team, but the NHL has a history of gambling scandals. Some readers who are avid fans of Wayne Gretzky may remember this case. In May 2007, former NHL player Rick Tocchet pleaded guilty to running a sports gambling ring while he was assistant coach for the Phoenix Coyotes under Gretzky. Dubbed "Operation Slapshot," Tocchet was one of three men to plead guilty in the case. Included in this triad was New Jersey state trooper James Harney, who, according to authorities, took bets in his patrol car while watching traffic. Gretzky's wife, Janet Jones, was also publicly implicated for placing bets in the ring. She was subpoenaed to testify but never faced charges. Nor did her husband affectionately known to millions of hockey fans as "the Great One."[103] Returning to the often repeated, but highly problematic, second chance narrative, Tocchet was allowed to return to the NHL one year later, on the condition that he refrain from gambling.

Tocchet is not the first NHL employee to be nailed for illegal gambling, and he won't be the last. In 1948, the NHL imposed a lifetime ban on players Don Gallinger and Billy Taylor for betting on their own teams, but then reinstated them in 1970. In January 1946, Toronto Maple Leafs defenseman Walter "Babe" Pratt was suspended by the NHL for betting on games that didn't involve his team. Initially, his banishment was forever, but he only missed nine games because he admitted his "evil ways" and promised never to do them again. He was also later inducted into the Hockey Hall of Fame.[104]

The NHL prohibits players from betting on hockey, but they can wager on other sports, and sometimes the consequences are financially devastating. That the legendary Jaromír Jágr owed more than USD$500,000 to an internet gambling site might be the key reason for his longevity in the world of professional hockey. Thomas Vanek, too, had hundreds of thousands of dollars in gambling debts.[105]

As stated before, nothing is exempt from pornification, including sports betting. Sexualized scenes of women are now integral parts of sports gambling marketing strategies, just as they are in other types of advertising. In Australia, for example, one Sportsbet television ad recently described the bikini as "one of man's greatest inventions" while a man poked the breast of a woman as she sat poolside. Another Australian ad produced by Betfair featured a James Bond–type character playing ping-pong with a woman in a bikini while a background voice said, "When you have the power, you can do what you want. With whoever you want, whenever you want, wherever you want, as many different ways as you want."[106]

But wait, there's more! In June 2021, the shirt sponsor of the English Premier League Norwich City Football Club was an Asian gambling company called BK8. It used pornographic images of women in social media promotions that violated the regulations of the UK's Advertising Standards Authority. BK8 used YouTube images of women simulating sexual acts and a marketing campaign involving young women in their underwear placing BK8 stickers on their breasts. These marketing strategies, after much criticism, were removed after three days, but many fans enjoyed them.[107]

More examples of porn in sports betting advertisements could be supplied here, but one of the most important points that readers should take away is that visual commercials featuring sexual images of women are explicitly designed to appeal to what film theorist Laura Mulvey has coined "the male gaze." Put another way, they empower heterosexual men and privilege their perceived sexual desires while simultaneously objectifying women.[108] More specifically, in advertisements shot from the male gaze, the camera forces the viewer to stare at women's body parts, usually freezing on their breasts and buttocks.[109]

The NHL held its annual All-Star Game in Las Vegas on February 5, 2022. Broadcast by ESPN+ and ABC, not only were sports betting ads driven by the male gaze prominently featured in this televised event but so was the popular singer Machine Gun Kelly (MGK), who performed during the second intermission. Recall from chapter 2 that women's rights groups are deeply uncomfortable, to say the least, with the NHL's relationship with Snoop Dogg. Well, its relationship with MGK is just as, if not more, problematic from the perspective of those who oppose the pornification of our culture and the glorification of statutory rape (sexual relations involving someone below the age of consent). In a 2013 interview with *FUSE*, MGK made some "controversial" statements about Kendall Jenner. He said that she was his first celebrity crush, and when asked if he was "counting down the days" until she turned eighteen, MGK answered:

> I'm not waiting til she's 18; I'll go now. I'm 23, dog, like, I'm not like a creepy age, like, you know what I'm saying? I'm 23 bro, she's 17, and she's, like, a celebrity. Like, there's no limits right there.
>
> Robert Plant, who was one of the greatest lead singers ever, for all y'all don't know he's from Led Zeppelin, dated a girl that was 14. Axl Rose, who was one of the biggest badasses ever, dated a girl that was 16 and wrote a song on his first album about the girl that was 16.
>
> I don't care. Say what you want, man. If Kendall Jenner was in your bedroom naked, and you're 50, you're going.[110]

The NFL is not much better, as proven by the 2022 Super Bowl. Snoop Dogg performed during the half-time show despite being sued for sexual assault and battery two days prior to the game, and he faced similar allegations in December 2021. This show also featured Eminem, whose song "Superman" includes these misogynistic lyrics: "Put Anthrax on a Tampax and slap you till you can't stand." Yes, Super

Bowl ads "were pretty safe" this time around, but the women featured in them, though much less sexualized than in previous years, were primarily given "sidekick roles."[111] For the trained eye, there were also some examples of more blatant sexism during parts of the broadcast, which is not surprising in today's raunch culture.

What are the solutions to the problems pointed out in this book and elsewhere? The first thing to do is to come to grips with the fact that there is no quick fix. Yet, there are copious reasons to be optimistic, one of which is that the public, government agencies, the mass media, and sports organizations are now much more knowledgeable about the amount and consequences of various types of violence against women than ever before. Meanwhile, fictional and nonfictional stories about the abuse of women, including harms committed by athletes, are commonplace in the media.

Given the persistence of patriarchy and the ongoing multipronged assault on efforts to advance gender and racial/ethnic equality, these are amazing achievements. Still, Dr. Claire Renzetti, University of Kentucky professor of sociology, editor of the widely read and cited scientific journal *Violence against Women*, and close friend of Walter DeKeseredy and Martin Schwartz, alerts us to this sad reality: "It is astounding that we are still fighting some of the same battles as we were 25 – even 40 – years ago, and there is still much work to be done."[112]

To reiterate what we said in chapter 1, it is essential to move beyond initiatives designed "only to stop the bleeding." The central argument of chapter 5 is that those seeking meaningful change in the world of professional hockey and other elite male sports must, at the same time, struggle for short-term victories and major structural and cultural changes within not only revenue-generating sports but also throughout our broader society. The nature of sport cannot be changed without changing the nature of society.

Likewise, as the late German sociologist Norbert Elias would have put it, studies of the relationship between professional hockey, rape culture, and violence against women that are not studies of society "are studies out of context."[113] Therefore, following in his footsteps and those of Kevin Young, Varda Burstyn, Michael D. Smith, and others who have had a major bearing on our critical thinking about male-dominated sports, we co-authored a book that situates professional hockey within the wider context of society at large.

Broadening the study of hockey players' abuse of women is of little, if any, value unless it informs policies and practices that prevent women from being victimized. Chapter 5, then, includes what we and our brothers- and sisters-in-arms strongly believe are highly effective means of eliminating hockey's violent, sexist, homophobic, and racist attributes, all of which are highly injurious symptoms of the ways in which our society is politically, socially, and economically configured. Chapter 5 also compels us to ask ourselves, "Do we really want to live this way?"

5

The Puck Drops Here: Prevention and Control Strategies

It is important to remember that the system by which men reproduce their dominance in sport (or any other social institution) is not seamless. Women continue to make grounds at undoing formal sexism and the institutionalization of men's privilege. In sport, women have made considerable progress in gaining the right to play, albeit in their own segregated sporting spaces. Lesbian women have been, more recently and increasingly, accepted into the female-sport fold, and women are beginning to use the legislative processes, along with shaming, to combat the abuse of their bodies at the hands of mostly team-sport athletes.

– Eric Anderson and Adam White[1]

It was a sad day on February 20, 2022, for many people around the world – the end of the XXIV Olympic Winter Games. Viewers saw some incredible athletic achievements and became familiar with an international cadre of people who exemplified the best that sport has to offer. The Games offered many hours of temporary relief from a variety of social and public health problems, including COVID-19. Plenty of viewers deeply appreciated the Olympians' camaraderie, dedication, and spirit.

Some people, however, were sad for reasons other than the closing of the Games. *Toronto Star* columnist Heather Mallick took the view that it "was the saddest Olympics ever. It was a symphony of bad." Here is why:

> Sadness leaked into so many events and into the Olympic concept itself … Communist China, a nation sensitive to mockery and desperate for medals, searched worldwide for people of vaguely Chinese origin to play for China. It was horribly awkward. Was that a win for China or for U.S. training? The medals were tainted.
>
> A lot of things were tainted at this Olympics. In the midst of an unwinding doping scandal, the Russian Kamila Valieva gamely skated. It was a showpiece, not for the 15-year-old's characteristic grace and courage but for child abuse. She looked terrified, fell and nearly fell repeatedly, and kept on going – one suspects out of terror.
>
> Her Russian coach, Eteri Tutberidze, already notorious for cruelty, berated Valieva in front of the cameras. The child wept. That was the Beijing Olympics image that will linger, salty tears on ice.
>
> The Russians, famous for doping, shouldn't have been there, even as the "Russian Olympic Committee," shorthand for Vladimir Putin. They are Russian government

athletes as opposed to Russians, just as the Communist Chinese athletes don't compete alone. They represent an authoritarian government that tortures Uyghur minorities in concentration camps, pollutes with wild abandon, and whose secrecy and dishonesty have alienated much of the world.[2]

Montreal Gazette columnist Jack Todd's view of the Games is equally negative for reasons like Mallick's. For him, these are "the Olympics that should have never been." Todd's post-mortem, however, also includes much praise for the gold-winning Canadian women's hockey team. Its match against the US team, notes Todd, averaged 3.54 million viewers on NBC, which is more than any NHL game played prior to this event. In fact, this event was the second-most viewed hockey game in the US since 2019.[3]

We are big fans of Mallick and Todd, and we greatly appreciate their keen insight, especially in today's era characterized by a rabid war on both critical thinking and those who publicly point out the harms done by racist, sexist, homophobic, and classist governments and corporations. Consider the war on critical race theory (CRT) that is currently going on in the US in the wake of recent Black Lives Matter protests. Those leading the charge against CRT are totally unfamiliar with this body of legal scholarly thought that emerged largely out of Harvard Law School in the 1970s and 1980s. There are variations in CRT, and no single summary of this school of thought can easily be presented here. What we can comfortably say, though, is that what all leading experts in the field have in common is their emphasis on identifying the outcomes of subtle and overt racism throughout contemporary society and a reinterpretation of civil rights laws to expose "legal claims of neutrality, objectivity, color-blindness and meritocracy as mere camouflages for the self-interest of powerful entities in society."[4]

It is not an exaggeration to say that right-wing critics of CRT like Texas senator Ted Cruz know nothing about CRT.[5] What they do know, nonetheless, is that racism is very much alive and well in the US and other parts of the world and that their attacks on CRT are, as *Boston Review* columnist David Theo Goldberg recently put it, a highly effective way

> to stoke white resentment while distracting from the depredations of conservative policies for all by the wealthy ... [I]t is a cynical ploy to keep power and privilege in the hands of those who have always held it. Meanwhile, the outcome remains what Marvin Gaye sang – to brothers and sisters, mothers and fathers – a half century ago: "there are far too many of you dying."[6]

Often quoted in this turbulent epoch is this excerpt from Dr. Martin Luther King Jr.'s famous 1965 sermon delivered at Temple Israel of Hollywood: "We shall overcome. We shall overcome. Deep in my heart I do believe we shall overcome. And I believe it because somehow the arc of the moral universe is long, but it bends towards justice." While the previous chapters of this book are likely to have given numerous readers the evidence-based impression that positive changes are not soon forthcoming in professional hockey and other all-male sports, there is hope, some of which was provided by the 2022 Winter Olympics. For instance, returning to Jack Todd's appraisal of this event, he reminds us that Marie-Philip Poulin – captain of the Canadian women's Olympic hockey team – "cemented her claim to be the greatest Canadian athlete of the past 12 years, beginning with her golden goal at the Vancouver Olympics, and carrying through Sochi and Beijing, with an overtime beauty at the IIHF World Championships in August."[7]

The achievements of two Black US women – Erin Jackson and Elana Meyers Taylor – will also be cemented in history. Prior to February 2022, only two Black Americans had ever won an individual medal in nearly 100 years of Winter Olympics. It took these two women less than a day to double that record. Jackson also became the first Black woman in the world to win an individual gold medal in a Winter Olympics event. Shortly after, Meyers Taylor won a silver medal in the inaugural monobob event and a bronze medal in the two-woman bobsled event, which makes her the most decorated Black athlete in the history of the Winter Olympics.[8]

Despite these and other notable changes, many sports will continue to uphold various types of inequality unless the ongoing and ever-changing struggle to end them continues, strengthens, and becomes more widespread. How do we move beyond simply using ineffective bandages and failed NHL strategies in responding to the harms covered in this book and in other critiques of all-male team sports? This chapter answers this question. We propose several strategies that target the broader social forces that propel male hockey players to abuse women and that buttress a system that promotes and rewards toxic masculinity, corporate greed, racism, and homophobia.

Our recommendations are based not only on many years of hands-on social scientific research, but also on DeKeseredy and Schwartz's decades of work in the battered women's movement, with other activist groups, and doing government research. Our policy proposals, too, are heavily informed by Stu Cowan's keen insight into the everyday world of professional hockey. If readers don't know this by now, hockey is an integral part of his life. He has been a member of the *Montreal Gazette*'s sports department for close to forty years and has held basically every position in that division during his tenure there. The advanced visions of others, including numerous people cited throughout this book, are also represented in this chapter.

We do not merely repeat what has already been recommended but rather supplement previous suggestions with more contemporary initiatives. Nevertheless, there is brief coverage of some of the "usual suspects," such as creating and putting into action effective equity, diversity, and inclusion plans. It is to these approaches we turn first because they garnered much media attention at the time of writing this chapter.

That there is so much male violence against women in the world today and that women are marginalized in professional hockey organizations shows that men's and women's lives are valued differently throughout society, a sad reality demonstrated by this book and other bodies of research, including recent alarming studies of *sex selection*. As defined by

statistician and health economist Howard Steven Friedman,
sex selection

> is driven by the motive of son preference and is highlighted
> by situations of declining fertility. Son preference refers to
> circumstances where parents place a higher value on having
> a son than on having a daughter. It has many roots. Many
> societies are historically male dominated, with property
> rights, inheritance laws, and dowry systems all designed to
> favor men ... It creates regional ripple effects throughout Asia,
> Europe, and even parts of America, where some prospective
> parents are selecting boys rather than girls.[9]

It is not only in the NHL that women's worth is less than
that of men. Men and women are valued differently in a
wide variety of sports, with soccer being one notable example. Consider that in March 2020, Carlos Cordeiro had
to quit his position as president of the United States Soccer
Federation (US Soccer) after publicly claiming, in defense
of paying female soccer players less than men, that female
soccer players had fewer physical skills and responsibilities
than their male counterparts.[10] Justice did, however, prevail.
On February 22, 2022, a six-year legal battle over equal
pay ended with US women soccer players being promised
USD$24 million plus bonuses matching those of the men.
US Soccer also committed to giving an equal pay rate for
the women's and men's national teams, including World
Cup bonuses.

The words expressed by veteran midfielder Megan
Rapinoe in her interview with the Associated Press are worth

repeating in light of our discussion about assigning value to human life:

> The additional hours and stress and outside pressures and discriminations we face, I mean sometimes you think why the hell was I born a female? And then sometimes you think how incredible it is to be able to fight for something that you actually believe in and stand alongside these women ... There was something more than stepping on the field and wanting to be a starter or wanting to score goals or wanting to win or wanting to have glory.[11]

Male professional athletes, their coaches, and their employers need to change, an issue to be addressed at length later in this chapter. Even so, the path toward meaningful and sustainable improvement also requires what happened to the US women soccer players. In other words, as recommended by two of the world's leading social scientific experts on sport, Eric Anderson and Adam White, team sports like hockey need to be gender-integrated, and this entails providing "women with the same social training, the same access, and the same symbols that men currently have associated with their formal participation in sport."[12]

Professional hockey is starting to show signs of effective listening, as examined in chapter 2. Some NHL teams, such as the Montreal Canadiens, are making serious moves toward gender integration, and in January 2022, the Premier Hockey Federation (PHF), formerly the National Women's Hockey League, announced that it is adding a seventh franchise in Montreal. The PHF will invest more than USD$25 million in direct payments and benefits to its players over the following three years, and its pledge includes more than USD$7.5 million in salary and benefits for the 2022–3 season. The PHF's investment gives players complete health-care benefits supplied by each franchise, as well as 10 percent equity of each team and control over their own likeness, which lets players profit from the use of their images.[13]

Some scholars informed by the *sports protection hypothesis* assert that all-female organizations, such as the PHF and the professional women's Australian rules football league mentioned in chapter 3, not only provide elite female athletes with employment opportunities but also enhance their self-esteem and confidence and protect them against male violence.[14] It is also argued that women's participation in sport helps woman abuse survivors heal.[15] Even so, a recent study of twenty women who regularly took part in sport in New Zealand uncovered contradictory evidence. Put differently, study participants described sport as an empowering context while simultaneously perceiving sporting environments as places that exacerbate their feelings of risk and defenselessness.[16]

Women's sport participation can play a partial, albeit small, role in protecting women from male violence, but some caution is necessary. An overarching emphasis on women's involvement in sport as a key solution is highly problematic because it implicitly blames women for their victimization by placing on them the burden of trying to prevent various attacks by men. The researchers who conducted the above New Zealand study expand on this point: "Positioning women's sports participation in this way reinforces the narrative that women can resist victimization if they are just empowered enough, while responsibility is shifted away from perpetrators."[17] No policy attention is given to the structural, social psychological factors that motivate men to abuse women.

What about the value of skills taught in combative sports and self-defense courses? Some studies found that they boost many women's confidence and self-esteem, but what is taught in these environments reveals a major disconnect between the lessons and the reality of male assaults on women and girls. Many, if not most, self-defense courses emphasize protection from strangers rather than the people most likely to attack them – male intimate partners, co-workers, friends, and acquaintances. What's more, combative sports and self-defense classes only deal with physical attacks and thus do not prevent new electronic means of sexual assault, coercive control, psychological abuse, and some other digital means of harming women (e.g., cyberstalking).[18]

Hockey and soccer still have a long way to go before they are truly gender-integrated and before deeply ingrained sexism is completely eradicated, but the NFL hasn't even left the starting gate yet. Super Bowl LVL, played on February 13, 2022, raked in millions of dollars, but the Cincinnati Bengals and Los Angeles Rams organizations paid their cheerleaders measly stipends for the time and effort they spent performing at the world's most profitable annual sporting event. These women are not alone. NFL cheerleaders in general only make a few thousand dollars a year, even though they work thirty to forty hours a week when you factor in rehearsals, workouts, charity events, and working at games. To make matters worse, some sources report that cheerleaders are required to pay for their own equipment, uniforms, and hair and nail treatments. As is repeatedly stated in corny TV commercials, "And that's not all!" Cheryl Cooky, Purdue University professor of American studies and women's, gender, and sexuality studies, reports the following:

> The paltry amounts the cheerleaders do receive have frequently come only after battles hard fought. Of the 26 NFL teams with cheerleaders, at least 10 have been sued by cheerleaders for wage theft, unsafe working conditions, harassment, or discrimination. The cheerleaders who filed these lawsuits often made less than minimum wage. In at least one case, a cheerleader claimed she was paid significantly less than her team's mascot, who made more than [USD]$60,000 a year.
>
> In a landmark case against the Oakland Raiders in 2014, the team paid out [USD]$1.25 million in back wages. Raiderette cheerleaders were subsequently paid [USD]$9 an hour, minimum wage at the time, for mandatory events, which they said was double what they had been paid prior to the lawsuit.[19]

Valuing male and female athletes equally not only requires equal pay but also equal protection from non-economic forms of abuse. Made explicit in this book are atrocities committed by coaches against male hockey players like Sheldon Kennedy. Many female athletes are also targeted by abusive coaches, and US women soccer players, again, necessitate attention. During 2021, five of the ten National Women's Soccer League (NWSL) teams fired white male coaches or forced them to resign because of sexual misconduct, verbal abuse, racist comments, and perpetuating a toxic work culture.[20] A few years prior, some Chicago Red Stars players reported their coach's (Rory Dames) abusive conduct to US Soccer, which oversaw the NWSL at that time but failed to act on the complaints. One former Red Stars player who spoke to *Washington Post* reporter Molly Hensley-Clancy on the condition of anonymity recalled how Dames

> pushed her into an "emotionally abusive" dynamic that made her deeply uncomfortable: texting her at all hours, asking her to spend significant time with him outside of soccer and retaliating against her when she eventually tried to pull away from him. When he asked her as a young player to frequent lunches and dinners, she said, she did not feel able to say no.[21]

Christen Press, a US national team star and former Red Stars player, said this of her decision to speak to US Soccer officials in 2014:

> I was terrified of what Rory would do and say if he found out this was something I'd said. And then I was made to feel by US Soccer that I was in the wrong, there was nothing to report, and that this was acceptable. For so many women in this league, you think you don't have any worth. And if you stand up and say what you think is right or wrong, nobody cares.[22]

North of the US border, in late July 2022, an independent review commissioned by Canada Soccer (CS) and conducted by McLaren Global Sport Solutions concluded that CS "mishandled" sexual harassment allegations in 2008 against then under-20 women's coach Bob Birarda, who, at that time, was awaiting sentencing on sexual assault charges. A 125-page report describes CS as "being dysfunctional and inefficient," with "significant leadership upheaval and transition at the highest levels" in 2007 and 2008. The report also concludes that "CS's press release that characterized Birarda's departure [in 2008] as being in the mutual interest of both parties without so much as addressing the harassment was a gross mischaracterization of the circumstances and failed the victims of the harassment, their teammates, and the organization as a whole."[23]

What is the solution? Obviously, major change needs to happen at the top, but additional steps are also necessary. First, as recommended by Eric Anderson and Adam White, radical change is needed in how coaches are hired, trained, and assessed. This entails the use of what they refer to as "super coaches" whose jobs are not to ensure that coaches lead their teams to victory, but who instead "examine how a coach trains his or her players for life." This would be a giant leap forward because most coaches lack careful supervision and thus are able to easily avoid accountability.[24]

The second step toward stopping what happened to the aforementioned soccer players, to Sheldon Kennedy, and to other athletes abused by coaches is the creation of what Anderson and White label a "coaches license,"[25] which would be regularly renewed by passing a biannual test that evaluates coaches' knowledge of the latest research on human development, ethics, education, injury prevention, sports medicine, and social justice issues related to sport. Furthermore, coaches who have been punished for abusing players and/or other members of their teams would have sanctions permanently recorded on their licenses so that they can't get a job with another team if they were fired for deviant or criminal conduct. Coaches would have to show their licenses to prospective employers, and they would be scanned to reveal any past wrongdoings.

Cynical readers may say, "Well, that's all fine and good, but what if some teams remain more concerned with winning and don't give a damn about a coach's past?" This point is well-taken, given that Grambling State University hired former Baylor University head football coach Art Briles as its offensive coordinator in February 2022. Baylor fired Briles in May 2016 after the investigation by the law firm Pepper Hamilton found that he and other Baylor employees mishandled cases of sexual violence described in chapter 3. Nonetheless, he was, not surprisingly, granted an all too familiar second chance. Trayvean Scott, Grambling's athletic director, told ESPN that "they did the homework" and were "able to move forward in support of Coach [Hue] Jackson's recommendation. We felt it (was appropriate) to give him a chance to really redeem himself after understanding where the facts lie."[26]

Much to the relief of thousands of woman abuse survivors, especially those who were sexually assaulted at Baylor while he worked there, Briles resigned from his position at Grambling just four days after he was hired. Many interpret this as the result of Briles being quickly forced to exit because many people were outraged by Grambling attaching its name to him.[27] Some argue, and there is evidence to support their claim, that he is "radioactive" and "forever unhireable."[28] After all these years, a growing cadre of people are storming the professional sports' second chance bastille, a social movement that is destined to gain even more momentum.

There is an old Italian saying: "a fish rots from the head." We couldn't agree more with leadership consultant Jon Gordon's Twitter posting on June 27, 2017: "So do teams and organizations. Leadership matters!"[29] It is not only coaches who need training and licenses but also hockey team owners like Rocky Wirtz, who, to quote *Chicago Sun-Times* reporter Ben Pope, "dropped a nuclear bomb on the concept of accountability" on February 2, 2022.[30] When, at a televised town-hall meeting, a reporter asked him about the Chicago Blackhawks efforts to guarantee that what happened to Kyle Beach would never occur again, Wirtz angrily replied:

> We're not going to talk about Kyle Beach. We're not going to talk about anything that happened. We're moving on. What we're going to do today is our business. I don't think it's any of your business. You don't work for the company. If somebody in the company asks that question, we'll answer it.

Asked the same question a few minutes later, Wirtz replied:

> I told you to get off the subject. I'm not going to bring up the Jenner & Block Report. I know you are talking about what the report was talking about, and I told you we're moving on. It's out of line to ask this line of questions. Why don't you ask about something else? Why don't you ask about the general manager search? Why do you bring up old business?[31]

Pope is right to opine that Wirtz cannot be trusted to ensure that atrocities like those experienced by Kyle Beach remain hideous events of the past. The same can be said about some other men in leadership positions within the NHL and other all-male sports leagues. Fortunately, the NHL has had the good sense to partner with Sheldon Kennedy's Respect Group for a training program for league and club employees to prevent bullying, abuse, harassment, and discrimination. It started in March 2022 and responds to the report on the Blackhawks' mishandling of Kyle Beach's case. The Respect Group's program is also part of phase one of the NHL's four-phase Respect Hockey initiative.[32]

But training programs alone are not enough. They must be accompanied by other initiatives we suggest, including placing visionary women from all walks of life in senior management positions. One example, mentioned in chapter 2, is France Margaret Bélanger. In a lengthy mid-February 2022 one-on-one interview with Stu Cowan, she clearly articulated a well-thought-out plan forward for the Montreal Canadiens, one that should be incorporated by the Blackhawks and other NHL teams. Stu asked Bélanger about the Logan Mailloux situation, and this was her response:

> Look, a lot has been said about Logan Mailloux and that dates back to July [2021]. I remember vividly because that Friday of the draft was the start of my two weeks holiday which, needless to say, changed. This whole series of events is unfortunate. My role here is to make sure that from that situation we try to get something positive out of it.
>
> We came out with this plan called Respect and Consent, led by Geneviève Paquette. It was presented by Geneviève and Rob Ramage when we opened training camp last September. My action is to make sure that through local organizations and through the investments we said we would

make we make a difference. It's not just about the money, but we said we would pledge $1 million, which is good money. But it's not about the money, it's about how can we invest in the community to make sure that these kids – not just guys, by the way, but girls and boys – understand what consent means and the very basic respect, which sometimes is not obvious to everyone.

What does respect mean? Hopefully, we have similar ideas of what it is. But if you're 15 or 17, depending on where you're from and what are your goals, that can become vague. So, this is our plan. It's to try through some teaching and some learning – starting with our hockey team, by the way – and eventually opening it to younger kids. For sure, we're going to be involved in sports, but are we going to open it up to other types of kids in schools? How do we train these guys, how do we make sure they understand there are things you simply cannot do?

I could dwell on the past and try to comment on that decision, but it's really not my role to comment on that decision. It's something that was done and it's looking for the future and trying to see how we can try to turn that into something positive. Sheldon Kennedy has his Respect Group and we've signed up for that and the NHL is supporting that program. We've signed up and we're going to start training probably in March. It's imminent. All our hockey team, everyone around our hockey team, and all the employees on the corporate side as well as a first step of training and education. We're starting with that.[33]

Bélanger should be commended for her leadership and for trying to make the NHL a safer place for women. Further, though the past can't be changed – and shouldn't be forgotten – as of July 2022, it seems that the CAD$1 million the Canadiens invested into the Respect and Consent Action Plan is making a difference and that Mailloux is working on making himself a better person. Noted previously, the Canadiens did not invite Mailloux to their rookie camp in 2021, and the OHL suspended him for the first twenty-six games with the London Knights. The Canadiens did, however, invite him to their development camp in July 2022, and he appears to be starting a new journey in his life.

On July 11, 2022, Mailloux spoke with the media in Brossard, Quebec, and revealed the process he has gone through since being drafted by the Canadiens:

> I've been working a lot over the past year. I want to be a Montreal Canadien. This is where I want to play in the future. It's definitely been a long journey to get here.
>
> It's been a lot of different stuff. A lot of meetings with therapists, professionals. I've done a lot of certification, education programs, training programs, stuff like that. So it's definitely been a lot.
>
> Respect, consent, the whole program they have going on here is unbelievable. I think every NHL team should have to do it, every junior team should have to do it, I think it should start in minor hockey as well. I think it's something that definitely needs to be done more often.
>
> I think (sexual consent) has a lot to do with communication. You have to communicate with your partner what's ok, what's not ok. It's an ongoing thing consent. I've definitely learned a lot over the past two years going through everything. So it's

something that can be taken away at any time during the act. So it's an ongoing, mutual agreement for sure.

I would have changed everything that I've done, 100 percent. I've definitely changed a lot as a person over the past two years. I've learned a lot. I wasn't educated back then, I feel like I am now.[34]

Sheldon Kennedy was also at the Bell Sports Complex on July 11, 2022, and was invited by the Canadiens to speak with the prospects. He, too, is optimistic about the Canadiens' Respect and Consent Action Plan and its impact on Mailloux. Here is what he said in an interview with Stu Cowan that day:

What I see from the Montreal Canadiens is a commitment to lead in this space and to me that's how we're going to have significant change. I don't think this is just a hockey issue. This is a societal issue. But if I look at the culture of hockey I think we've got some catching up to do.

The whole goal today was to be able to reach the new drafted players around the respect initiative, around what is respect, what are the issues. What is discrimination, harassment, abuse, equity, inclusion, and diversity? Basically, what is it and how do we communicate around that that's going to be the conversation today.

I don't know much about the Logan Mailloux story. I know a little bit about it. I just had a chance to meet Logan downstairs for the first time and we had a great conversation. I felt we could communicate about the issues at hand and to me that's huge. So many times you can never talk about these issues. People don't even know where to start.

We had a healthy conversation and I hope nothing but the best for Logan and that he continues to learn and be the best he can be in his space.

But for me, I'm here because I see leadership and I see an organization that wants to be the best they can be in this space.

We know about Mailloux's plans and the assistance he received, but what are the Canadiens doing to help the target of his abuse rebuild her life? Have the Canadiens reached out to her? What have they done to help make her feel safe after what Mailloux did to her? And what is Hockey Canada going to do to help the survivor of the 2018 group sexual assault besides paying her an out-of-court settlement?

Described in various parts of this book is the dismissal of the needs and concerns of women abused by elite hockey players, and this must stop. How many times do we need to hear about cases like this one involving former NHL player Reid Boucher before effective steps are taken? In 2011, Boucher, then age seventeen, sexually assaulted a twelve-year-old girl whose family hosted him as a billet family in Ann Arbor, Michigan, when Boucher played for the USA Hockey National Team Development Program. He was originally charged with first-degree criminal sexual assault but was allowed to plead guilty to third-degree criminal sexual conduct against a minor in a Washtenaw County Trial Court on December 13, 2021.

In February 2022, Boucher was sentenced to four years of probation with one year of suspended jail time if he success-fully completes the probation. Under the initial charge, he would have faced twenty-five years in prison. Circuit Judge Patrick Conlin let Boucher enter a plea for the lesser charge due to "unusual circumstances," such as his age at the time of the crime and when it occurred.

Was justice served? What about the survivor? Boucher played for Lokomotiv Yaroslavl of the KHL (after playing more than 130 NHL games) before the Russian team fired him on February 18, 2022. The girl he abused, on the other hand, is now twenty-three years old and has coped with intense trauma, self-harm, and substance abuse issues since the 2011 incident. When asked about her reaction to the judge's decision to accept Boucher's plea, she said she is "disgusted. I feel like a lot of the progress I've made over the last 10 years – that's been undone."[35] Sarah Rennie, executive director of the Michigan Coalition to End Domestic and Sexual Violence, was deeply disturbed by Judge Conlin's reference to the amount of time that had passed since Boucher's assault. She told the *Detroit Free Press*, "It's an outrageous, unacceptable and illegal plea."[36]

Boucher's abusive conduct, by the way, did not stop in 2011. On January 21, 2022, *The Athletic's* Katie Strang reported that in October 2014, Boucher, then twenty-one years old and a New Jersey Devils prospect, tried to get a fifteen-year-old Canadian girl to send him pictures over Facebook. Strang also details that in January of the same year, Boucher tried to get photos from a seventeen-year-old New Jersey girl by messaging her via Facebook.[37] What's more, Boucher fled from his Michigan-based team to play for the OHL's Sarnia Sting from 2011 to 2013 before joining the NHL.

In January 2022, shortly after Boucher pleaded guilty in the Michigan court, the OHL claimed that it was unaware of the allegations made against Boucher during his tenure with USA Hockey. Sting officials also declared ignorance. Team president Bill Abercrombie, who was vice president of operations during Boucher's time in Sarnia, told the press, "I'm sure the league and we're going to try to dig in and find out how it got overlooked and who's responsible."[38] Something's not right here. So, again following the advice of Anderson and White, players (like coaches) should be required to get licenses. This would greatly minimize the chances of abusive players like Boucher flying under the radar.

There are numerous reparations and conciliation-based strategies that the Canadiens and other sports teams should examine, many of which are suggested by a large cadre of criminologists. It is beyond the scope of this chapter to review them, but what they all have in common is an emphasis on parallel justice, an issue briefly discussed in chapter 1. This entails greater efforts by the NHL and the teams affiliated with it to help people like the young woman abused by Mailloux and the women sexually assaulted by members of the 2003 and 2018 Canadian World Junior teams. One promising approach is to give a woman a safe opportunity to confront an offender with her anger and pain (either face-to-face or through an intermediary) and to ask the offender to account for himself.[39] Of course, some survivors may not wish to participate, but for many, the opportunity to explain the harm they suffered would be welcome.

The term *parallel justice* was coined by Susan Herman, former executive director of the National Center for Victims of Crime. These are its guiding principles:

- Justice requires helping survivors of crime rebuild their lives.
- All victims deserve justice.

- All victims should be presumed credible unless there is reason to believe otherwise.
- Victims' safety should be a top priority.
- Victims should experience no further harm.
- Victims' rights should be implemented and enforced.
- Victims should be told what happened to them was wrong, and that every effort will be made to help them rebuild their lives.
- Victims' needs should be addressed through a comprehensive, coordinated community response.
- Decisions about how to address victims' needs should be based on sound information and research.[40]

We are unsure if Sheldon Kennedy's Respect Group training program and the Canadiens' Respect and Consent Action Plan include strategies aimed at preventing young men from consuming violent and dehumanizing porn. If not, for reasons provided in chapter 4 and elsewhere (e.g., Nick T. Pappas's *The Dark Side of Sports*), any education and/or training program aimed at reducing hockey players' violence against women is incomplete without such initiatives. Research done by Walter DeKeseredy, Martin Schwartz, and others conclusively shows that the correlation between in-person violence against women and porn consumption is related to some types of pro-abuse male peer support.

Male peer support also motivates men to send women sexual pictures or messages (including porn) that female recipients do not want. Further, male peer support influences many vindictive men to distribute sexual pictures of their former female partners on the internet without their consent. And there are male sexist online communities with members who never come into face-to-face contact with each other but often exchange violent pornographic written, audio, and visual communication with their peers.[41] Sociologist Michael Kimmel describes one variant of this subculture:

> Online chat rooms are, by their nature, spaces of social interaction among men. These chat rooms are the closest thing to a pornographic locker room in which bonding is often accomplished by competing with other guys. In the online chat rooms, a description of a violent sexual encounter might be followed by another user's "Oh yeah, well last night I did this to the woman I was with ..." which would be followed by another response designed to even top that. The competition can become heated – and violent – rather quickly. What we had stumbled on was the "homosocial" element in heterosexual porn viewing, the way in which anything, including intimacy with a member of the opposite sex, can be turned into a competitive moment with other guys.[42]

Added to trainings about respect, consent, bullying, intimidation, abuse, and harassment should be modules that help hockey players develop what Laurie Mandel, founder and director of the Get a Voice project, refers to as *collective courage*. She directs us to the fact that, on their own, young men, including those who are athletes, "won't stand up and say something." Programs like hers help them "use voices of courage and leadership – and to work together, so that if they see something happening and speak up, someone will say something too. When they do it together, it really works well."[43] Curricula like Mandel's teach athletes to challenge their peers' use of porn. They also teach them that, to quote what Nick Pappas says about keeping company with fellow athletes who use porn, "choosing to walk with a herd that engages in unhealthy behavior increases the likelihood of stepping in its residual dung sooner or later."[44]

More will soon be said in this chapter about collaborating with men and boys. As a prelude, we must say that there are more than a few good men in the hockey world, including in the NHL, who "do the right thing"[45] by standing up to toxic masculinity, rape culture, and their accompanying harms. In fact, there may be more than we realize. Social psychologists have a concept that is relevant here: *pluralistic ignorance.*[46] This concept refers to situations where individuals think that they are the only ones who oppose the majority position because no one else is speaking up. In a locker room, for example, or a hangout, or any place where men gather, a popular topic is bragging about sexual prowess and achievements. Yet, many times it is only one or two loud braggarts making claims of sexual aggression, and a group of other men who assume that they are the only opposition. So, the group ethos is sexual aggression, and everyone goes along with it. It might even affect behavior, as boys or men who think that they are loners might behave in a way to conform to the group, not realizing that most of the group might actually be feeling the same way. A program, then, that encourages boys and men to speak up against toxic masculinity might have more support than many realize.

Professional sports leagues that actually care for the friends, relatives, and romantic partners of their employees will reduce the conditions that lead to the harms described throughout this book and prove that there are better ways to treat women, racial/ethnic minorities, members of the LGBTQ+ community, and others who are routinely subjected to what Anderson and White see as hostile forms of "out-grouping."[47] In a section of her book calling for the hiring of more female sports journalists, Jessica Luther states, "If we can one day get football and empathy in the same conversation on a regular basis, we will have a sure sign that we are doing something right."[48] The same can be said about hockey, but we have a long way to go. For example, ESPN reporter Emily Kaplan asked former Florida Panthers GM Dale Tallon if he believed the NHL should adopt a specific domestic violence policy and his answer was: "It's something I never even thought of …"[49]

As of May 2023, the NHL was the only one of four major North American professional sports leagues without a specific violence against women policy. Hopefully, one will soon be developed, but it should not only hold perpetrators accountable. When asked about the need for such an NHL policy, Terry O'Neill, executive director of the National Employment Lawyers Association, echoed our words and told Emily Kaplan: the league must pay equal attention to the needs of the women abused by NHL employees.[50] Note, too, that Jeff Benedict strikes a chord by stating that if professional sports leagues can create strict guidelines about substance abuse, they can certainly create rules that govern other off-the-field conduct such as woman abuse.[51]

Today more than ever, social justice advocates know that progressive people of all walks of life cannot eliminate one form of inequality, like patriarchy, by ignoring others. One type, in particular, that has historically plagued hockey and received scant attention is racism. Some critics, such as R. Renee Hess, founder and executive director of Black Girl Hockey Club, contend that white supremacy "runs rampant" throughout hockey, as it does in the NFL and other all-male elite sports leagues.[52] Recent evidence of this is San Jose Barracuda forward Krystof Hrabik's imitation of monkey movements in a January 12, 2022, taunt that targeted Bokondji Imama (who is Black) of the Tucson Roadrunners.[53] The AHL suspended Hrabik for thirty games, but many people maintain that not enough is being done to curtail racism in the hockey world.

Ponder these statistics. In the NHL's 105-year history, there has never been a Black general manager until the San Jose Sharks hired Mike Grier in July 2022, and there has only ever been one Black head coach. Dirk Graham stood behind the Chicago Blackhawks' bench for fifty-nine games in 1998–9 and was fired shortly thereafter. Also, only two Black assistant coaches have ever raised the Stanley Cup: Tampa Bay Lightning video coach Nigel Kirwan (2002 and 2020) and goalie coach Frantz Jean (2020). The on-ice situation isn't much better. Only eighteen Black players appeared in more than five games in 2019–20, and there were just a few more who identify as Asian (eight), Indigenous (six), Hispanic/Latino (four), or Arab/Middle Eastern (four).[54] As if you don't already know – hockey is the whitest of North American sports.

Homophobia is also rampant in the world of hockey. While the NHL is the lone major professional sports league in the world in which every franchise hosts a Pride Night, only one openly gay player (Luke Prokop) is currently under contract to an NHL team (the Nashville Predators) and no openly gay men are currently playing. Not surprisingly, other hockey leagues are homophobic. For example, a study of semi-professional male hockey players in Australia (none of whom identified as gay or bisexual) found that 68 percent reported teammates using homophobic slurs in the previous two weeks and 60 percent reported using such slurs themselves. The players surveyed are from eleven different countries, including 25.3 percent from Canada and the US.[55]

What is to be done? One obvious and often-stated answer to this question is education. Most people would agree, but they might also call for rule changes as well as the public shaming of sexist, racist, and homophobic hockey teams. There are other possible solutions too numerous to review in one short chapter. Regardless of what steps are taken, always heed these words of caution based on Kevin Young's many years of studying sports violence:

> Even when challenged, embarrassed and disciplined, we know from the past that sport changes slowly and that its powerful hegemonic structures display astounding elasticity that allows it to bounce back and enable [hurtful] practices ... to persist, even flourish. Examples are all around us, hiding in plain sight. If this were not true, how else could we explain what, on the one hand, is argued to be a transformed, more responsible and more modern world of ice hockey whose values and practices, on the other hand, don't seem to have changed much over the past 40 years? Despite some undeniable changes on the ice and in the commentary booth, the NHL remains a dangerous place to work.[56]

Changes, though, as said before in reference to Grambling's hiring of Art Briles (followed by his quick resignation), are happening, and there are signs of powerful gatekeepers skating on thin ice. Keep in mind that Sportsnet fired Don Cherry in 2019 for his on-air claim that recent immigrants to Canada ignore Remembrance Day. This was an especially important historic event because, since 1982, Cherry constantly used his role on the television program *Hockey Night in Canada* to, as sociologist Kristi Allain frames it, "valorize the experiences of white working-class men – men that he ... feels are at risk from new social forces (for example feminism, immigration, and the movement away from physical labor) that look to devalue their cultural positions."[57]

More transitions are coming. In the words of John Gerdy:

Sports' influence and standing in our culture will change. Nothing can grow unabated forever. Even a star burns brightest just before it explodes. The institution of sport in [North America] is like a house of cards, ever in danger of collapsing from its own weight. It is like a runaway freight train that will surely derail at the next great bend in the tracks. It has become grossly distorted from what it was meant to be and indeed from what we want and need it to be. How much more of organized sports' negative influence can we continue to absorb as a culture before we rise up and scream, "Enough!"[58]

Transforming the toxic professional hockey culture is not easy, and the problems we have outlined will not be eliminated by regulatory changes or education alone. A massive overhaul is necessary, and those seeking social justice in the NHL and other professional sports should be mindful of Audre Lorde's scolding of those who think that minor tweaks of the status quo will make a difference: "The master's tools will never dismantle the master's house."[59] Related to this point, and following Elliott Currie's critique of hurtful political developments that occurred during Donald Trump's term as president of the United States, those seeking change in profit-generating, all-male sports need to think *systemically* – that is, they need to view the racist, sexist, and homophobic practices that exist within these contexts as consequences of broader social forces rather than simply the injurious outcomes of decisions made by particularly insensitive individuals like Gary Bettman.[60]

One of the most important steps in solving the problems identified in this book is creating solidarity among various groups who want to make elite hockey leagues better places for people of all walks of life. Structured social inequality, whether it is in hockey or other institutions, thrives on fragmentation and divisions. Hence, it is vital to develop what Currie coins as "an alliance of broader constituencies."[61] This means working closely with women's groups, LGBTQ+ coalitions, communities of color, and other progressive organizations that want to be "hockey's agents of change."[62]

Academics, too, especially sociologists and criminologists, need to be part of this alliance. In the second edition of his book *Sport, Violence and Society*, Kevin Young reveals that while there is a voluminous social scientific literature on various types of violence and aggression, mainstream sociologists and criminologists have not been fleet of foot in dealing with violence in sport, and there are several reasons for this, including the fact that many, if not most, sociologists do not treat the study of sport as a worthy scholarly enterprise. Hockey violence expert Michael D. Smith frequently expressed his frustration with the marginalization of his work to Walter DeKeseredy and his other close colleagues.

Hockey is not completely outside the purview of academic inquiry. Since the 1990s, as uncovered by Julie Stevens and Andrew C. Holman, it has garnered more scholarly attention, but the bulk of the work done to date, as noted in their review of contemporary relevant literature, comes from

> historians and literary scholars whose interests focus on the lost or misunderstood meanings of signal past events in the sport. They have been concerned chiefly with the ways that hockey represents symbolically and figuratively – the identities of the communities that sponsor the game. The literature is rich and growing and intellectually profound ... The field of hockey studies would benefit from getting closer to the game, from making connections with those who experience the sport daily or weekly at rink side.[63]

The connections called for by Stevens and Holman are clear in this book. No one can accuse Stu Cowan of not spending enough time rink side. He lives and breathes hockey, and sociologists who study long-ignored problems in this sport can learn much from him, as well as from others whose lives are deeply entrenched in hockey arenas. Additionally, Walter DeKeseredy spent much time playing and watching hockey, and he learned many lessons about the damage done to both women and men by sexism, racism, homophobia, and hegemonic masculinity as a competitive hockey goaltender during his teenage years. His ice-level and rink-side experiences played a key role in his transition from a well-meaning man to a feminist man. Martin Schwartz made the same transition, but his changeover is grounded in life events that transpired in other social contexts.

Our personal and political journeys are not over, and we are prepared for the long haul. Regardless of how long it takes to get there, the hard, time-consuming journey toward a truly egalitarian hockey world is worth it, and we encourage all men to become our fellow travelers and allies with women in their struggle to end male violence. Also, as our friend and colleague Rus Funk points out, always keep in mind that working collaboratively with women is as much about "liberating men from the constraints of masculinity" as it is about helping to save women's lives and supporting their inherent right to live in peace.[64]

There are major disagreements among progressive men working to prevent violence against women, but they all agree with this observation: "Since it is men who are the offenders, it should be men – not women – who change their behavior."[65] This may sound like a rather simplistic point, but it is an essential one to repeatedly bring forward: male-on-female violence will not stop until men stop abusing women. What, then, can men do?

Perhaps first and foremost, following the advice of social scientists who specialize in the dark side of sport, male coaches and men in senior sports management and ownership positions need to publicly speak out against woman abuse, bullying, homophobia, racism, and sexual harassment, as well as strictly prohibit these and other hurtful behaviors. Second, as stated earlier in this chapter, men in these positions should have ongoing training in social justice issues and so should male athletes. Of special relevance here is what sports sociologist Michael Messner uncovered in his research:

> A few of the heterosexual men whom I interviewed objected to – and eventually rejected – the sexism and homophobia of the jock subculture. But they were rare exceptions to the rule. For young men who truly wanted athletic careers, rejecting one of the key bonds to the male peer group would have ruined their chances of success. So, whether they like the sexism and homophobia or not, most went along with these things. And when verbal sparring and bragging about sexual conquests led to actual behavior, peer group values encouraged these young men to treat females as objects of conquest. This sort of masculine peer group dynamic is at the heart of what feminists called the "rape culture."[66]

You are already aware of these problems, and we would be remiss if we didn't say that Messner's observation is now nearly thirty years old. But this is not to say that what he witnessed is non-existent today, especially given the breadth of the harms covered in previous chapters. All the same, there has been considerable growth in the number of male allies in the feminist movement to end woman abuse over the past thirty to forty years. More hope is provided by the availability of effective anti-sexist training that focuses on male athletes' roles as leaders instead of perpetrators. One that stands out for leading experts in the field is the Mentors in Violence Prevention (MVP) model. It was conceived and co-developed by Jackson Katz in 1993 at Northeastern University's Center for the Study of Sport in Society. Although MVP is primarily used in US colleges and high schools, it could be tailored to be applied in other countries including Canada.

MVP is a multi-ethnic, mixed-sex, and mixed-gender identity program, and it has made inroads into professional sports as part of the broader struggle to end violence against women. Deemed successful by many leading experts in the field, MVP, according to Jackson Katz,

> expands the number of men willing to take a stand to prevent sexual assault and relationship abuse. MVP has been especially effective at challenging and inspiring male leaders in the dominant and multiracial cultures of athletics, fraternities, and the military to partner with women to reduce gender violence.
>
> In highly interactive MVP workshops, everything is fair game for discussion: the difference between prevention and "risk reduction" strategies; the pleasures and perils of hook-up culture; victim-blaming; the role of alcohol in sexual assault; the role of porn culture in shaping social and sexual norms; the symbiotic relationship between sexism and heterosexism; the many intersections of race, sex and gender; harassment and abuse directed toward members of LGBTQ communities, and ways to prevent it; and the role of women as bystanders when women are the perpetrators of harassment and abuse.[67]

Some readers may say, "Well that sounds good, but can you be more specific about the lessons taught by the MVP program?" Previous work published by us, and others, lists many things men and boys are taught to do individually or collectively in dressing rooms, on the bench, and elsewhere, but it is beyond the reach of this book to repeat all these strategies. Below, however, are a few examples informed by strategies developed by Donald Sabo and Michael Messner:

- Resist locker-room sexism, homophobia, and racism. This not only includes refusing to laugh at hurtful jokes and challenging racist, sexist, and homophobic practices in the locker room, but also bullying tactics used against other men.
- Teach young athletes social justice values and practices. Parents and community members can help children to recognize harmful stereotypes and to question practices such as making fun of an athlete because he "throws like a girl."
- Fight sexism, racism, and homophobia in sports media. It is, for example, worthwhile to phone or email to object to images of female athletes as sex objects, or male athletes as dumb jocks.[68]

Some communities and teams may want to start their own men's organizations, and that is warmly welcomed. In doing so, avoid reinventing the wheel and search for organizations that are already doing social justice and anti-violence work and find out how they are doing it. Also, to avoid simply duplicating what others are doing, contact women's organizations to determine what type of new work is required. This helps avoid "burnout," which typically happens when people take on too much work, and it addresses the serious problem of time demands.

The insights of Indigenous men, men of color, lower-class men, men who are disabled, gay men, and men who represent other marginalized groups should be considered when developing a progressive men's group. There may be several other collectives that can provide what Australian feminist legal scholar Skye Saunders defines as male "champions of change" with new insights that can help them serve as role models for hockey players and other types of athletes.[69] The insights of women who belong to these groups should also be counted. Unfortunately, most progressive men's anti-violence groups mainly consist of those who are white, middle class, and heterosexual. At every training session, regardless of which philosophy informs it, coaches, owners, managers, athletic directors, and others involved in the educational process must be conscious of who is not there and that their perspectives are not being heard.[70]

Mahatma Gandhi is well known for leading the people of India to independence from British rule in 1947. He is also famous for making this statement: "You must be the change you want to see in the world." Similarly, US author and speaker John C. Maxwell wrote, "most people want to change the world to improve their lives, but the world they need to change first is the one inside themselves."[71] Feminist men agree. To join other male champions of change, men must first, as Jackson Katz states, "have the courage to look inward."[72] Agents of change in all-male athletics also need to stay involved in the ongoing process of self-examination, self-discovery, and transforming themselves, with the ultimate goal of shedding their toxic masculine baggage.

Much, if not most, of this book emphasizes that one of the most important determinants of male hockey players' violence against women is male peer support. Yet, as demonstrated by the MVP program and research done in countries outside of North America like Sweden and Australia, male peer groups can also be important means of violence prevention if their members are actively and effectively encouraged to challenge other men and disrupt toxic peer norms.[73] In fact, we are starting to see what Swedish researchers Kalle Berggren and Lucas Gottzén describe as a growth in *transformative responses* within all-male friendship networks. These are unambiguous emphases on ending male-on-female violence while simultaneously supporting an individual group member by encouraging him to seek help.[74]

Hundreds of suggestions could be added to the inventory of useful means of changing oneself and sexist men, but Ron Thorne-Finch makes the most important point of all:

> Men can no longer excuse themselves and pretend it does not happen. They are all responsible in some way – even only indirectly. Distancing themselves from the issue will not accomplish anything; only active involvement will bring about the needed changes. The time has come. The longer men procrastinate, the most they jeopardize the emotional and physical well-being of millions of women.[75]

In chapter 3, we introduced Lee Bowker's standards of gratification thesis, which asserts that fathers teach boys that women and children are subordinate to the man of the family. It is unclear exactly how many North American fathers (and fathers in other countries) do this, but we can safely conclude that well-meaning men outnumber abusive men. Nevertheless, how many of these men have meaningful discussions with their sons about woman abuse, racism, heteronormativity, and other major symptoms of inequality in our society? We assume the answer is "not many." This is worrisome and must change. Equally troubling are "angry hockey dads" like this one, described by Ed Condran:

> A few seasons ago, my older son's ice hockey team, comprised of 9- and 10-year-old children, only had one goalie on the roster. The concern was what would happen to the team if he were injured or was stricken with an illness. A quarter of the way through the season, a second netminder was added. The goalies split time during a game.
>
> The new goalie played the entirety of the next game and the other goalie's father lost it. After the contest, he grabbed his son's stick and marched out onto the ice. The referees witnessed the bad intent and grabbed the incensed parent, who promptly hurled the stick which struck another dad on the arm. The hothead then tried to pick a fight with the new goalie's dad, who (wisely) didn't take the bait. The out-of-control hockey father and his son left the organization the next day.[76]

Some readers may recall former professional hockey player Patrick O'Sullivan.[77] His father, nicknamed "Crazy John," took the label "angry hockey dad" to a new level. Below are atrocities O'Sullivan recalled in an interview with *Sportsnet*:

• Several times, when Patrick was eight years old, Crazy John served him a dinner of Spam and baked beans. When Patrick vomited up the meal, Crazy John forced him to eat it.

- There were nights when Patrick was locked outside until morning. He was forced to run, weighed down by his sweaty equipment, behind his dad's van after games. He was woken up in the night to do "pushups until my arms gave out ... situps until my stomach cramped."
- "When I came off the ice after practice or a game, I never knew exactly what was next, but I knew it was going to be bad."
- "I'd be looking at an hour or two or more of my father's conditioning program, running the steps in the arena stands like a hamster on a treadmill or chasing after the van for two or three miles. If he didn't think that was toughening me up, he'd slap me around. Every year he was ramping it up: slap in the face when I was eight; a slap with more force and a kick in the ass when I was nine; a punch when I was 10; a big right hook on my jaw and a kick in the gut or ribs until I was gasping when I was eleven, twelve and thirteen."
- Patrick was regularly beaten after cutting the lawn if his job was not up to Crazy John's impossible standards.[78]

Patrick O'Sullivan's experiences give a whole new meaning to Crosby, Stills, Nash, & Young's song "Teach Your Children." Obviously, then, on top of making it clear in more ways than one that behaviors like Crazy John's are unacceptable, the entire minor league hockey community needs to repeatedly send this message to all hockey dads:

What could possibly be worth doing so much emotional, physical and mental damage to your son or daughter? A college scholarship? A cup of coffee in the NHL? Hope you didn't say yes to either of these. No matter how far your player goes in hockey, a tortured childhood is never worth it. Youth hockey is supposed to be a fun, nurturing environment for a child, where they learn motor skills, teamwork, and a sense of camaraderie with their peers. They're supposed to be getting exercise and hanging out with their friends – not working towards an ultimate goal.[79]

All hockey dads and every type of father also need to hear this:

Clearly one of the most important roles a father – or a father figure – can play in his son's life is to teach by example. If men are always respectful toward women and never verbally or physically abuse them, their sons in all likelihood will learn to be similarly respectful. Nevertheless, every man who has a son should be constantly aware that how he treats women is not just between him and the women – there is a little set of eyes that is always watching him and picking up cues about how a man is supposed to act. If a man says demeaning and dismissive things about women, his son hears it. If he laughs at sexist jokes and makes objectifying comments about women's bodies as he watches TV, his son hears it.[80]

What happens when our sons get older? Adolescence is a time when young people's peers become progressively more important and when they distance themselves to some degree from their parents and/or receive more independence from them.[81] This is one of the key reasons why having patriarchal peers is a strong predictor of woman abuse and other types of deviant behavior. Yet, many young men still live at home and have close relationships with their parents who supply transformative responses. This was the case with Andreas, a twenty-two-year-old Swedish man interviewed by Berggren and Gottzén. He told his stepfather about his violence against his girlfriend, and his stepfather responded, "What the hell are you doing? If you love her as much as you say you do, then why do you behave like that?" Andreas's mother also provided transformative responses. During quarrels with his girlfriend, he would seek her advice, and she told him to try to calm down by counting to ten as a means of reducing relationship conflicts and coping with his anger. Andreas recalls:

I have never had any self-awareness to change myself except for this with my mom, because my mom had figured out that it was wrong, what I was doing ... This situation where I grabbed my girlfriend, then mom said: "Maybe it's best you start going to [anti-violence organization]. They can help you. [82]

The above example demonstrates that mothers, too, have a key role to play in the anti-violence and anti-sexist educational process. One interesting approach proved to be very successful for Walter DeKeseredy's friend Darlene Murphy. She had frank, ongoing discussions with her sons about sexuality and healthy intimate relationships (something fathers should do too). She emphasized that when a woman says "No," she means "No." She also stressed that sex is a powerful source of energy, but one that can be, and should be, controlled. Darlene is a highly skilled and well-respected mediator in Ontario's Durham Region,[83] and boys raised by strong, assertive women like her who have close relationships with their mothers during their teenage years grow up to be kind, successful men. They have learned to see the world through a progressive female gaze.

The time has come for more male teachers and school administrators to "step up to the plate" and demonstrate some progressive leadership by offering programs on social justice in their schools. They can also do several things on a personal level, such as talking to male students and male faculty in assemblies, classes, at sporting events, in faculty and staff training, and in private conversations. School staff should also employ these strategies informed by Ron Thorne-Finch and Robin Warshaw:[84]

- Confront students, teachers, and athletic staff who speak about racism, sexism, homophobia, or violent and dehumanizing pornography in an approving manner.
- Confront students and staff who perpetuate and legitimate rape myths.
- Take every opportunity to speak out against the injustices covered in this book.
- Use social media to encourage discussion about the harms examined in this book and how men and boys can work together to reduce them.

Much more can be done, and we know that the initiatives recommended here are simply not enough to reshape professional hockey and other all-male sports riddled with toxic masculinity, racism, and other highly injurious symptoms of living in an unjust society. Again, these proposals are intended to be meaningful additions to what has already been recommended in previous books on the dark side of hockey, such as Laura Robinson's *Crossing the Line* and Evan F. Moore and Jashvina Shah's *Game Misconduct*. We want to work together with people like them to help change the rules of the game not only because we love the sport, but also because, as Colin D. Howell, retired director of the Centre for the Study of Sport and Health at Saint Mary's University in Halifax, Nova Scotia, observes, attempts to fix hockey are strongly connected to the broader struggle for both social justice and the empowerment of those who are marginalized by society in general (e.g., members of the LGBTQ+ community).[85]

The problems with hockey that we explored are sustained, in part, by four widely held beliefs: (1) inevitability; (2) resignation; (3) intimidation; and (4) dismissal. The first belief is that hockey players' violence against women is "just one of those ugly, painful things" thrown at women. The second is that the NHL and other elite hockey leagues will never change for the better given the massive benefits they garner from the current status quo. The third is that elite hockey organizations are too powerful to overcome. The last belief sees sport as an inconsequential element of society.[86] These beliefs, however, are being contested, and those doing so are commended for their courage. Based on our own experiences and those of our friends and colleagues involved in the struggle for social justice, we believe that the prevention of violence against women in the world of hockey and elsewhere is both a profound act of bravery and a dramatic act of revolution. Fortunately, we are not alone. Echoing our conviction are the recent words of

National Post columnist Sabrina Maddeaux. In her commentary on the 2022 gang rape allegations against the 2003 and 2018 Canadian World Junior hockey teams, she rightfully observes that "hockey doesn't need an action plan as much as it needs a revolution. The era of boy-kings must end."[87]

Now that you have read this book, what do you make of the connection between professional hockey, rape culture, and violence against women? What is missing for you? What did you struggle with? What insights excited you? What information enriched your understanding of the sordid features of hockey? What part will you choose to play in the growing movement to curb the vast amount of pain and suffering identified in this book? It is always necessary to keep in mind this line of reasoning raised by Renate Klein: "Ending abuse is not only about specialized services delivered by trained professionals. It is perhaps more importantly about 'humdrum' cultural change in which everyone does things a little differently every day."[88] Also remember that *you* will be part of the evolving story of violence against women. This problem is part of *your* history, directly or indirectly. It will also affect *your* future. Please don't be a bystander.

Afterword

The NHL draft is a tedious event at the best of times. Unlike the slim, trim, high-definition approach taken by the NFL and the NBA, the NHL parades everyone from the assistant GM to the owner's ten-year-old grandson onto the stage before announcing the pick.

The 2021 draft, however, was worse than usual. It was conducted over Zoom because of the COVID-19 pandemic, so there was no hometown crowd to cheer the local pick or boo commissioner Gary Bettman. It also took place on July 23–4, a month late because the pandemic-wrecked season had run late, so hockey journalists were condemned to a tedious parade of gangly, pimply faced eighteen-year-olds in the company of their extended families, either jumping up to cheer when they were chosen or putting on a long face as their draft stock fell.

It was too much for this aging scribe. With the Canadiens drafting thirty-first out of thirty-two teams, I decided to hit the sack. At some point in the night, I woke and fumbled for my phone, curious to see whom the Canadiens had drafted.

I scrolled down and scrolled down – and there it was. Logan Mailloux, defenseman, the London Knights. Even in my befuddled state, it only took about thirty seconds to process the news. The fabled Montreal Canadiens, winners of twenty-four Stanley Cups and renowned as the class of the National Hockey League, had drafted a young man convicted of image-based sexual abuse in Sweden. An athlete whose own stated preference was that he not be drafted.

There was zero doubt – the Canadiens had just generated a firestorm. How could GM Marc Bergevin and assistant GM Trevor Timmins not have anticipated what was coming? How could they wreck the organization's reputation for the thirty-first pick in a relatively weak draft?

The answers are embedded in the hockey culture that is the subject of this book. It is a culture that treats women as disposable objects to be used and discarded, that has been excusing such behavior with the "boys will be boys" mantra for so long now that even highly paid and experienced executives such as Bergevin and Timmins can fail to see what a sportswriter who was barely half awake could process in half a minute: the shit was going to hit the fan.

At every step after that, Bergevin and Timmins made things worse. Clearly unprepared for the fallout, they left it to ham-fisted vice president of public relations Paul Wilson to handle the response, which consisted mostly of trying to manipulate reporters by favoring some while shutting out those who were too critical or too aggressive in their questioning. The approach backfired completely. When the team struggled terribly at the beginning of the following season, Bergevin, Timmins, and Wilson all lost their jobs as part of the ongoing fallout from the Mailloux draft.

How could the executives have made such decisions? I believe the answer is that it's because they operate in a hockey culture that, at heart, sees nothing wrong with what Mailloux did, nor with the Chicago Blackhawks purposely ignoring video coach Brad Aldrich sexually abusing prospect Kyle Beach, nor with the 2018 alleged gang sexual assault involving members of Canada's World Junior gold-medal team, in which an inebriated young woman had consensual sex with one junior player, who then invited several of his junior hockey buddies to join them in the hotel room. What happened that night led to a CAD$3.55-million lawsuit that was settled by Hockey Canada acting, for reasons that still remain unclear, on behalf of the perpetrators.

That led to a series of explosive revelations from investigative reporters Rick Westhead, Katie Strang of *The Athletic*, and others, culminating in the news that Hockey Canada had settled twenty-one sexual misconduct claims since 1989 for a total of CAD$8.9 million. That such an approach was obviously routine (and a blatant misuse of funds from sponsors, parents, and the government) gives some indication of the depth of the misogyny behind decisions taken by Hockey Canada's directors, the actions of some NHL executives, and the players themselves, who operate with the brazen entitlement of those who know they will never be held accountable.

As *Skating on Thin Ice* makes clear, the decision-makers and the actors in these dramas act as they do on the basis of *aggrieved entitlement*, the sense that well-to-do white males are somehow unfairly treated by society and are therefore entitled to act as they please and take what they want. The status quo, in other words.

It wouldn't be possible if the victims of rape and domestic abuse weren't ignored, belittled, abused, or subject to nightmarish interrogations at every turn. Investigators don't investigate, they cover up. As of this writing, it has been ten months since Westhead's shocking revelations about the payoff to hide the alleged gang rape in London, Ontario. During that time, the NHL has supposedly been investigating the very short list of current NHL players who were known to be (1) among the junior players at the hotel in London that night, and (2) who have not, like Cale Makar, Victor Mete, and several others, made it clear that they were not participants.

It has been two months since commissioner Gary Bettman declared that the investigation was "getting really close to the end" and still – no ending.

The investigators initially hired by Hockey Canada to look into the assault were no better, and police department investigators in London have left the impression that they couldn't find a squad car if it cruised into a swimming pool at a police picnic.

All this, of course, is deliberate. The point is not to find out exactly what happened but to stall, obfuscate, and buy time for the story to fade from the 24/7 news cycle.

The abuse is almost as old as the NHL itself. In 1918, more than 100 years ago, Canadiens defenseman Sprague Cleghorn was arrested for beating his wife with a crutch. (This begs the question: Would Cleghorn have been arrested had he *not* used a crutch?) The authors of *Skating on Thin Ice* make very clear that despite studies, newspaper reports, television exposés, and empty promises, nothing in hockey has changed since the late Blackhawks star Bobby Hull was treating his three wives (and who knows how many other women) as punching bags and getting away with it, simply because he was the biggest star in the game in the 1960s.

There are millions of fans who still believe that's as it should be. Boys will be boys, don't ya know? Like Stu Cowan, I received a raft of hate mail after criticizing the Canadiens for drafting Mailloux. Most was of the "your a fucken fagot" variety penned by anonymous, semiliterate trolls, but the most persistent of the abusers was a former professor of animal science at McGill University. In one lengthy rant after another, he accused me of ruining poor Mailloux's life. Of the fate of the young woman, whose life in a small Swedish town had been torched when she was only eighteen years old, the professor had nothing to say. He was too busy weeping over a young athlete who, after the usual slap on the wrist punishment, still stood to make millions of dollars playing a kid's game.

That's why this book is so very necessary. The toxic male culture in the world of hockey is real, and until the dark side of the sport is exposed and challenged, no one in its glare will be entirely safe. But it takes courage to write a book like this. As the authors make clear, *Skating on Thin Ice* is by no means the only book on the subject, but it goes well beyond a mere catalog of atrocities to point the way to a solution.

A prime example of movement in the right direction is the Respect and Consent Action Plan conceived in the wake of the Mailloux draft controversy by France Margaret Bélanger, president of sports and entertainment for Groupe CH, the Canadiens' parent company.

Much of it comes down to education. If boys as young as thirteen or fourteen have never been confronted with the idea that forced sexual encounters or battering women is not just wrong but criminally wrong, it's too much to expect that young athletes facing peer pressure to degrade women will depart from what they know. Mailloux himself has become one of the more articulate supporters of Bélanger's initiative.

It's still an uphill struggle – but if there's hope, it lies in everyone who loves the game supporting Bélanger's approach and moving in the opposite direction from the Chicago Blackhawks and their chairperson, Rocky Wirtz, by espousing change and following up on commitments. There is, of course, more to it than that, but I will leave it to authors who have spent their lives studying one of the more intractable problems in our society: the sexual, physical, and psychological abuse of women.

Jack Todd
Columnist and Author
Special to the *Montreal Gazette*

Acknowledgments

We must first thank our editor, Jodi Lewchuk, for encouraging us to take on this project. Jodi deeply cares about her authors, and we count ourselves lucky to have had the pleasure of working closely with her and hope to do so again one day. We would be remiss, too, if we didn't make explicit that her keen insight made this book far better than it otherwise would have been.

It is impossible to mention all those who inspired us to author this book, but special thanks to some whose support was especially important: Elliott Currie, Gail Dines, and Claire Renzetti. Other folks also deserve special recognition. MeKaila Blackwell, Mackenzie Freeman, and Danielle Stoneberg spent many hours gathering materials we were not aware of, and they are among the best research assistants we have ever worked with. Two colleagues who do much for West Virginia's Department of Sociology and Anthropology – Barbara Reiprich and Pim Trommelen – also helped us gather the literature cited in this book and facilitated the book's production in other ways too numerous to mention here.

We wrote much of this book in isolation due to the COVID-19 pandemic, but we were very lucky to be able to regularly communicate with the following amazing folks via our smartphones, email, and Zoom – both to get their thoughts on issues covered here and to learn about events and studies with which we were unfamiliar: Michael Braswell; Henry Brownstein; Fran Buntman; Gail Caputo; Dennis Cloud; Joseph Donnermeyer; David Friedrichs; Rosemary Gido; Carol Gregory; Rebecca Hayes; Brian Hudzick; Hiromi Ishizawa; Gary Keveles; Peter Kraska; Emily Lenning; Alison Marganski; Bill Miller; Warren Morgan; Steven Muzzatti; James Nolan; Leah C. Oldham; Barbara Owen; Adam Pritchard; James Ptacek; Brandie Pugh; Jill Rosenbaum; Robert Savelle; Donna Selman; Jim Taylor; Jack Todd; Ron Weitzer; and Joshua Woods. Because some of these people disagree with each other, we assume full responsibility for the material presented in this book.

Skating on Thin Ice could not have been completed without the ongoing support of our loved ones. Walter DeKeseredy is deeply appreciative of Pat and Andrea DeKeseredy, Daniel O'Brien, his grandson Oliver O'Brien, and his five fur children, Bennie, Captain, George, Higgins, and Jinksie. Martin Schwartz would particularly like to reaffirm the importance in his life of his long-suffering partner, Carol Blum, and his more recently suffering sister-in-law, Elizabeth Blum.

Stu Cowan would like to thank the late, great Red Fisher for his willingness to take a chance on a young kid when he was sports editor at the *Montreal Gazette*, hiring Stu to edit the scoreboard statistics page and giving him a start in the sports journalism business. Fisher and Michael Farber, the *Gazette* sports columnist at the time who would later go on to write for *Sports Illustrated*, would become important mentors during Stu's career. Stu would also like to thank his wife, Sylvia Haley, for her constant support and understanding when it comes to his crazy work schedule, as well as his two children, Haley-May and Scott.

Notes

1. More Than a Few Bad Men

1 Laura Robinson, *Crossing the Line: Violence and Sexual Assault in Canada's National Sport* (Toronto: McClelland & Stewart, 1998), 64.

2 Michael McKinley, "Montreal Canadiens; A Religion," in *Encyclopedia of French Cultural Heritage in North America*, accessed October 8, 2021, http://www.ameriquefrancaise.org/en/article-335/Montreal_Canadiens;_a_Religion.html.

3 Brendan Kelly, "What the Puck: Carey Price's Health Is the Most Important Thing," *Montreal Gazette*, October 7, 2021, https://montrealgazette.com/sports/hockey/nhl/hockey-inside-out/what-the-puck-carey-prices-health-is-the-most-important-thing.

4 Carey Price (@cp0031), Instagram photo, November 9, 2021, https://www.instagram.com/p/CWEhywHvjmx.

5 The term *hegemonic masculinity* was coined by R.W. Connell in his book *Masculinities* (Berkeley: University of California Press, 1995).

6 Michael D. Smith, *Violence and Sport* (Toronto: Butterworths, 1983), 50.

7 Lucy Crossley, "LSE Rugby Club Banned after 'Misogynistic, Sexist and Homophobic' Behaviour," *Mail Online*, October 9, 2014, https://www.dailymail.co.uk/sport/rugbyunion/article-2786833/LSE-Rugby-Club-banned-misogynistic-sexist-homophobic-behaviour.html.

8 The OHL, WHL, and QMJH operate under the umbrella of the CHL.

9 Ken Campbell, "More Explosive and Shocking Allegations against Junior Hockey in Newly Filed Lawsuit," *Hockey News*, June 18, 2020,

https://www.si.com/hockey/news/more-explosive-and-shocking
-allegations-against-junior-hockey-in-newly-filed-lawsuit.

10 Todd Crosset, "Athletic Affiliation and Violence against Women: Toward
    a Structural Prevention Program," in *Masculinities, Gender Relations, and
    Sport*, ed. Jim McKay, Michael A. Messner, and Don Sabo (Thousand
    Oaks, CA: Sage Publications, 2000), 147–61.

11 Michael A. Messner, "Still a Man's World? Studying Masculinities and
    Sport," in *Handbook of Studies on Men and Masculinities*, ed. Michael
    Kimmel, Jeff Hearn, and R.W. Connell (Thousand Oaks, CA: Sage
    Publications, 2005), 317.

12 See, for example, Alberto Godenzi, Martin D. Schwartz, and Walter S.
    DeKeseredy, "Toward a Gendered Social Bond/Male Peer Support The-
    ory of University Woman Abuse," *Critical Criminology* 10, no. 1 (January
    2001): 1–16, https://doi.org/10.1023/A:1013105118592.

13 Andrew Beaton, "Jon Gruden Used Racial Trope to Describe NFLPA
    Chief DeMaurice Smith in 2011 Email," *Wall Street Journal*, October 8,
    2021, https://www.wsj.com/articles/jon-gruden-email-demaurice
    -smith-11633721045.

14 Quoted in Barry Werner, "NFL Investigates Raiders Head Coach
    Jon Gruden for Racist Comment about DeMaurice Smith in 2011,"
    Touchdown Wire, October 8, 2021, https://touchdownwire.usatoday
    .com/2021/10/08/nfl-investigates-raiders-head-coach-jon-gruden-for
    -racist-comment-about-demaurice-smith-in-2011.

15 Nancy Armour, "Opinion: Getting Rid of Jon Gruden Was Easy: How Will
    NFL Root Out Other Bigots?," *USA Today*, last modified October 12, 2021,
    https://www.usatoday.com/story/sports/columnist/nancy-armour
    /2021/10/11/jon-gruden-raiders-coach-out-leaving-more-questions-nfl
    -owners/6098711001.

16 House Committee on Oversight and Reform, "Ahead of Hearing, Over-
    sight Committee Releases New Evidence of Dan Snyder's Role in Cre-
    ating a Hostile Workplace and His Efforts to Undermine Investigation,"
    news release, June 22, 2022, https://oversightdemocrats.house.gov
    /news/press-releases/ahead-of-hearing-oversight-committee-releases
    -new-evidence-of-dan-snyder-s-role.

17 Jenny Vrentas, "Panel Finds Daniel Snyder Interfered with Sexual Har-
    assment Investigation," *New York Times*, June 22, 2022, https://www
    .nytimes.com/2022/06/22/sports/football/dan-snyder-harassment
    -news-congress.html.

18 Quoted in Ken Belson and Katherine Rosman, "Jon Gruden Resigns
    after Homophobic and Misogynistic Emails," *New York Times*, last mod-
    ified October 28, 2021, https://www.nytimes.com/2021/10/11/sports
    /football/what-did-jon-gruden-say.html.

19 As of February 2022, more than two-thirds of NFL players were Black,
    but there was only one Black head coach. For more information on the
    NFL's poor diversity record, see Nancy Armour, "Another Black Coach
    Is Fired, and the NFL Goes On Acting Like It's Inclusive," *USA Today*,

January 13, 2022, https://www.usatoday.com/story/sports/columnist
/nancy-armour/2022/01/13/texans-fired-david-culley-and-nfl-goes
-acting-like-its-inclusive/6518405001.

20 For more detailed information on the extent, distribution, causes, and
consequences of image-based sexual abuse, see Nicola Henry, Clare
McGlynn, Asher Flynn, Kelly Johnson, Anastasia Powell, and Andrea J.
Scott, *Image-Based Sexual Abuse: A Study on the Causes and Consequences
of Non-consensual Nude or Sexual Imagery* (London: Routledge, 2021).

21 Readers are encouraged to watch Nancy Schwartzman's film *Roll Red
Roll* (2018), which vividly documents this case.

22 Amy Davidson Sorkin, "Life after Steubenville," *The New Yorker*,
March 18, 2013, https://www.newyorker.com/news/amy-davidson
/life-after-steubenville.

23 Quoted in Steven Psihogios, "Some NHL Teams Reportedly Won't
Draft Prospect after 'Offensive Photography' Charge," *Yahoo! Sports*,
July 16, 2021, https://news.yahoo.com/some-nhl-teams-reportedly
-wont-draft-prospect-after-offensive-photography-charge-025707263
.html.

24 Montreal Canadiens, "Statement on the Selection of Logan Mailloux,"
news release, July 23, 2021, https://www.nhl.com/canadiens/news
/statement-on-the-selection-of-logan-mailloux/c-325764184.

25 Quoted in Stu Cowan, "Logan Mailloux a Polarizing Pick by Canadiens in First Round of Draft," *Montreal Gazette*, July 24, 2021, https://
montrealgazette.com/sports/hockey/nhl/hockey-inside-out
/canadiens-select-logan-mailloux-with-first-round-pick-at-nhl-draft.

26 Katie Strang and Corey Pronman, "Woman Victimized by NHL Prospect
in Sweden: 'All I Wanted Was a Heartfelt Apology,'" *The Athletic*, July 20,
2021, https://theathletic.com/2716093/2021/07/20/woman-victimized
-by-nhl-prospect-in-sweden-all-i-wanted-was-a-heartfelt-apology.

27 Quoted in "OHL Set to Reinstate Canadiens First-Round Pick Logan
Mailloux," *Sportsnet*, December 29, 2021, https://www.sportsnet.ca
/juniors/article/ohl-set-reinstate-canadiens-first-round-pick-logan
-mailloux-saturday.

28 Susan Herman, "Is Restorative Justice Possible without a Parallel System for Victims?," in *Critical Issues in Restorative Justice*, ed. Howard
Zehr and Barb Toews (Monsey, NY: Criminal Justice Press, 2004), 75–83.

29 Quoted in Tim Daniels, "Marc Bergevin Says He Wasn't Aware of Brad
Aldrich Allegations While with Blackhawks," *Bleacher Report*, June 27,
2021, https://bleacherreport.com/articles/10006587-marc-bergevin
-says-he-wasnt-aware-of-brad-aldrich-allegations-while-with-blackhawks.

30 Reid J. Schar, *Report to the Chicago Blackhawks Hockey Team regarding the
Organization's Response to Allegations of Sexual Misconduct by a Former
Coach* (Chicago: Jenner & Block, 2021), https://www.jenner.com/a/web
/8kmbgFUEYWcNnvzFTa5h8H/4HRMZQ/Report%2520to%2520the%
2520Chicago%2520Blackhawks%2520Hockey%2520Team%2520-%2520
October%25202021.pdf.

31 NHL Public Relations, "Chicago Blackhawks Fined $2 Million for Inadequate Procedures and Mishandling of the 2010 Matter Related to the Conducts of Former Video Coach Brad Aldrich," news release, October 26, 2021, https://media.nhl.com/public/news/15337.

32 TSN, "Kyle Beach Speaks with Rick Westhead about His Lawsuit against the Chicago Blackhawks Organization," YouTube, October 27, 2021, 26:55, https://www.youtube.com/watch?v=OBpRpaNR2tg.

33 Brendan Kelly, "What the Puck: Kudos to Molson for Cleaning Canadiens' House," Montreal Gazette, November 29, 2021, https://montrealgazette.com/sports/hockey/nhl/hockey-inside-out/what-the-puck-kudos-to-molson-for-cleaning-canadiens-house.

34 NHL Public Relations, "Statement from NHL Commissioner on Resignation of Joel Quenneville," news release, October 28, 2021, https://www.nhl.com/news/commissioner-gary-bettman-statement-joel-quenneville-resignation/c-327342922.

35 Chris Bumbaca, "Blackhawks Captain Jonathan Toews Says Executives Out in Wake of Investigation Are 'Good People,'" USA Today, October 28, 2021, https://www.usatoday.com/story/sports/nhl/blackhawks/2021/10/27/jonathan-toews-comments-kyle-beach-investigation-chicago-blackhawks/8578775002.

36 Nancy Armour, "Opinion: Blackhawks and NHL Continue to Fail Sexual Abuse Victim, Just as They Did in 2010," USA Today, October 28, 2021, https://www.usatoday.com/story/sports/columnist/nancy-armour/2021/10/28/kyle-beach-blackhawks-nhl-continue-fail-sexual-abuse-victim/8580321002.

37 Chris Johnston, "The NHL's Toxic Culture Is No Longer a Secret: The Hotline Is Helping," Toronto Star, November 10, 2021, https://www.thestar.com/sports/hockey/opinion/2021/11/10/the-nhls-toxic-culture-is-no-longer-a-secret-the-hotline-is-helping.html.

38 Deloitte is a large company that provides audit, consulting, financial advisory, risk advisory, tax, and legal services. It is the third largest privately owned company in the US. For more information on Deloitte, see Deloitte, "About Deloitte," accessed November 11, 2021, https://www2.deloitte.com/us/en/pages/about-deloitte/articles/about-deloitte.html.

39 Johnston, "NHL's Toxic Culture."

40 Robinson, Crossing the Line, 231.

41 Rachel Doerrie, "The Logan Mailloux Draft Pick Confirms Worst Fears of Who Is and Is Not Welcome in the NHL," EP Rinkside, July 29, 2021, https://eprinkside.com/2021/07/29/logan-mailloux-column.

42 Gianluca Agostinelli, "The Montreal Canadiens Have Legitimized Rape Culture by Drafting Logan Mailloux," The Conversation, July 26, 2021, https://theconversation.com/the-montreal-canadiens-have-legitimized-rape-culture-by-drafting-logan-mailloux-165047.

43 The Canadian Press, "Two Quebec Major Junior Hockey Players Formally Charged with Sexual Assault," CTV News, October 5, 2021,

https://montreal.ctvnews.ca/two-quebec-major-junior-hockey-players
-formally-charged-with-sexual-assault-1.5611774.

44 Sabrina Maddeaux, "Hockey Canada Encouraged a Celebrity Culture
That Made Players Feel Untouchable," *National Post*, July 29, 2022,
https://nationalpost.com/opinion/sabrina-maddeaux-hockey-canada
-encouraged-a-celebrity-culture-that-made-players-feel-untouchable.

45 Kevin McGran and Kieran Leavitt, "TSN Reports on Shocking Video
from 2003 as Hockey Canada Confirms Two Police Investigations of
Sex-Assault Claims," *Toronto Star*, July 22, 2022, https://www.thestar
.com/sports/hockey/2022/07/22/hockey-canada-says-2003-world
-junior-team-also-accused-of-group-sexual-assault.html.

46 Joe Friesen, Colin Freeze, and Robyn Doolittle, "Canadian World Junior
Player Asked Woman Whether She Had Gone to Police after Alleged Sexual Assault," *Globe and Mail*, July 19, 2022, https://www.theglobeandmail
.com/canada/article-hockey-canada-sexual-assault-lawsuit-police.

47 Recent research supporting this claim is provided by Martin D. Schwartz,
"Masculinities, Sport, and Violence against Women: The Contribution
of Male Peer Support Theory," *Violence against Women* 27, no. 5 (April
2021): 688–707, https://doi.org/10.1177/1077801220958493.

48 Evan F. Moore and Jashvina Shah, *Game Misconduct: Hockey's Toxic
Culture and How to Fix It* (Chicago: Triumph Books, 2021), 1.

49 Jashvina Shah, "Hockey Has Never Cared about Survivors, and It's
Getting Worse," *Russian Machine Never Breaks* (blog), July 27, 2021,
https://russianmachineneverbreaks.com/2021/07/27/jashvina-shah
-hockey-care-about-survivors.

50 Kieran Leavitt, "21 Victims. $8.9M in Compensation. Hockey Canada
Reveals Its History of Settling Sexual Misconduct Claims," *Toronto Star*,
July 27, 2022, https://www.thestar.com/news/canada/2022/07/27
/hockey-canada-scandal-president-former-ceo-to-appear-before
-committee.html.

51 Jack Todd, "Change at Hockey Canada Needs to Come at the Top,"
Montreal Gazette, July 25, 2022, https://montrealgazette.com
/sports/hockey/nhl/hockey-inside-out/jack-todd-change-at-hockey
-canada-needs-to-come-at-the-top.

52 See Michael Kimmel, *Angry White Men: American Masculinity at the End
of an Era* (New York: Nation Books, 2017), 18; emphasis in original.

53 Jackson Katz, *Man Enough? Donald Trump, Hillary Clinton, and the
Politics of Presidential Masculinity* (Northampton, MA: Interlink Books,
2016), ix.

54 Mike Freeman, "Jon Gruden's Emails Not Just an NFL Problem. They're
Symbolic of Societal White Grievance," *USA Today*, October 12, 2021,
https://www.usatoday.com/story/sports/columnist/mike-freeman
/2021/10/12/jon-gruden-raiders-emails-nfl-issue-symbolic-white
-grievance/6103857001.

55 "'When Does It Stop?' P.K. Subban Asks after Black Teen Reports
Abuse at Hockey Tournament," *Montreal Gazette*, December 2, 2021,

https://montrealgazette.com/sports/hockey/when-does-it-stop-p-k -subban-asks-after-black-teen-reports-abuse-at-hockey-tournament.

56 Quoted in Luke Fox, "Simmonds Rails against Racism, Says Denyskin Should Be 'Banned for Life,'" *Sportsnet*, September 30, 2021, https:// www.sportsnet.ca/nhl/article/simmonds-rails-racism-says-denyskin -banned-life.

57 Quoted in Fox, "Simmonds Rails against Racism."

58 Quoted in Hemal Jhaveri, "The Disorderly Conduct Charges against Auston Matthews Are No Laughing Matter," *USA Today*, September 25, 2019, https://ftw.usatoday.com/2019/09/maple-leafs-auston-matthews -disorderly-conduct-charges-are-no-laughing.

59 See, for example, F. Vera-Gray, *The Right Amount of Panic: How Women Trade Freedom for Safety* (Bristol: Policy Press, 2018).

60 Liz Kelly and Jill Radford, "The Problem of Men: Feminist Perspectives on Sexual Violence," in *Law, Order and the Authoritarian State*, ed. Phil Scranton (Philadelphia: Open University Press, 1987), 242.

61 "Leafs' Matthews Addresses Disorderly Conduct Charges," *Reuters*, September 25, 2019, https://www.reuters.com/article/us-icehockey-nhl -tor-matthews/leafs-matthews-addresses-disorderly-conduct-charges -idUSKBN1WA2ZP.

62 Hockey Hall of Fame, "Lady Byng Memorial Trophy," accessed April 17, 2023, https://www.hhof.com/thecollection/ladybyngmemorialtrophy .html.

63 Chris Baud, "NHL Announces Thoughtless Jerk Auston Matthews as Lady Byng Trophy Finalist," *Deadspin* (blog), July 16, 2020, https:// deadspin.com/nhl-announces-thoughtless-douchebag-auston-matthews -as-1844409576.

64 Baud, "NHL Announces."

65 Abbey Mastracco, "Women in Sports Experience Widespread Harassment – How Can That Change?," *Bleacher Report*, January 22, 2021, https://bleacherreport.com/articles/2927699-women-in-sports -experience-widespread-harassment-how-can-that-change.

66 Velgey, "Under the Surface: Sexual Harassment and Assault in Sports," *SB Nation* (blog), December 5, 2017, https://www.hockeywilderness .com/2017/12/5/16732830/under-the-surface-sexual-harassment-and -assault-in-sports-weinstein-and-the-nhl.

67 Jackson Katz, *The Macho Paradox: Why Some Men Hurt Women and How All Men Can Help* (Naperville, IL: Sourcebooks), 141.

68 James E. Sutton, "Athlete Multiple Perpetrator Rape (MPR) as Interactional and Organizational Deviance: Heuristic Insights from a Multilevel Framework," *Violence against Women* 28, no. 14 (November 2022): 3609, https://doi.org/10.1177/10778012211070312.

69 Pat Hickey, "NHL Needs to Reinforce Fighting Deterrents," *Montreal Gazette*, last modified January 16, 2022, https://montrealgazette.com /sports/hockey/nhl/hockey-inside-out/hickey-on-hockey-nhl-needs-to -reinforce-fighting-deterrents.

70   Katz, *Macho Paradox*, 143.
71   A.J. Perez, "Sharks Star Evander Kane Facing a New Set of Allegations," *Front Office Sports*, September 22, 2021, https://frontofficesports.com /sharks-star-evander-kane-facing-a-new-set-of-allegations.
72   Art Jahnke, "Hockey Task Force Finds Oversight Deficiencies, Culture of Entitlement," *BU Today*, September 5, 2012, https://www.bu.edu /articles/2012/hockey-task-force-finds-oversight-deficiencies-culture -of-entitlement.
73   Mary Carmichael, "Sex, Drinking Detailed in Report on BU Hockey," *Boston Globe*, September 7, 2012, https://www.bostonglobe.com /metro/2012/09/06/salacious-details-emerge-from-hockey -subcommittee-reports/E7I6SS0sBHrNKeXVzY2b9N/story.html.
74   Reading Group Center, "*Our Guys* Reading Group Guide," Knopf Doubleday Publishing Group, accessed October 19, 2021, http:// knopfdoubleday.com/2010/01/09/our-guys-reading-group-guide.
75   Bernard Lefkowitz, *Our Guys* (New York: Vintage Books, 1997), 5–6.
76   Lefkowitz, *Our Guys*, 487.
77   Lefkowitz, *Our Guys*, 486.
78   Associated Press, "Roy Cleared in Domestic Violence Case," *New Haven Register*, February 1, 2001, https://www.nhregister.com/news/article /Roy-cleared-in-domestic-violence-case-11712395.php.
79   Lefkowitz, *Our Guys*, 167.
80   Ken Maguire, "Four Braintree High Students Face Rape Charges," *Southcoast Today*, last modified January 12, 2011, https://www .southcoasttoday.com/article/20020203/News/302039969.
81   National Republican Congressional Committee (NRCC), "Slaps on the Wrist for Sex Offenders Who 'Destroyed Innocence and Trust,'" NRCC, October 23, 2010, https://www.nrcc.org/2010/10/23/slaps-on-the -wrist-for-sex-offenders-who-destroyed-innocence-and-trust.
82   Those who attend middle schools (typically grades 6–8) are preadolescents and young adolescents.
83   Kathleen C. Basile, Dorothy L. Espelage, Katherine M. Ingram, Thomas R. Simon, and Faith L. Berrier, "The Role of Middle School Sports Involvement in Understanding High School Sexual Violence Perpetration," *Journal of Interpersonal Violence* 37, no. 3/4 (February 2022): 1514–39, https://doi.org/10.1177/0886260520922357.
84   See Futures without Violence, "Coaching Boys into Men," accessed October 25, 2021, https://www.futureswithoutviolence.org/engaging -men/coaching-boys-into-men.
85   Gary Alan Fine, *With the Boys: Little League Baseball and Preadolescent Culture* (Chicago: University of Chicago Press, 1987).
86   In Canada, minor hockey is amateur hockey played by people who are twenty years old and younger. Generally, players are categorized into these playing levels according to age: Novice (ages seven and eight), Atom (ages nine and ten), Bantam (ages thirteen and fourteen), Midget (ages fifteen to seventeen), and Junior/Juvenile (ages eighteen and

nineteen). There is also non-competitive and competitive minor hockey. For more information, see "Levels of Minor (Youth) Hockey," The Hockey Fanatic, accessed October 26, 2021, https://www.thehockeyfanatic.com /hockey-parents/levels-of-minor-hockey.

87 Robinson, *Crossing the Line*, 13–14.

88 Schwartz, "Masculinities."

89 Walter S. DeKeseredy, "Woman Abuse in Dating Relationships: The Relevance of Social Support Theory," *Journal of Family Violence* 3, no. 1 (1988): 1–13, https://doi.org/10.1007/BF00994662.

90 For more detailed information on male peer support research, see Walter S. DeKeseredy and Martin D. Schwartz, *Male Peer Support and Violence against Women: The History and Verification of a Theory* (Boston: Northeastern University Press, 2013).

91 Lee H. Bowker, *Beating Wife-Beating* (Lexington, MA: Lexington Books, 1983), 135–6.

92 See Walter S. DeKeseredy, *Understanding the Harms of Pornography: The Contributions of Social Scientific Knowledge* (Sterling, MA: Culture Reframed, 2020), https://www.culturereframed.org/wp-content/uploads /2020/02/CR_Harms_of_Porn_Report_2020.pdf.

93 This study was commissioned by the Lauren's Kids Foundation, a South Florida organization that educates adults and children about sexual abuse prevention. For more information on this survey, see Lauren Book, "College Athletes Report High Incidence of Sexual Abuse by Campus Authority Figures, Survey Finds," Lauren's Kids, August 31, 2021, https://laurenskids.org/college-athletes-report-high-incidence -of-sexual-abuse-by-campus-authority-figures-survey-finds.

94 Brian L. Withrow, *Research Methods in Criminal Justice* (London: Routledge, 2104), 393.

95 Quoted in "The Sheldon Kennedy/Graham James Case: Sexual Abuse in Canadian Junior Hockey," Silent Edge, accessed October 27, 2021, https://www.silent-edge.org/kennedy.html.

96 Quoted in Bruce Arthur, "Kyle Beach, like Sheldon Kennedy before Him, Fights Back against 'Culture of Silence' in Hockey," *Toronto Star*, last modified October 28, 2021, https://www.thestar.com/sports /hockey/opinion/2021/10/27/kyle-beach-like-sheldon-kennedy-before -him-fights-back-against-culture-of-silence-in-hockey.html.

97 Jack Todd, "Blackhawks Dynasty Is Forever Tainted by Mishandling of Kyle Beach's Case," *Montreal Gazette*, October 31, 2021, https:// montrealgazette.com/sports/hockey/nhl/hockey-inside-out/jack-todd -blackhawks-dynasty-is-forever-tainted-by-mishandling-of-kyle-beachs -case.

98 Jeff Benedict, *Public Heroes, Private Felons: Athletes and Crimes* (Boston: Northeastern University Press, 1997).

99 Now deleted comment on Stu Cowan, "Canadiens Drafting Mailloux 'Reflects Deep Insensitivity': Expert," *Montreal Gazette*, July 27, 2021,

https://montrealgazette.com/sports/hockey/nhl/hockey-inside
-out/cowan-canadiens-drafting-mailloux-reflects-deep-insensitivity
-expert.
100 Dick Labete, September 18, 2021, comment on Brendan Kelly, "What
the Puck: Habs' Decision to Draft Logan Mailloux Remains Baffling,"
Montreal Gazette, September 17, 2021, https://montrealgazette.com
/sports/hockey/nhl/hockey-inside-out/what-the-puck-still-no-real
-explanation-why-the-habs-picked-mailloux.
101 Stu estimates that there were over 100 negative online comments on his
coverage of Logan Mailloux.
102 See Susan Faludi, *Backlash: The Undeclared War against American Women*
(New York: Crown Publishers, 1991), xix.
103 See Michael Flood, Molly Dragiewicz, and Bob Pease, "Resistance and
Backlash to Gender Equality," *Australian Journal of Social Issues* 56, no. 3
(2020): 393–408, https://doi.org/10.1002/ajs4.137.
104 See Walter S. DeKeseredy, "Defenders of Freedom or Perpetrators and
Facilitators of Crimes? Beyond Progressive Retreatism in the Trump
Era," *Victims & Offenders* 14, no. 8 (2019): 925–39, https://doi.org/10.1080
/15564886.2019.1671282.
105 Mark Potok and Evelyn Schlatter, "Men's Rights Movement Spreads
False Claims about Women," *Intelligence Report* 145 (March 2012),
https://www.splcenter.org/fighting-hate/intelligence-report/2012
/men's-rights-movement-spreads-false-claims-about-women.
106 philliskessel13 and Achariya, "Toxic Masculinity, Domestic Violence,
and Hockey: All Signs Are Indicating That Canadiens Forward Alex
Galchenyuk Has Been Abused by His Partner. Why Is This Not Being
Taken Seriously?," *SB Nation* (blog), January 13, 2016, https://www
.pensionplanpuppets.com/2016/1/13/10758630/toxic-masculinity
-domestic-violence-and-hockey.
107 "Galchnyuk Mocked for Roll in Domestic Violence Case," *Duquesne
Duke*, January 28, 2016, http://www.duqsm.com/galchenyuk-mocked
-for-roll-in-domestic-violence-case.
108 Allan Muir, "Patrick Kane Remains NHL's Most Polarizing Figure,"
Sports Illustrated, March 10, 2016, https://www.si.com/nhl/2016/03/10
/patrick-kane-sex-assault-case-reaction-sports-illustrated-story.
109 Will Maule, "Youth Pastor Arrested for 'Sexual Battery' after Slapping
News Reporter in the Rear," *Christian Headlines*, December 16, 2019,
https://www.christianheadlines.com/contributors/will-maule/youth
-pastor-arrested-for-sexual-battery-after-slapping-news-reporter-in-the
-rear.html.
110 Erin Ash, Jimmy Sanderson, Chenjerai Kumanyika, and Kelly
Gramlich, "'Just Goes to Show How These Hoes Try to Tear Me
Down': Investigating Twitter and Cultural Conversations on Athletic
Ability, Race, and Sexual Assault," *Journal of Sports Media* 12, no. 1
(Spring 2017): 65–87, https://doi.org/10.1353/jsm.2017.0003.

111 See Martin D. Schwartz and Walter S. DeKeseredy, *Sexual Assault on the College Campus: The Role of Male Peer Support* (Thousand Oaks, CA: Sage Publications, 1997).

112 See Henry et al., *Image-Based Sexual Abuse*.

113 For more feminist criticisms of this movement, see Bianca Fileborn and Rachel Loney-Howes, eds., *#MeToo and the Politics of Social Change* (New York: Palgrave Macmillan, 2019).

114 Tarana Burke, "I Founded 'Me Too' in 2006. The Morning It Went Viral Was a Nightmare," *Time*, September 14, 2021, https://time.com/6097392 /tarana-burke-me-too-unbound-excerpt.

115 Many victim advocates also contend that the #MeToo moment in the NHL has passed. See, for example, Kristin Raworth, "Has the #MeToo Moment Passed?," *The Line* (blog), November 4, 2021, https://theline .substack.com/p/kristin-raworth-has-the-metoo-moment.

116 Neil Gilbert, "The Phantom Epidemic of Sexual Assault," *Public Interest* 103 (Spring 1991): 54–65.

117 Secoya Freedman, August 29, 2021, comment on Brendan Kelly, "What the Puck: Druoin, Mailloux Put Focus on Habs' Mental-Health Support," *Montreal Gazette*, August 24, 2021, https://montrealgazette .com/sports/hockey/nhl/hockey-inside-out/what-the-puck-drouin -mailloux-put-focus-habs-mental-health-support.

118 Varda Burstyn, *The Rites of Men: Manhood, Politics, and the Culture of Sport* (Toronto: University of Toronto Press, 2000), 192.

119 For the since deleted exchange, see Bryan Bicknell, "Former London, Ont. Hockey Star and NHL Player Brandon Prust in Trouble over 'Force You into the Sex Trade' Tweet," *CTV News*, August 25, 2021, https:// www.ctvnews.ca/mobile/sports/former-london-ont-hockey-star -and-nhl-player-brandon-prust-in-trouble-over-force-you-into-the-sex -trade-tweet-1.5561790.

120 Lee H. Bowker, "Introduction," in *Masculinities and Violence*, ed. Lee H. Bowker (Thousand Oaks, CA: Sage Publications, 1988), xi–xviii.

2. In Their Own Words: Giving Voice to Survivors of Professional Hockey Violence and Sexism

1 Quoted in Evan F. Moore and Jashvina Shah, *Game Misconduct: Hockey's Toxic Culture and How to Fix It* (Chicago: Triumph Books, 2021), 81.

2 Gary Ronberg, *The Ice Men* (New York: Crown Publishers, 1973), 221.

3 Known as the "Golden Jet," Bobby Hull is widely considered the best Chicago Blackhawks player of all time. In the fifteen years he played in Chicago, he had five seasons with fifty or more goals, and he won the Hart Memorial Trophy twice, the Art Ross Trophy three times, the Lady Byng Trophy, and a Stanley Cup. In 2017, the NHL generated a list of the 100 Greatest NHL Players of all time and Hull is one of them (the list is alphabetical rather than ranked).

4　Steven Lewis, quoted in Brian Vallée, *The War on Women: Elly Armour, Jane Hurshman, and Criminal Violence in Canadian Homes* (Toronto: Key Porter Books, 2007), 22.
5　For a review of these studies, see Walter S. DeKeseredy, *Contemporary Critical Criminology*, 2nd ed. (London: Routledge, 2022).
6　Lacrosse was declared Canada's national sport in 1859, but in 1994, the Canadian government passed Canada's National Sport Act, which made lacrosse the national summer sport and hockey the national winter sport.
7　Jeffrey Simpson, *Star-Spangled Canadians: Canadians Living the American Dream* (Toronto: HarperCollins, 2000), 95.
8　U.S. News & World Report, "Canada Is the No. 1 Country in the World, According to the 2021 Best Countries Report," news release, April 13, 2021, https://www.usnews.com/info/blogs/press-room/articles/2021-04-13/canada-is-the-no-1-country-in-the-world-according-to-2021-best-countries.
9　See, for example, John Lancaster, "Court Documents Reveal More Details about 2017 Homicides of Barry and Honey Sherman," *CBC News*, last modified June 12, 2021, https://www.cbc.ca/news/canada/toronto/barry-honey-sherman-murder-2021-1.5860527.
10　W.E.B. Du Bois, *The Philadelphia Negro: A Social Study* (New York: Schoken Books, 1967), 163.
11　Kevin M. Swartout and William F. Flack Jr., "Campus Sexual Assault," in *The Routledge International Handbook of Violence Studies*, ed. Walter S. DeKeseredy, Callie Marie Rennison, and Amanda K. Hall-Sanchez (London: Routledge, 2018), 291.
12　See Walter S. DeKeseredy, "Defenders of Freedom or Perpetrators and Facilitators of Crime? Beyond Progressive Retreatism in the Trump Era," *Victims & Offenders* 14, no. 8 (2019): 925–39, https://doi.org/10.1080/15564886.2019.1671282.
13　"Former University of Ottawa Hockey Players Not Guilty of Sexual Assault," *CTV News*, June 25, 2018, https://www.ctvnews.ca/canada/former-university-of-ottawa-hockey-players-not-guilty-of-sexual-assault-1.3988142.
14　Matthew Kupfer, "Ex-Gee-Gees Hockey Players Found Not Guilty of Sexual Assault," *CBC News*, June 25, 2018, https://www.cbc.ca/news/canada/ottawa/guillaume-donovan-david-foucher-verdict-1.4717857.
15　"Toronto Police Investigating Jian Ghomeshi Allegations," *CBC News*, last modified November 1, 2014, https://www.cbc.ca/news/canada/toronto-police-investigating-jian-ghomeshi-allegations-1.2820337.
16　Kevin Donovan and Jesse Brown, "CBC Fires Jian Ghomeshi over Sex Allegations," *Toronto Star*, last modified July 12, 2017, https://www.thestar.com/news/canada/2014/10/26/cbc_fires_jian_ghomeshi_over_sex_allegations.html.
17　"Jian Ghomeshi to Plead Not Guilty to Sex Assault, Choking Charges," *CBC News*, November 26, 2014, https://www.cbc.ca/news/canada

/jian-ghomeshi-to-plead-not-guilty-to-sex-assault-choking-charges
-1.2850661.

18 Quoted in Adam Miller, "Jian Ghomeshi Trial: Former CBC Radio
Host Found Not Guilty of All Charges," *Global News*, March 24, 2016,
https://globalnews.ca/news/2595443/jian-ghomeshi-trial-former
-cbc-radio-host-found-not-guilty-of-all-charges.

19 Kevin Donovan, "Jian Ghomeshi: 8 Women Accuse Former CBC Host of
Violence, Sexual Abuse or Harassment," *Toronto Star*, October 29, 2014,
https://www.thestar.com/news/gta/2014/10/29/jian_ghomeshi
_8_women_accuse_former_cbc_host_of_violence_sexual_abuse_or
_harassment.html.

20 DeKeseredy, *Contemporary Critical Criminology*, 6.

21 See, for example, Kristen Zaleski, *Understanding and Treating Military
Sexual Trauma* (New York: Springer, 2015).

22 Tom Blackwell, "Q Producer Who Alleges Ghomeshi Threatened to
'Hate F---' Her Says She Complained to Boss in 2010," *National Post*,
October 30, 2014, https://nationalpost.com/news/canada/q-journalist
-who-alleges-ghomeshi-threatened-to-hate-f-her-says-she-complained
-to-boss-in-2010.

23 Elliott Currie, *A Peculiar Indifference: The Neglected Toll of Violence on
Black America* (New York: Metropolitan Books, 2020), 17.

24 Currie presents disturbing data showing that homicide is the *leading*
cause of death for Black males from age fifteen to thirty.

25 The entire field of violence against women research would greatly
benefit from devoting more attention to abused women's protective
and resistance strategies. See, for example, the important points made
in Susan Dewey's review of *Woman Abuse in Rural Places* by Walter S.
DeKeseredy, *International Review of Victimology* 28, no. 1 (2021): 134–5,
https://doi.org/10.1177/02697580211046749.

26 This is the subtitle of Sherry Hamby's book *Battered Women's Protective
Strategies: Stronger Than You Know* (Oxford: Oxford University Press, 2014).

27 Matthew Cohen, "10 Rules NHL Hockey Wives Have to Follow," *The
Sportster*, November 18, 2018, https://www.thesportster.com
/hockey/10-rules-nhl-hockey-wives-have-to-follow.

28 At the time of writing this chapter in November 2021, Meyer is the
head coach of the NFL Jacksonville Jaguars.

29 Quoted in Scooby Axson, "Report: Texts Show Urban Meyer Knew of
Domestic Violence Allegations against Assistant in 2015," *Sports Illustrated*, August 1, 2018, https://www.si.com/college/2018/08/01
/urban-meyer-zach-smith-domestic-abuse-text-messages-ohio-state.

30 The approach is common in the feminist literature on woman abuse.
See, for instance, Walter S. DeKeseredy and Linda MacLeod, *Woman
Abuse: A Sociological Story* (Toronto: Harcourt Brace Canada, 1997).

31 Moore and Shah, *Game Misconduct*, 93.

32 Quoted in Kevin Draper, "A Disparaging Video Prompts Explosive
Fallout within ESPN," *New York Times*, last modified August 25, 2021,

https://www.nytimes.com/2021/07/04/sports/basketball/espn
-rachel-nichols-maria-taylor.html.

33 Draper, "Disparaging Video."

34 Quoted in Draper, "Disparaging Video."

35 Mary Daly, *Gyn/Ecology: The Metaethics of Radical Feminism* (Boston: Beacon Press, 1978).

36 Walter S. DeKeseredy, Andrea DeKeseredy, and Patricia DeKeseredy, "Understanding *The Handmaid's Tale*: The Contribution of Radical Feminism," in *Crime TV: Streaming Criminology in Popular Culture*, ed. Johnathan A. Grubb and Chad Posick (New York: New York University Press, 2021), 82–95.

37 Sgadmin, "My Least Favorite Hawk – Bobby Hull," *Faxes from Uncle Dale* (blog), August 19, 2014, https://www.faxesfromuncledale.com /least-favorite-hawk-bobby-hull.

38 Walter S. DeKeseredy, Molly Dragiewicz, and Martin D. Schwartz, *Abusive Endings: Separation and Divorce Violence against Women* (Oakland: University of California Press, 2017).

39 Lenore E. Walker, *Terrifying Love: Why Battered Women Kill and How Society Responds* (New York: Harper & Row, 1989), 5.

40 For more information on the Danger Assessment, see Jacquelyn C. Campbell and Jill Theresa Messing, eds., *Assessing Dangerousness: Domestic Violence Offenders and Child Abusers*, 3rd ed. (New York: Springer, 2017).

41 See DeKeseredy, Dragiewicz, and Schwartz, *Abusive Endings*.

42 In 2002, Hull's daughter Michelle told viewers of an ESPN profile on her father, "A lot of bad memories stem from how my dad acted when he was drinking. When he had been drinking, you'd just know that you didn't want to be around here." Michelle is now a lawyer defending survivors of abuse like her mother Joanne. See also David Shoalts, "Bobby Hull's Golden Hockey Career Diminished by His Troubling Dark Side," *New York Times*, January 30, 2023, https://www.nytimes .com/2023/01/30/sports/hockey/bobby-hull-death-nhl.html.

43 Quoted in Mike Repplier and Lauren Effron, "NY Officer's Body Camera Reveals Horrific Crime Scene in Murder-for-Hire Plot Aftermath," *ABC News*, August 30, 2019, https://abcnews.go.com/US/ny-officers -body-camera-reveals-horrific-crime-scene/story?id=46358994.

44 Quoted in Repplier and Effron, "NY Officer's Body Camera."

45 Edward G. Gondolf, "MCMI-III Results for Batterer Program Participation in Four Cities: Less 'Pathological' Than Expected," *Journal of Family Violence* 14, no. 1 (March 1999): 1–17, https://doi.org/10.1023 /A:1022843324943.

46 DeKeseredy, Dragiewicz, and Schwartz, *Abusive Endings*, 2.

47 See, for example, Ola W. Barnett, *A Neuroscientific Approach to Family Violence* (San Diego, CA: Congnella, 2021).

48 J.J. Gayford, "Battered Wives," *Medicine, Science and the Law* 15, no. 4 (October 1975): 237–45, https://doi.org/10.1177/002580247501500404.

49 See, for instance, R. Emerson Dobash and Russell Dobash, *Violence against Wives: A Case against the Patriarchy* (New York: Free Press, 1979).

50 See Claire M. Renzetti and Raquel Kennedy Bergen, "Introduction: The Emergence of Violence against Women as a Social Problem," in *Violence against Women*, ed. Claire M. Renzetti and Raquel Kennedy Bergen (Lanham, MD: Rowman & Littlefield, 2005), 1–12.

51 C. Wright Mills, *The Sociological Imagination* (New York: Oxford University Press, 1959).

52 DeKeseredy, *Contemporary Critical Criminology*, 6.

53 Matt DeLisi and Michael G. Vaughn, "Correlates of Crime," in *The Handbook of Criminological Theory*, ed. Alex R. Piquero (Malden, MA: John Wiley & Sons, 2016), 18–36.

54 "Hooking up" is an ambiguous term and it means different things to different people. It is primarily used in the US and generally refers to a casual sexual encounter (with no promise of commitment) ranging from kissing to sexual intercourse. For more information on this type of sex, see Lisa Wade, *American Hookup: The New Culture of Sex on Campus* (New York: W.W. Norton, 2017).

55 Barbara J. Costello and Trina L. Hope, *Peer Pressure, Peer Prevention: The Role of Friends in Crime and Conformity* (London: Routledge, 2016).

56 For more information on the Human Relations Area Files, see "About HRAF," Human Relations Area Files, accessed April 4, 2023, https://hraf.yale.edu/about.

57 Laura Robinson, *Crossing the Line: Violence and Sexual Assault in Canada's National Sport* (Toronto: McCelland & Stewart, 1998), 120.

58 Quoted in Bill Harris, "'Hockey Wives' Star Noureen DeWulf on Why Many NHL Players Marry Young," *Toronto Sun*, March 17, 2015, https://torontosun.com/2015/03/17/hockey-wives-star-noureen-dewulf-on-why-many-nhl-players-marry-young.

59 Colette Allred, "Age Variation in the Divorce Rate, 1990 and 2017," Family Profiles FP-10-13 (Bowling Green, OH: National Center for Family and Marriage Research, 2019), https://doi.org/10.25035/ncfmr/fp-19-13.

60 DeKeseredy, Dragiewicz, and Schwartz, *Abusive Endings*, 132–3.

61 Rick Westhead, "Alumni Association Seeking Improved Benefits for Retired NHLers," *TSN*, December 14, 2017, https://www.tsn.ca/alumni-association-seeking-improved-benefits-for-retired-nhlers-1.944241.

62 Pablo S. Torre, "How (and Why) Athletes Go Broke," *Sports Illustrated Vault*, March 23, 2009, https://vault.si.com/vault/2009/03/23/how-and-why-athletes-go-broke.

63 Dominic Nguyen, "Divorce Rate by Country: The World's 10 Most and Least Divorced Nations," *Unified Lawyers* (blog), last modified February 2, 2022, https://www.unifiedlawyers.com.au/blog/global-divorce-rates-statistics.

64 "15 NBA Stars Who Married Gold Diggers," *The Sportster*, October 30, 2017, https://www.thesportster.com/basketball/15-nba-stars-who-married-gold-diggers.

65 Jeff Benedict, *Public Heroes, Private Felons: Athletes and Crimes* (Boston: Northeastern University Press, 1997), 193.

66 Quoted in Katina Goulakos, "Anonymous Confessions from a Montreal Canadiens Wife, Ex-Girlfriend, and Former Mistress," *MTL Blog*, November 12, 2019, https://www.mtlblog.com/montreal /anonymous-confessions-from-a-montreal-canadiens-wife-ex -girlfriend-and-former-mistress.

67 Kevin Draper, "Kobe Bryant and the Sexual Assault Case That Was Dropped but Not Forgotten," *New York Times*, January 27, 2020, https://www.nytimes.com/2020/01/27/sports/basketball/kobe -bryant-rape-case.html.

68 Men's consumption of, and addiction to, internet pornography can negatively affect their female partners in similar ways. See Anna J. Bridges and Robert Jensen, "Pornography," in *Sourcebook on Violence against Women*, ed. Claire M. Renzetti, Jeffrey Edleson, and Raquel Kennedy Bergen, 2nd ed. (Thousand Oaks, CA: Sage Publications, 2011), 133–48.

69 Michael Busby, "When Does Infidelity Become a Form of Domestic Abuse?," Busby & Associates, June 29, 2017, https://www.busby-lee .com/familylawblog/when-does-infidelity-become-a-form-of-domestic -abuse.

70 Walter S. DeKeseredy, Danielle M. Stoneberg, and Gabrielle L. Lory, "Polyvictimization in the Lives of North American Female University/ College Students: The Contribution of Technology-Facilitated Abuse," in *The Emerald International Handbook of Technology-Facilitated Violence and Abuse*, ed. Jane Bailey, Asher Flynn, and Nicola Henry (Bingley, UK: Emerald, 2021), 65–81.

71 Benedict, *Public Heroes, Private Felons*, 196.

72 See Steven Lee Myers, "A Chinese Tennis Star Accuses a Former Top Leader of Sexual Assault," *New York Times*, November 15, 2021, https://www.nytimes.com/2021/11/03/world/asia/china-metoo -peng-shuai-zhang-gaoli.html.

73 Quoted in D'Arcy Maine, "What We Know about Tennis Player Peng Shuai's Sexual Assault Allegation and Current Whereabouts," *ESPN*, November 19, 2021, https://www.espn.com/tennis/story/_/id /32656323/what-know-tennis-player-peng-shuai-sexual-assault -allegations-current-whereabouts.

74 Quoted in Maine, "What We Know."

75 Quoted in Maine, "What We Know."

76 Katie Campione, "Serena Williams Speaks Out about Missing Player Peng Shuai as UN Asks China for Proof of Whereabouts," *People*, November 19, 2021, https://people.com/crime/serena-williams-joins -athletes-speaking-out-about-missing-chinese-tennis-player-as-un -asks-for-proof-of-whereabouts.

77 Chris Johnston, "Inside the NHL: Why Olympic Participation Is in Peril, Rogers Aftershocks and Dion Phaneuf Gets His Due," *Toronto Star*,

November 22, 2021, https://www.thestar.com/sports/hockey/opinion/2021/11/22/inside-the-nhl-why-olympic-participation-is-in-peril-rogers-aftershocks-and-dion-phaneuf-gets-his-due.html.

78 Quoted in Johnston, "Inside the NHL."

79 Tony Porter, *Well-Meaning Men: Breaking Out of the Man Box* (Charlotte, NC: A Call to Men, 2006), 1.

80 Ontario Women's Directorate, *Neighbors, Friends, and Families: How to Talk to Men Who Are Abusive* (Toronto: Ontario Women's Directorate, 2006), 8–9.

81 Quoted in Nicki Jhabvala, "After Hearing a Survivor's Story, This NFL Player Joined Her Efforts against Sexual Violence," *Washington Post*, November 24, 2021, https://www.washingtonpost.com/sports/2021/11/24/james-smith-williams-brenda-tracy-domestic-violence.

82 Moore and Shah, *Game Misconduct*, 133.

83 Quoted in Jhabvala, "After Hearing a Survivor's Story."

84 Pat Hickey, "Canadiens Will Rely on Front-Office Tandem Led by Jeff Gorton," *Montreal Gazette*, November 29, 2021, https://montrealgazette.com/sports/hockey/nhl/hockey-inside-out/canadiens-will-rely-on-front-office-tandem-led-by-jeff-gorton.

85 Pat Hickey, "Hickey on Hockey: Canadiens' Value Has Little to Do with Good Management," *Montreal Gazette*, December 11, 2021, https://montrealgazette.com/sports/hockey/nhl/hockey-inside-out/hickey-on-hockey-canadiens-value-has-little-to-do-with-good-management.

86 Moore and Shah, *Game Misconduct*, 49.

87 Moore and Shah, *Game Misconduct*, 70.

88 Kalina Laframboise and Dan Spector, "Montreal Canadiens Launch 'Consent and Respect' Action Plan after Controversial Draft Pick," *Global News*, September 15, 2021, https://globalnews.ca/news/8192274/montreal-canadiens-consent-plan-mailloux.

89 Quoted in Jack Todd, "Habs Take Another Concrete Step in Aftermath of Mailloux Mess," *Montreal Gazette*, September 19, 2021, https://montrealgazette.com/sports/hockey/nhl/hockey-inside-out/jack-todd-habs-take-another-concrete-step-in-aftermath-of-mailloux-mess.

90 Quoted in Laframboise and Spector, "Montreal Canadiens."

91 Peter G. Jaffe, Marlies Suderman, Deborah Reitzel, and Steve. M. Killip, "An Evaluation of a Secondary School Primary Prevention Program on Violence in Intimate Relationships," *Violence and Victims* 7, no. 2 (1992): 129–46, https://psycnet.apa.org/doi/10.1891/0886-6708.7.2.129.

92 Todd, "Habs Take Another Concrete Step."

93 Moore and Shah, *Game Misconduct*, 115.

94 Robinson, *Crossing the Line*, 230.

95 Laureen Snider, *Bad Business: Corporate Crime in Canada* (Toronto: Nelson Canada, 1993), 57.

96 Montreal Canadiens, "France Margaret Bélanger Appointed President, Sports and Entertainment," news release, August 24, 2021, https://

www.nhl.com/canadiens/news/france-margaret-belanger-appointed
-president-sports-and-entertainment/c-326017294.

97 Stu Cowan, "Canadiens Score Big by Hiring Chantal Machabée Away
from RDS," *Montreal Gazette*, January 5, 2022, https://montrealgazette
.com/sports/hockey/nhl/hockey-inside-out/stu-cowan-canadiens
-score-big-by-hiring-chantal-machabee-away-from-rds.

98 Montreal Canadiens, "Poulin: 'Hopefully, It Opens More Doors for the
Next Generation,'" news release, June 7, 2022, https://www.nhl.com
/canadiens/news/marie-philip-poulin-hopefully-it-opens-more
-doors-for-the-next-generation/c-334531520.

99 "NHL Trailblazer Is 'Delighted,'" *Gamesdone*, January 24, 2022, https://
gamesdone.com/2022/01/24/nhl-trailblazer-is-delighted.

100 Scott Williams, "Listening Effectively," College of Business, Wright
State University, accessed November 30, 2021, http://www.wright
.edu/~scott.williams/skills/listening.htm.

101 Jhabvala, "After Hearing a Survivor's Story."

102 *A Few Good Men* is the title of a popular 1992 Hollywood film (based on
an earlier Broadway play of the same name written by Aaron Sorkin)
that centers on the court-martial of two US marines charged with the
murder of a fellow marine.

103 These and other interviews with rural Ohio survivors of separation/
divorce presented in this book were originally published in Walter S.
DeKeseredy and Martin D. Schwartz, *Dangerous Exits: Escaping Abusive
Relationships in Rural America* (New Brunswick, NJ: Rutgers University
Press, 2009). Names have been changed for anonymity.

104 This case and excerpts from the lawsuit are included in Jackie Spiegel,
"Penguins Sexual Assault Scandal, Explained: Former AHL Assistant
Coach, Wife File Lawsuits Alleging Assault, Retaliation," *Sporting News*,
November 9, 2021, https://www.sportingnews.com/us/nhl/news
/penguins-sexual-assault-scandal-explained-former-ahl-assistant
-coach-wife-lawsuits-retaliation/8s3omdvt1vfh1wrd8beuebzt8.

105 "Penguins Reach Agreement with Former Assistant and His Wife following Sex Abuse Claims," *CBS News Pittsburgh*, November 9, 2021,
https://pittsburgh.cbslocal.com/2021/11/09/penguins-minor-league
-sex-abuse-lawsuit-settlement.

106 Antonia Noori Farzan, "Former American Hockey League Coach Clark
Donatelli Indicted on Four Counts of Sexual Assault," *Providence Journal*, November 16, 2021, https://www.usatoday.com/story/sports
/nhl/2021/11/16/clark-donatelli-ahl-indictment-sexual-assault
/8638759002.

107 Ann Goetting, *Getting Out: Life Stories of Women Who Left Abusive Men*
(New York: Columbia University Press, 1999), 16.

108 Rebecca Solnit, "Listen Up, Women Are Telling Their Story Now,"
The Guardian, December 30, 2014, https://www.theguardian.com
/news/2014/dec/30/-sp-rebecca-solnit-listen-up-women-are-telling
-their-story-now.

109   This concluding sentence is heavily informed by arguments presented in this dated, but still widely cited, article: Mary E. Gilfus, Susan Fineran, Deborah J. Cohan, Susan A. Jensen, Lisa Hartwick, and Robin Spath, "Research on Violence against Women: Creating Survivor-Informed Collaborations," *Violence against Women* 5, no. 10 (October 1999): 1194–1212, https://doi.org/10.1177/10778019922183327.

3. With a Little Help from Their Friends: Male Peer Support and Violence against Women

1   Llowell Williams, "The 'Boys Will Be Boys' Defense of Sexual Misconduct Is Deeply Insulting to Good Men," *Medium*, July 23, 2019, https://llowell.medium.com/the-boys-will-be-boys-defense-of-sexual-misconduct-is-deeply-insulting-to-good-men-d449d97f5719.

2   See Chad Posick and Johnathan Hall, "Insane Violence Has Meaning: Psychopathy and Abuse in *The Fall*," in *Crime TV: Streaming Criminology in Popular Culture*, ed. Johnathan A. Grubb and Chad Posick (New York: New York University Press, 2021), 56–67. See also Walter S. DeKeseredy, Molly Dragiewicz, and Martin D. Schwartz, *Abusive Endings: Separation and Divorce Violence against Women* (Oakland: University of California Press, 2017), 1–3.

3   Quoted in Walter S. DeKeseredy and Martin D. Schwartz, *Dangerous Exits: Escaping Abusive Relationships in Rural America* (New Brunswick, NJ: Rutgers University Press, 2009), 70.

4   Anthony Ellis, *Men, Masculinities and Violence* (London: Routledge, 2016), 18.

5   See, for example, Martin Wilson and Margo Daly, *Homicide* (Hawthorne, NY: Aldine de Gruyter, 1988).

6   See Ann Innis Dagg and Lee Harding, *Human Evolution and Male Aggression: Debunking the Myth of Man and Ape* (Amherst, NY: Cambria Press, 2012).

7   Ilan Dar-Nimrod, Steven J. Heine, Benjamin Y. Cheung, and March Schaller, "Do Scientific Theories Affect Men's Evaluations of Sex Crimes?," *Aggressive Behavior* 37, no. 5 (2011): 440–9, https://doi.org/10.1002/ab.20401.

8   Michael Kimmel, *The Gendered Society* (New York: Oxford University Press, 2000), 244.

9   Walter S. DeKeseredy, *Contemporary Critical Criminology*, 2nd ed. (London: Routledge, 2022), 56.

10   Dagg and Harding, *Human Evolution*, 209.

11   Edward W. Morris and Kathleen Ratajczak, "Critical Masculinity Studies and Research on Violence against Women: An Assessment of Past Scholarship and Future Directions," *Violence against Women* 25, no. 16 (December 2019): 1980–2006, https://doi.org/10.1177/1077801219875827.

12   Barbara J. Costello and Trina L. Hope, *Peer Pressure, Peer Prevention: The Role of Friends in Crime and Conformity* (London: Routledge, 2016), 1.

13 Ronald L. Akers, Christine S. Sellers, and Wesley G. Jennings, *Criminological Theories: Introduction, Evaluation, and Application*, 8th ed. (New York: Oxford University Press, 2021), 1.

14 Michael Kimmel, *Angry White Men: American Masculinity at the End of an Era* (New York: Nation Books, 2017), 32.

15 Barbara J. Costello and Trina L. Hope, *Peer Pressure, Peer Intervention: The Role of Friends in Crime and Conformity* (London: Routledge, 2016), 1.

16 Costello and Hope, *Peer Pressure, Peer Prevention*, 1.

17 Quoted in M. Goldstein, "When Did You Stop Beating Your Wife?," *Long Island Magazine*, September 18, 1977, 10.

18 Angela R. Gover, Tara N. Richards, and Maria J. Patterson, "Explaining Violence against Women within the Context of Intimate Partner Violence (IPV)," in *Sourcebook of Violence against Women*, ed. Claire M. Renzetti, Jeffrey L. Edleson, and Raquel Kennedy Bergen, 3rd ed. (Thousand Oaks, CA: Sage Publications, 2018), 31–50.

19 DeKeseredy, Dragiewicz, and Schwartz, *Abusive Endings*, 121.

20 Peggy Reeves Sanday, *Fraternity Gang Rape* (New York: New York University Press, 1990), 135.

21 Lee H. Bowker, *Beating Wife-Beating* (Lexington, MA: Lexington Books, 1983), 135.

22 Derek H. Suite, "Intimate Partner Violence in Male-Dominant Sport Culture," in *Intimate Partner Violence: An Evidence Based Approach*, ed. Rahn Kennedy Baily (New York: Springer, 2021), 169.

23 Kurt Lewin, *Field Theory in Social Science: Selected Theoretical Papers* (New York: Harper & Row, 1951), 169.

24 Eugene J. Kanin, "An Examination of Sexual Aggression as a Response to Sexual Frustration," *Journal of Marriage and the Family* 29, no. 3 (1967): 428–33, https://doi.org/10.2307/349577.

25 Quoted in Robin Warshaw, *I Never Called It Rape* (New York: Harper & Row, 1988), 106–7.

26 Warshaw, *I Never Called It Rape*, 93.

27 Stu Cowan, "Canadiens Drafting Mailloux 'Reflects Deep Insensitivity': Expert," *Montreal Gazette*, July 27, 2021, https://montrealgazette .com/sports/hockey/nhl/hockey-inside-out/cowan-canadiens -drafting-mailloux-reflects-deep-insensitivity-expert.

28 Laura Robinson, *Crossing the Line: Violence and Sexual Assault in Canada's National Sport* (Toronto: McCelland & Stewart, 1998), 118.

29 Gary Crawford and Victoria K. Gosling, "The Myth of the 'Puck Bunny': Female Fans and Men's Ice Hockey," *Sociology* 38, no. 3 (2004): 477–93, https://doi.org/10.1177/0038038504043214.

30 Robinson, *Crossing the Line*, 148.

31 Quoted in Robinson, *Crossing the Line*, 103.

32 Quoted in Robinson, *Crossing the Line*, 103–4.

33 "What Percentage of Youth Ice Hockey Players Make It to the NHL?" Stickhandling Pro, accessed January 12, 2022, https://www

.stickhandlingpro.com/blog/What-Percentage-of-Youth-Ice-Hockey
-Players-Make-it-to-the-NHL.

34 The roots of male peer support (MPS) are more fully described in
Walter S. DeKeseredy and Martin D. Schwartz, *Male Peer Support and
Violence against Women: The History and Verification of a Theory* (Boston:
Northeastern University Press, 2013), 44–68.

35 Walter S. DeKeseredy and Martin D. Schwartz, "Male Peer Support
and Woman Abuse: An Expansion of DeKeseredy's Model," *Sociological
Spectrum* 13, no. 4 (1993): 393–413, https://doi.org/10.1080/02732173
.1993.9982041.

36 Claire M. Renzetti, *Feminist Criminology* (London: Routledge,
2013), 8.

37 Evan F. Moore and Jashvina Shah, *Game Misconduct: Hockey's Toxic
Culture and How to Fix It* (Chicago: Triumph Books, 2021), 115.

38 Varda Burstyn, *The Rites of Men: Manhood, Politics, and the Culture of
Sport* (Toronto: University of Toronto Press, 2000), 27.

39 Erica Frydenberg and Ramon Lewis, "Boys Play Sport and Girls Turn
to Others: Age, Gender and Ethnicity as Determinants of Coping,"
Journal of Adolescence 16, no. 3 (September 1993): 253–66, https://doi
.org/10.1006/jado.1993.1024.

40 Steve Dempster, "Having the Balls, Having It All? Sport and Constructions of Undergraduate Laddishness," *Gender and Education* 21, no. 5
(2009): 481–500, https://doi.org/10.1080/09540250802392299.

41 Eric Anderson, "'I Used to Think Women Were Weak': Orthodox
Masculinity, Gender Segregation, and Sport," *Sociological Forum* 23,
no. 2 (April 2008): 257–80, https://doi.org/10.1111/j.1573-7861.2008
.00058.x.

42 Laura Robinson, "Hockey Night in Canada," in *Sexual Assault in Canada:
Law, Legal Practice and Women's Activism*, ed. Elizabeth A. Sheehy
(Ottawa: University of Ottawa Press, 2012), 73–86.

43 Erving Goffman, "On the Characteristics of Total Institutions," in *Asy-
lums: Essays on the Social Situation of Mental Patients and Other Inmates*
(New York: Random House, 1961), 73.

44 Steven M. Ortiz, "Traveling with the Ball Club: A Code of Conduct for
Wives Only," *Symbolic Interaction* 20, no. 3 (1997): 225–49, https://doi
.org/10.1525/si.1997.20.3.225.

45 Robinson, "Hockey Night in Canada," 76.

46 Robinson, "Hockey Night in Canada," 76.

47 Jack Levin and Jim Nolan, *The Violence of Hate: Understanding Harmful
Forms of Bias and Bigotry*, 4th ed. (Lanham, MD: Rowman & Littlefield,
2017), 41–5.

48 David Kauzlarich, foreword to *Contemporary Critical Criminology*, by
Walter S. DeKeseredy, viii.

49 Joe Helm, "Recounting a Day of Rage, Hate, Violence and Death,"
Washington Post, August 12, 2017, https://www.washingtonpost.com
/graphics/2017/local/charlottesville-timeline.

50 Spencer coined the term *alternative right* in 2008. He heads the National Policy Institute, which is a white nationalist "think tank" based in Arlington, Virginia.

51 "Full Text: Trump's Comments on White Supremacists, 'Alt-Left' in Charlottesville," *POLITICO*, August 15, 2017, https://www.politico.com/story/2017/08/15/full-text-trump-comments-white-supremacists-alt-left-transcript-241662.

52 Bridget Steel, Mackenzie Martin, Alexa Yakubovich, David K. Humphreys, and Elizabeth Nye, "Risk and Protective Factors for Men's Sexual Violence against Women at Higher Education Institutions: A Systematic and Meta-Analytic Review of the Longitudinal Evidence," *Trauma, Violence, & Abuse* 23, no. 3 (2020): 716–32, https://doi.org/10.1177/1524838020970900.

53 Pierre McGuire, "Alcohol Is Hockey's 'Dirty Little Secret,'" *Montreal Gazette*, May 9, 2007, https://www.pressreader.com/canada/montreal-gazette/20070905/282179351700713.

54 Emily Redenbach, "Varlamov, Voynov, and Domestic Violence in Sports," *CaliSports News*, July 3, 2015, http://www.calisportsnews.com/varlamov-voynov-domestic-violence-sports.

55 Quoted in Sadie Gurman, "Woman Says Avalanche Star Semyon Varlamov Laughed While He Beat Her," *Denver Post*, last modified April 28, 2016, https://www.denverpost.com/2013/10/31/woman-says-avalanche-star-semyon-varlamov-laughed-while-he-beat-her.

56 Nathan Fenno, "Ex-Kings Player Slava Voynov Spent Two Months in Jail for Domestic Abuse, but Is at Olympics Representing Russia," *Los Angeles Times*, February 19, 2018, https://www.latimes.com/sports/olympics/la-sp-olympics-voynov-assault-20180219-story.html.

57 Antonia Abbey, "Alcohol-Related Sexual Assault on College Campuses," in *Addressing Violence against Women on Campus*, ed. Catherine Kaukinen, Michelle Hughes Miller, and Rachel A. Powers (Philadelphia: Temple University Press, 2017), 78–94.

58 See, for example, DeKeseredy and Schwartz, *Male Peer Support*, 56–9.

59 Thomas Vander Ven, *Getting Wasted: Why College Students Drink So Much and Party So Hard* (New York: New York University Press, 2011).

60 Nick T. Pappas, Patrick C. McKenry, and Beth Skilken Catlett, "Athlete Aggression on the Rink and off the Ice: Athlete Violence and Aggression in Hockey and Interpersonal Relationships," *Men and Masculinities* 6, no. 3 (2004): 291–312, https://doi.org/10.1177/1097184X03257433.

61 Pappas, McKenry, and Catlett, "Athlete Aggression," 309.

62 Justin Bourne, "On Booze, and the Hockey Players That Love It," *Yahoo! Sports*, March 17, 2011, https://sports.yahoo.com/blogs/puck-daddy/bourne-blog-booze-hockey-players-love-180213034.html.

63 Jessica Luther, *Unsportsmanlike Conduct: College Football and the Politics of Rape* (New York: Edge of Sports, 2016), 130–51.

64 US Bureau of Labor Statistics, "2020 American Time Use Survey," accessed December 20, 2021, https://www.bls.gov/tus.

65 Rick Porter, "TV Long View: How Much Network TV Depends on Cop Shows," *Hollywood Reporter*, June 20, 2020, https://www.hollywoodreporter.com/tv/tv-news/heres-how-network-tv-depends-cop-shows-1299504.

66 Eamonn Carrabine, preface to *Crime TV: Streaming Criminology in Popular Culture*, ed. Johnathan A. Grubb and Chad Posick (New York: New York University Press, 2021), vii.

67 Kevin Young, *Sport, Violence and Society*, 2nd ed. (London: Routledge, 2019), 247.

68 Rick Westhead, "Penguins Told AHL Coach to 'Stay Quiet' about Wife's Sexual Assault, Lawsuit Says," *TSN*, December 8, 2020, https://www.tsn.ca/pittsburgh-penguins-told-ahl-coach-to-stay-quiet-about-wife-s-sexual-assault-lawsuit-says-1.1561342.

69 Institutional betrayal is frequently discussed in the social scientific literature on sexual assault in institutions of higher learning. It occurs when survivors experience rejection and disbelief when they turn to powerful institutional stakeholders (e.g., university administrators) for support. There is also evidence of institutional betrayal being strongly associated with *athlete multiple perpetrator rape*. For more information on this connection, see James E. Sutton, "Athlete Multiple Perpetrator Rape (MPR) as Interactional and Organizational Deviance: Heuristic Insights from a Multilevel Framework," *Violence against Women* 28, no. 14 (November 2022): 3608–30, https://doi.org/10.1177/10778012211070312.

70 National Collegiate Athletic Association (NCAA), Baylor University Public Infractions Decision, August 11, 2021, 2, https://ncaaorg.s3.amazonaws.com/infractions/decisions/Aug2021INF_BaylorDecision Public.pdf.

71 Paula Lavigne and Mark Schlabach, *Violated: Exposing Rape at Baylor University amid College Football's Sexual Assault Crisis* (New York: Center Street, 2017), 2.

72 Lavigne and Schlabach, *Violated*, 3.

73 Nicole Chavez and Jay Croft, "Ex-frat Leader's Plea Deal Is the Latest in a Series of Baylor Sex Assault Scandals," *CNN*, December 12, 2018, https://www.cnn.com/2018/12/12/us/baylor-sex-assault-cases-timeline/index.html.

74 Quoted in Joe Hernandez, "NCAA Won't Punish Baylor for Failing to Report Sexual Assault Claims against Players," *NPR*, August 12, 2021, https://www.npr.org/2021/08/12/1027070133/ncaa-baylor-sexual-assault-claims-failure-to-report.

75 For the collective bargaining agreement between the NHLPA and the NHL, see https://www.nhlpa.com/the-pa/cba.

76 Jon Garcia, "How the Predators and NHL Have Handled Allegations of Domestic Violence, Sexual Assault," *The Tennessean*, June 20, 2018, https://www.tennessean.com/story/sports/nhl/2018/06/20/austin-watson-nhl-domestic-violence-sexual-assault-hockey/718223002.

77 Young, *Sport, Violence and Society*, 247.
78 Luther, *Unsportsmanlike Conduct*, 130.
79 Rick Woods, September 21, 2021, comment on Jack Todd, "Habs Take Another Concrete Step in the Aftermath of Mailloux Mess," *Montreal Gazette*, September 19, 2021, https://montrealgazette.com/sports /hockey/nhl/hockey-inside-out/jack-todd-habs-take-another -concrete-step-in-aftermath-of-mailloux-mess.
80 "Excerpts from Skidmore Hazing Paper," *USCHO*, November 30, 2004, https://www.uscho.com/2004/11/30/excerpts-from-skidmore -hazing-paper.
81 Betsy Powell, "Family Speaks Out over Alleged Sexual Assault at Hockey Camp," *Toronto Star*, August 9, 2022, https://www.thestar .com/news/gta/2022/08/09/family-speaks-out-over-alleged-sexual -assault-at-hockey-camp.html.
82 Quoted in John Kryk, "Target in 2005 McGill Hazing Horror Speaks Out," *Toronto Sun*, November 9, 2013, https://torontosun .com/2013/11/09/target-in-2005-mcgill-hazing-horror-speaks-out.
83 Kryk, "Target in 2005 McGill Hazing."
84 Quoted in Gare Joyce, "The Full Cost," *Sportsnet*, accessed December 22, 2021, https://www.sportsnet.ca/hockey/nhl/akim-aliu-hockey -hazing-big-read.
85 Quoted in Joyce, "Full Cost."
86 Sutton, "Athlete Multiple Perpetrator Rape (MPR)," 3622.
87 Mothers Against Drunk Driving (MADD), "The Rate of Impaired Driving in Canada," accessed January 10, 2022, https://madd.ca/pages /impaired-driving/overview/statistics.
88 Tristin Hopper, "Drunk Driving Is Canada's Deadliest Crime – and One of Our Most Lightly Punished," *National Post*, February 16, 2021, https://nationalpost.com/news/canada/drunk-driving-is-canadas -deadliest-crime-and-one-of-our-most-lightly-punished.
89 Hopper, "Drunk Driving."
90 National Center for Health Statistics, "NVSS Vital Statistics Rapid Release," Centers for Disease Control and Prevention, accessed January 10, 2022, https://www.cdc.gov/nchs/nvss/vsrr/mortality-dashboard .htm.
91 Quoted in Moore and Shah, *Game Misconduct*, 129–30.
92 Lindsay Munschauer, "Is the NHL's 'Strongly-Held Policy' on Domestic Violence Just Empty Words?," *University of Buffalo Law Sports and Entertainment Forum* (blog), April 10, 2019, https://ublawsportsforum .com/2019/04/10/is-the-nhls-strongly-held-policy-on-domestic -violence-just-empty-words.
93 Moore and Shah, *Game Misconduct*, 125–6.
94 Joshua Clipperton, "Oilers GM Ken Holland on Evander Kane: 'I Believe in Second Chances,'" *Toronto Star*, January 11, 2022, https://www .thestar.com/sports/hockey/2022/01/11/oilers-gm-ken-holland-on -evander-kane-i-believe-in-second-chances.html.

95 See, for example, Moore and Shah, *Game Misconduct*, 120–7.
96 Justin Cuthbert, "Oilers Find New Way to Fail Connor McDavid amid Evander Kane Speculation," *Yahoo! Sports*, January 13, 2022, https://ca.sports.yahoo.com/news/oilers-find-new-way-to-fail-connor-mc -david-204234260.html.
97 Quoted in Arun Srinivasan, "Connor McDavid Downplays Evander Kane's Off-Ice Issues amid Oilers Rumors," *Yahoo! Sports*, January 12, 2022, https://sports.yahoo.com/connor-mc-david-downplays -evander-kanes-off-ice-issues-amid-oilers-rumours-025828754.html.
98 Ken Dryden, *Scotty: A Hockey Life Like No Other* (Toronto: McClelland & Stewart, 2019), 119.
99 Shawna Lee June Marks, "The Sexual Politics of Australian Football: Social Constructions of Masculinity, Sex, and Sexual Violence" (PhD diss., Flinders University, 2020), 47.
100 Martin D. Schwartz, "Masculinities, Sport, and Violence against Women: The Contribution of Male Peer Support Theory," *Violence against Women* 27, no. 5 (April 2021): 699, https://doi.org/10.1177 /1077801220958493.
101 Brent Schrotenboer, "NFL Teams Cut Rate of Second Chances for Players Charged with Domestic Violence," *USA Today*, June 10, 2021, https://www.usatoday.com/in-depth/sports/nfl/2021/06/10/nfl-players -charged-domestic-violence-fewer-second-chances/7508294002.
102 Quoted in Gavin Lee, "Los Angeles Kings Hire Marc Bergevin," *Pro Hockey Rumors*, January 9, 2022, https://www.prohockeyrumors.com /2022/01/los-angeles-kings-hire-marc-bergevin.html.
103 Lisa Dillman, "What Were the Kings Thinking in Hiring Marc Bergevin, and What Does It Mean for the Front Office?," *The Athletic*, January 10, 2022, https://theathletic.com/3061012/2022/01/10/dillman-what -were-the-kings-thinking-in-hiring-marc-bergevin-and-what-does-it -mean-for-the-front-office.
104 Luther, *Unsportsmanlike Conduct*, 19.
105 Bowker, *Beating Wife-Beating*, 135.
106 Michael D. Smith, *Violence and Sport* (Toronto: Butterworths, 1983), 75.

4. Other Key Elements of a Rape-Supportive Culture in Professional Hockey

1 Jessica Luther, *Unsportsmanlike Conduct: College Football and the Politics of Rape* (New York: Edge of Sports, 2016), 33.
2 Liz Kelly, *Surviving Sexual Violence* (Minneapolis: University of Minnesota Press, 1988), 76.
3 Liz Kelly, "The Continuum of Sexual Violence," in *Women, Violence and Social Control*, ed. Jalna Hanmer and Mary Maynard (Atlantic Highlands, NJ: Humanities Press International, 1987), 48.
4 Walter S. DeKeseredy, *Woman Abuse in Rural Places* (London: Routledge, 2021), 14.

5 Liz Kelly and Jill Radford, "The Problem of Men: Feminist Perspectives on Sexual Violence," in *Law, Order and the Authoritarian State*, ed. Phil Scranton (Philadelphia: Open University Press, 1987), 242.

6 James Ptacek, "Rape and the Continuum of Sexual Abuse in Intimate Relationships: Interviews with US Women from Different Social Classes," in *Marital Rape: Consent, Marriage, and Social Change in Global Context*, ed. Kersti Yllö and M. Gabriela Torres (New York: Oxford University Press, 2016), 123–38.

7 F. Vera-Gray, *The Right Amount of Panic: How Women Trade Freedom for Safety* (Bristol: Policy Press, 2018), 5–7.

8 Elizabeth Stanko is one of the first feminist scholars and activists to raise awareness about men's obliviousness to the precautions women take to protect themselves. See her book *Everyday Violence: How Women and Men Experience Sexual and Physical Danger* (London: Pandora, 1990).

9 Jackson Katz, *The Macho Paradox: Why Some Men Hurt Women and How All Men Can Help* (Naperville, IL: Sourcebooks), 2–3.

10 Quoted in Karen G. Weiss, *Party School: Crime, Campus, and Community* (Boston: Northeastern University Press, 2013), 90.

11 Weiss, *Party School*, 91.

12 This question is informed by research summarized in Meda Chesney-Lind and Lisa Pasko, *The Female Offender: Girls, Women, and Crime*, 3rd ed. (Thousand Oaks, CA: Sage Publications, 2013).

13 Meda Chesney-Lind and Michele Eliason, "From Invisible to Incorrigible: The Demonization of Marginalized Women and Girls," *Crime, Media, and Culture* 2, no. 1 (2006): 37, https://doi.org/10.1177/1741659006061709.

14 Jasmine Hirst, "Aileen Wuornos Killed. I Knew Her. And I Know Why," *Ozy*, accessed January 21, 2022, https://www.ozy.com/true-and-stories/aileen-wuornos-killed-i-knew-her-and-i-know-why/396729 (site discontinued).

15 Varda Burstyn, *The Rites of Men: Manhood, Politics, and the Culture of Sport* (Toronto: University of Toronto Press, 2000), 243.

16 For more on this case, see Peter Goffin, "New Trial Begins for Latest Allegations against Maple Leaf Gardens Sex Abuser Gordon Stuckless," *Toronto Star*, October 4, 2017, https://www.thestar.com/news/crime/2017/10/02/gordon-stuckless-stands-trial-on-new-charges-related-to-complaints-of-sex-abuse-at-maple-leaf-gardens.html.

17 Michael Salter, "Child Sexual Abuse," in *Routledge Handbook of Critical Criminology*, 2nd ed., Walter S. DeKeseredy and Molly Dragiewicz (London: Routledge, 2018), 316–33.

18 Pavla Miller, *Patriarchy* (London: Routledge, 2017), 3.

19 D. Scharie Tavcer and Walter S. DeKeseredy, "Female Crime: Theoretical Perspectives," in *Women and the Criminal Justice System: A Canadian Perspective*, 2nd ed., Jane Barker and D. Scharie Tavcer (Toronto: Emond, 2018), 33.

20 Tavcer and DeKeseredy, "Female Crime," 33.

21 Angus Reid Institute, "Game Misconduct: Canadians May Love Their Hockey, but They Also See Serious Problems with Its Culture," May 5, 2021, https://angusreid.org/wp-content/uploads/2021/05/2021.05.03 _Hockey_Culture.pdf.

22 John Hernandez, "Misogyny, Racism and Bullying Prevalent across Canadian Youth Hockey, Survey Finds," *CBC News*, last modified May 5, 2021, https://www.cbc.ca/news/canada/british-columbia /misogyny-racism-bullying-across-canadian-youth-hockey-1.6014070.

23 Canadian Hockey League (CHL), "Update on Player Wellbeing," Independent Review Panel, January 21, 2022, https://cdn.chl.ca/uploads /chl/2022/01/21095713/PlayerWellbeingUpdate_FINAL.pdf.

24 CHL, "Update on Player Wellbeing," 3.

25 Quoted in Paul Kasabian, "Daniel Carcillo, Garrett Taylor Detail Alleged Abuse in Junior Hockey Lawsuit," *Bleacher Report*, June 18, 2020, https://bleacherreport.com/articles/2896776-daniel-carcillo -garrett-taylor-detail-alleged-abuse-in-junior-hockey-lawsuit.

26 Kathleen Custers and Jenna McNallie, "The Relationship between Television Sports Exposure and Rape Myth Acceptance: The Mediating Role of Sexism and Sexual Objectification of Women," *Violence against Women* 23, no. 7 (June 2017): 813–29, https://doi.org/10.1177 /1077801216651340.

27 Nicole L. Johnson and Dawn M. Johnson, "An Empirical Exploration into the Measurement of Rape Culture," *Journal of Interpersonal Violence* 36, no. 1–2 (January 2017): 70–95, https://doi.org/10.1177/0886260517732347.

28 Postmedia News, "SIN BIN: Porn Star Marks Return of NHL, Invites Fans to 'Slide in My DMs,'" *Toronto Sun*, August 9, 2020, https:// torontosun.com/sports/other-sports/sin-bin-porn-star-celebrates-hockeys -return-by-inviting-players-fans-to-slide-into-her-dms.

29 JamieD, "Hockey or Sex: 7 In-Game Comments That Will Make You Think," *Total Pro Sports*, May 12, 2009, https://www.totalprosports .com/2009/05/12/hockey-or-sex-7-in-game-comments-that-will-make -you-think (site discontinued).

30 Nick T. Pappas, *The Dark Side of Sports: Exposing the Sexual Culture of Collegiate and Professional Athletes* (Maidenhead, UK: Meyer & Meyer Sport, 2012), 60.

31 Quoted in Pappas, *Dark Side of Sports*, 60.

32 Michael Kimmel, *Guyland: The Perilous World Where Boys Become Men* (New York: Harper, 2008), 181.

33 Kimmel, *Guyland*, 187.

34 David Slayden, "Debbie Does Dallas Again and Again: Pornography, Technology, and Market Innovation," in *Porn.com: Making Sense of Online Pornography*, ed. Feona Attwood (New York: Peter Lang, 2010), 54–68.

35 Peter Lehman, "Introduction: 'A Dirty Little Secret' – Why Teach and Study Pornography?," in *Pornography: Film and Culture*, ed. Peter Lehman (New Brunswick, NJ: Rutgers University Press, 2006), 4.

36 Chloe Papas, "How a Perth Hockey Team Got Sponsored by the World's Biggest Porn Site," *Vice*, March 8, 2017, https://www.vice.com/en/article/ez8vkm/how-a-perth-hockey-team-got-sponsored-by-the-worlds-biggest-porn-site.

37 See examples of this in Feona Attwood, *Sex Media* (Cambridge: Polity Press, 2018).

38 As stated on its website (https://culturereframed.org), this nonprofit organization provides "education and resources to build resilience and resistance to hypersexualized media and porn."

39 Gail Dines, *Pornland: How Porn Has Hijacked Our Sexuality* (Boston: Beacon Press, 2010), 100.

40 Pornhub, "Gives America Wood," Pornhub Events, accessed April 12, 2023, https://www.pornhub.com/event/arborday.

41 Gresham M. Sykes and David Matza, "Techniques of Neutralization: A Theory of Delinquency," *American Sociological Review* 22, no. 6 (December 1957): 664–70, https://doi.org/10.2307/2089195.

42 Scharon Hardling, "Pornography Meets Environmentalism: Porn Site Is Planting Trees When Users Watch Big D*** Videos to Celebrate Arbor Day 2014," *Latin Post*, April 28, 2014, https://www.latinpost.com/articles/11350/20140428/pornography-meets-environmentalism-porn-site-planting-trees-when-users-watch.htm.

43 Hardling, "Pornography Meets Environmentalism."

44 Nick Schager, "How Pornhub Became Public Enemy Number One for Crusaders," *Yahoo! News*, March 10, 2023, https://uk.news.yahoo.com/pornhub-become-public-enemy-number-034606672.html.

45 Nicholas Kristof, "The Children of Pornhub: Why Does Canada Allow This Company to Profit off Videos of Exploitation and Assault?," *New York Times*, December 4, 2020, https://www.nytimes.com/2020/12/04/opinion/sunday/pornhub-rape-trafficking.html.

46 Pamela Paul, *Pornified: How Pornography Is Damaging Our Lives, Our Relationships, and Our Families* (New York: Owl Books, 2005), 5.

47 Barton is referring to Melania Trump, wife of former US president Donald Trump. In 2000, she was featured naked in a *GQ* profile shoot on Donald Trump's Boeing 727 wearing handcuffs and holding a pistol. This and other pictures of her are still posted on *GQ*'s website: "Melania Trump: The First Lady in Our Nude Photo Shoot," *GQ*, November 8, 2016, https://www.gq-magazine.co.uk/article/donald-trump-melania-trump-knauss-first-lady-erections.

48 Here, Barton is referring to Donald Trump himself.

49 Bernadette Barton, *The Pornification of America: How Raunch Culture Is Ruining Our Society* (New York: New York University Press, 2021), 2.

50 "Pure Tenderness and Sincerity: Russian Female Hockey Players Strip Off for Annual Calendar," *RT*, December 22, 2019, https://www.rt.com/sport/476608-whl-calendar-2020-female-players.

51 Phoebe Jackson-Edwards, "Having a Field Day! Women's Hockey Team Strip Off as They Practice Their Drills for Cheeky Charity Calendar,"

Daily Mail, October 19, 2015, https://www.dailymail.co.uk/femail/article
-3279302/Women-s-hockey-team-strip-practice-drills-cheeky
-charity-calendar.html.

52 See World Population Review, "Teacher Pay by State 2023," accessed
May 3, 2023, https://worldpopulationreview.com/state-rankings
/teacher-pay-by-state.

53 Quoted in Kristopher J. Brooks, "'Dash for Cash' Stunt Demeans Teachers, Critics Say," *CBS News*, December 14, 2021, https://www.cbsnews
.com/news/south-dakota-teachers-dash-for-cash.

54 Libby Page, "What's Wrong with Naked Calendars?," *The Guardian*,
October 17, 2013, https://www.theguardian.com/education/2013
/oct/17/what-s-wrong-with-university-naked-calendars.

55 "Naked Calendar in National Backlash," *The Boar*, December 23, 2012,
https://theboar.org/2012/12/naked-calendar-makes-national-news.

56 Diana E.H. Russell, *Against Pornography: The Evidence of Harm* (Berkeley,
CA: Russell Publications, 1993), 3.

57 Linette Etheredge and Janine Lemon, "Pornography, Problem Sexual
Behavior and Sibling on Sibling Sexual Violence," Royal Commission
into Family Violence 2015, 4, http://rcfv.archive.royalcommission.vic
.gov.au/getattachment/B8A6174A-6C6F-495F-BF7B-9CA9BF902840
/Etheredge,-Linette.pdf.

58 Dines, *Pornland*, ix.

59 Niki Fritz, Vinny Malic, Bryant Paul, and Yanyan Zhou, "A Descriptive
Analysis of the Types, Targets, and Relative Frequency of Aggression in
Mainstream Pornography," *Archives of Sexual Behavior* 49, no. 8 (Novem-
ber 2020): 3041–53, https://doi.org/10.1007/s10508-020-01773-0.

60 This is a personal communication included in John Foubert, *Protecting Your Children from Internet Pornography: Understanding the Science,
Risks, and Ways to Protect Your Kids* (Chicago: Northfield Publishing,
2022), 11.

61 Robert Jensen, *Getting Off: Pornography and the End of Masculinity* (Cambridge, MA: South End Press, 2007), 38.

62 Alia E. Dastagir, "'Secrets of Playboy': Hugh Hefner's Former Girlfriends, Playmates and Employees Allege a Culture of Abuse," *USA
Today*, January 24, 2022, https://www.usatoday.com/story/life/health
-wellness/2022/01/24/secrets-playboy-hugh-hefner-playmates-abuse
-trauma/6623453001.

63 Here, Dines is referring to the late US millionaire and convicted sex
offender Jeffrey Epstein. He was arrested in July 2019 on charges of sex
trafficking and conspiracy to engage in sex trafficking. He died in jail
while awaiting trial, and his death was officially ruled a suicide. His
high-profile social circle included former US presidents Bill Clinton
and Donald Trump as well as Queen Elizabeth's son Prince Andrew.

64 For more information on how Hefner and his company abused
women, see Gail Dines and Eric Silverman, "Hugh Hefner's Playboy
Empire Was Built on the Abuse of Women," *Ms.*, January 28, 2022,

https://msmagazine.com/2022/01/28/hugh-hefner-playboy
-feminist-women-rape-abuse-sexual-assault.

65 Rowan Pelling, "What Did Playboy Ever Do for Women?," *UnHerd*, April
17, 2020, https://unherd.com/2020/04/what-did-playboy-ever-do-for
-women.

66 Paul, *Pornified*, 127.

67 *Soul Train* was a very popular, syndicated US musical variety television
show that aired for thirty-five years (October 2, 1971, to March 27,
2006). It mainly featured performances by Black R&B, soul, and hip-
hop artists.

68 Quoted in Rogani Araya, "*Soul Train* Creator Don Cornelius Allegedly
Tied Up Two Playboy Bunnies and Sexually Assaulted Them," *Jasmine
Brand*, February 1, 2022, https://thejasminebrand.com/2022/02/01
/soul-train-creator-don-cornelius-allegedly-tied-up-two-playboy
-bunnies-and-sexually-assaulted-them.

69 Dines, *Pornland*, 102.

70 See Roland Atkinson and Thomas Rodgers, "Pleasure Zones and Murder Boxes: Online Pornography and Violent Video Games as Cultural
Zones of Exception," *British Journal of Criminology* 56, no. 6 (November
2016): 1291–307, https://doi.org/10.1093/bjc/azv113.

71 Bob Duff, "Iconic Red Wings Goalie Masks," *Detroit Hockey Now*, October
31, 2021, https://detroithockeynow.com/2021/10/31/five-iconic-red
-wings-goalie-masks.

72 For the Amazon listing, see https://www.amazon.com/Wen-XinRong
-Halloween-Costume-Masquerade/dp/B07X6MZS6Z/ref=sr_1_6?crid=
2WN7RN1JFARAF&keywords=jason+masks&qid=1643393867&sprefix
=jason+masks%2Caps%2C87&sr=8-6 (accessed January 28, 2022).

73 Walter S. DeKeseredy, Stephen L. Muzzatti, and Joseph F. Donnermeyer,
"Mad Men in Bib Overalls: Media's Horrification and Pornification of
Rural Culture," *Critical Criminology* 22, no. 2 (2014): 179–97, https://
doi.org/10.1007/s10612-013-9190-7.

74 Ellie Hall, "The Dayton Shooter Was the Lead Singer of a 'Pornogrind'
Metal Band," *BuzzFeed News*, August 5, 2019, https://www.buzzfeednews
.com/article/ellievhall/dayton-shooter-pornogrind-band.

75 Dines, *Pornland*, 131.

76 Dines, *Pornland*, xiii.

77 Kaveh Waddell, "How Porn Leads People to Upgrade Their Tech," *The
Atlantic*, June 7, 2016, https://www.theatlantic.com/technology
/archive/2016/06/how-porn-leads-people-to-upgrade-their-tech
/486032.

78 Foubert, *Protecting Your Children*, 13.

79 Jason Hahn, "People Are Watching More Porn amid Coronavirus Out-
break, According to Pornhub," *People*, March 19, 2020, https://people
.com/human-interest/people-watching-more-porn-amid-coronavirus
-outbreak-says-pornhub.

80 "Sexts" are sexually explicit images sent from someone's smartphone.

81 Culture Reframed, "Home," accessed April 12, 2023, https://www
.culturereframed.org.
82 Natasha Vargas-Cooper, "Hard Core: The New World of Porn Is
Revealing Eternal Truths about Men and Women," *The Atlantic*,
January/February 2011, https://www.theatlantic.com/magazine
/archive/2011/01/hard-core/308327.
83 Rus Ervin Funk, *Reaching Men: Strategies for Preventing Sexist Attitudes,
Behaviors, and Violence* (Indianapolis: JIST Life, 2006), 120.
84 Pappas, *Dark Side of Sports*, 13.
85 John R. Gerdy, *Sports: The All-American Addiction* (Jackson: University
Press of Mississippi, 2002), 148–9.
86 Burstyn, *Rites of Men*, 117.
87 Danny Bennett, "A Look into the Financials of the NHL amid Raising
the Cap and Inking New Deals," *Bolts by the Bay* (blog), August 21,
2021, https://boltsbythebay.com/2021/08/21/a-look-into-the
-financials-of-the-nhl-amid-raising-the-cap-and-inking-new-deals.
88 Burstyn, *Rites of Men*, 120.
89 Quoted in "Golf Inc Pays for Tiger's Affairs with Millions in Lost Ads,"
Business Standard, January 20, 2013, https://www.business-standard
.com/article/companies/golf-inc-pays-for-tiger-s-affairs-with-millions
-in-lost-ads-109121800103_1.html.
90 "U.S. Sports Betting: Here's Where All 50 States Currently Stand on Le-
galizing Sports Gambling, Mobile Betting," *CBS Sports*, April 27, 2023,
https://www.cbssports.com/general/news/wanna-bet-explaining
-where-all-50-states-stand-on-legalizing-sports-gambling.
91 American Gaming Association, "Economic Impact of Legalized Sports
Betting," June 1, 2017, https://www.americangaming.org/resources
/economic-impact-of-legalized-sports-betting.
92 Greg Wyshynski and David Purdum, "Evander Kane Betting Allegations: What We Know and What We Don't," *ESPN*, August 2, 2021,
https://www.espn.com/chalk/story/_/id/31944608/evander-kane
-betting-allegations-know.
93 Wyshynski and Purdum, "Evander Kane and Betting Allegations."
94 DraftKings Sportsbook, "Hockey Betting Guide," accessed February 4,
2022, https://sportsbook.draftkings.com/help/how-to-bet/hockey
-betting-guide.
95 Erving Goffman, *Interaction Ritual: Essays in Face-to-Face Behavior*
(Garden City, NY: Doubleday, 1967), 185.
96 Michael D. Smith, *Violence and Sports* (Toronto: Butterworths, 1983), 100.
97 Smith, *Violence and Sports*, 101.
98 Philippe Cantin, *Serge Savard: Forever Canadien* (Montreal: KO, 2020), 105.
99 Quoted in Chris Lemon, "A True Love of the Game," *Trot*, June 2016,
https://standardbredcanada.ca/trot/june-2016/true-love-game.html.
100 Quoted in Lemon, "True Love of the Game."
101 Quoted in Scott Eden, "From the Archives: How Former Ref Tim
Donaghy Conspired to Fix NBA Games," *ESPN*, July 9, 2020, https://

www.espn.com/nba/story/_/id/25980368/how-former-ref-tim-donaghy
-conspired-fix-nba-games.
102 Quoted in Jacob Steinberg, "Match-Fixing Suspicions Raised in 1,100
Cases since Pandemic's Start," *The Guardian*, October 15, 2021, https://
www.theguardian.com/sport/2021/oct/15/match-fixing-suspicions
-raised-in-1100-cases-since-pandemic-start-sportradar.
103 "Tocchet Pleads Guilty, May Avoid Jail Time," *ESPN*, May 25, 2007,
https://www.espn.com/nhl/news/story?id=2882460.
104 Stephen Whyno, "How Leagues Investigate Gambling Allegations," *Associated Press*, August 6, 2021, https://apnews.com
/article/sports-nhl-nfl-san-jose-sharks-hockey-73293ff5e7d3b1fbe
152f84c51c15797.
105 See Wyshynski and Purdum, "Evander Kane Betting Allegations."
106 Farrah Tomazin, "Sports Betting Giants Turn to Sexual Imagery and
Mateship to Normalise Gambling," *The Age*, last modified April 3, 2016,
https://www.theage.com.au/national/victoria/sports-betting-giants
-turn-to-sexual-imagery-and-mateship-to-normalise-gambling
-20160402-gnwnen.html.
107 Joey D'Urso and Michael Bailey, "Norwich City's Asian Gambling Shirt
Sponsor Criticized for Using 'Women as Glorified Sexual Objects' in
Adverts," *The Athletic*, June 7, 2021, https://theathletic.com/2637224
/2021/06/07/norwich-citys-asian-gambling-shirt-sponsor-criticised
-for-using-women-as-glorified-sexual-objects-in-adverts.
108 Laura Mulvey, "Visual Pleasure and Narrative Cinema," *Screen* 16,
no. 3 (Autumn 1975): 6–18, https://doi.org/10.1093/screen/16.3.6.
109 Barton, *Pornification of America*, 29.
110 Quoted in Grace Turney, "Machine Gun Kelly Admitted He Would
Have Sex with an Underage Kendall Jenner: 'I'm Not Waiting til She's
18,'" *Showbiz CheatSheet*, October 23, 2021, https://www.cheatsheet.com
/entertainment/machine-gun-kelly-admitted-sex-underage-kendall
-jenner-not-waiting-18.html.
111 Lisa Lacy, "After 50 Years, the Era of Objectification in Super Bowl
Advertising Is (Hopefully) Over," *The Drum*, February 5, 2017, https://
www.thedrum.com/news/2017/02/05/after-50-years-the-era
-objectification-super-bowl-advertising-hopefully-over.
112 Claire M. Renzetti, "Editor's Introduction," *Violence against
Women* 25, no. 16 (December 2019): 1903–5, https://doi.org
/10.1177/1077801219876357.
113 Norbert Elias, "Introduction," in *Quest for Excitement: Sport and Leisure
in the Civilizing Process*, ed. Norbert Elias and Eric Dunning (Oxford:
Blackwell, 1986), 19–62.

5. The Puck Drops Here: Prevention and Control Strategies

1 Eric Anderson and Adam White, *Sport, Theory and Social Problems: A
Critical Introduction*, 2nd ed. (London: Routledge, 2018), 139.

2 Heather Mallick, "This Was the Saddest Olympics Ever. It Was a Symphony of Bad," *Toronto Star*, February 21, 2022, https://www.thestar.com/opinion/star-columnists/2022/02/21/this-was-the-saddest-olympics-ever-it-was-a-symphony-of-bad.html.
3 Jack Todd, "Dreadful TV Ratings for Beijing Games Should Send IOC a Message," *Montreal Gazette*, February 21, 2022, https://montrealgazette.com/sports/hockey/nhl/hockey-inside-out/jack-todd-dreadful-tv-ratings-for-beijing-games-should-send-ioc-a-message.
4 Lee E. Ross, "Critical Race Theory," in *The Routledge Companion to Criminological Theory and Concepts*, ed. Avi Brisman, Eamonn Carrabine, and Nigel South (London: Routledge, 2017), 259.
5 Nonetheless, in December 2021, Cruz released a free e-book that he claims is designed to help conservatives find and fight CRT in public schools.
6 David Theo Goldberg, "The War on Critical Race Theory," *Boston Review*, May 7, 2021, https://bostonreview.net/articles/the-war-on-critical-race-theory.
7 Todd, "Dreadful TV Ratings."
8 Bryan Armen Graham, "Jackson and Meyers Taylor Have Made History in Beijing for Black Americans," *The Guardian*, February 18, 2022, https://www.theguardian.com/sport/2022/feb/18/jackson-and-meyers-taylor-have-made-history-in-beijing-for-black-americans.
9 Howard Steven Friedman, *Ultimate Price: The Value We Place on Life* (Oakland: University of California Press, 2020), 144–5.
10 Anne M. Peterson and Ronald Blum, "US Women's Team Players See Settlement as Turning Point," *Toronto Star*, February 22, 2022, https://www.thestar.com/news/world/2022/02/22/american-women-players-settle-suit-vs-us-soccer-for-24m.html.
11 Quoted in Anne M. Peterson and Ronald Blum, "U.S. Soccer Federation and Women's Team Settle Lawsuit for $24 Million," *PBS News Hour*, February 22, 2022, https://www.pbs.org/newshour/nation/u-s-soccer-federation-and-womens-team-settle-lawsuit-for-24-million.
12 Anderson and White, *Sport, Theory and Social Problems*, 165.
13 Reuters, "Women's Hockey League to Expand to Montreal as Part of $25-Million Plan," *Montreal Gazette*, January 18, 2022, https://montrealgazette.com/sports/hockey/womens-hockey-league-to-expand-to-montreal-as-part-of-25-million-plan.
14 Kari Fasting, Stiliani Chroni, and Nada Knorre, "The Experiences of Sexual Harassment in Sport and Education among European Female Sports Science Students," *Sports, Education and Society* 19, no. 2 (2014): 115–30, https://doi.org/10.1080/13573322.2012.660477.
15 Hannah Mendelsohn, "Women's Sports: How Sport Helps Survivors of Violence against Women and Girls," *Give Me Sport*, November 14, 2019, https://www.givemesport.com/1521467-womens-sports-how-sport-helps-survivors-of-violence-against-women-and-girls.

16 Lynzi Armstrong and Abby Hutchison, "Participation in Sport, Empower-ment, and Safety from Violence: Critiquing the Connections through Wom-en's Experiences in Aotearoa/New Zealand," *Violence against Women* 28, no. 3–4 (March 2022): 801–22, https://doi.org/10.1177/10778012211008982.
17 Armstrong and Hutchison, "Participation in Sport," 817.
18 Walter S. DeKeseredy, "Thinking Critically about Campus-Based Self-Defense Programs: A Response to Christine Gidycz," *Trauma, Violence, & Abuse* 15, no. 4 (October 2014): 334–8, https://doi.org/10.1177/1524838014521024.
19 Cheryl Cooky, "At Super Bowl 2022, the NFL, Rams and Bengals Rake In Money. Cheerleaders Get Pennies," *NBC News*, February 12, 2022, https://www.nbcnews.com/think/opinion/super-bowl-2022-nfl-rams-bengals-will-rake-money-cheerleaders-ncna1289003.
20 Alex Azzi, "2021 NWSL Timeline: Five Male Coaches Ousted Due to Misconduct, Abuse Allegations," *NBC Sports*, November 23, 2021, https://onherturf.nbcsports.com/2021/11/23/2021-nwsl-timeline-five-male-coaches-ousted-allegations-of-abuse.
21 Molly Hensley-Clancy, "'Nobody Cares': NWSL Players Say US Soccer Failed to Act on Abuse Claims against Red Stars Coach," *Washington Post*, November 22, 2021, https://www.washingtonpost.com/sports/2021/11/22/rory-dames-chicago-red-stars-resigns.
22 Quoted in Hensley-Clancy, "'Nobody Cares.'"
23 Neil Davidson, "Review Says Canada Soccer Mishandled Sexual Assault Allegations against Coach," *CBC News*, July 28, 2022, https://www.cbc.ca/sports/soccer/canada-soccer-mishandles-sexual-harassment-allegations-1.6534967.
24 Anderson and White, *Sport, Theory and Social Problems*, 164.
25 Anderson and White, *Sport, Theory and Social Problems*, 164.
26 Quoted in Cydney Henderson, "Former Grambling Star Doug Wil-liams 'Very Disappointed' by School's Hiring of Art Briles," *USA Today*, February 24, 2022, https://www.usatoday.com/story/sports/ncaaf/2022/02/24/doug-williams-very-disappointed-grambling-hires-art-briles/6931193001.
27 Shehan Jeyarajah, "Art Briles Resigns at Grambling State after Hiring Sparks Outrage Stemming from Baylor Scandal," *CBS Sports*, March 1, 2022, https://www.cbssports.com/college-football/news/art-briles-resigns-at-grambling-state-after-hiring-sparks-outrage-stemming-from-baylor-scandal.
28 Dan Wolken, "Hue Jackson, Grambling State Latest to Learn Art Briles Lesson – He's Forever Radioactive," *USA Today*, March 1, 2022, https://www.usatoday.com/story/sports/college/columnist/dan-wolken/2022/03/01/hue-jackson-grambling-state-latest-learn-art-briles-lesson/9325499002.
29 Jon Gordon (@JonGordon11), "An old Italian saying: a fish rots from the head," Twitter, June 29, 2017, 1:22 p.m., https://twitter.com/JonGordon11/status/880476629025169408.

30 Ben Pope, "Rocky Wirtz Destroys Accountability with Outburst over Blackhawks' Sexual-Assault Scandal," *Chicago Sun-Times*, February 2, 2022, https://chicago.suntimes.com/blackhawks/2022 /2/2/22915387/rocky-wirtz-blackhawks-sexual-assault-scandal-kyle -beach-destroys-accountability.

31 Quoted in Pope, "Rocky Wirtz Destroys Accountability."

32 Associated Press, "Sheldon Kennedy Helping NHL with Training after Blackhawks Report," *NBC Sports*, February 11, 2022, https://nhl .nbcsports.com/2022/02/11/sheldon-kennedy-helping-nhl-with -training-after-blackhawks-report.

33 Quoted in Stu Cowan, "France Margaret Bélanger Making Her Mark with the Canadiens," *Montreal Gazette*, February 15, 2022, https:// montrealgazette.com/sports/hockey/nhl/hockey-inside-out /france-margaret-belanger-making-her-mark-with-canadiens.

34 Quoted in Thomas Ketko, "Mailloux Discusses Participation in Canadiens' Respect and Consent Program," *Sportsnet*, July 12, 2022, https:// www.sportsnet.ca/nhl/article/mailloux-discusses-participation-in -canadiens-respect-and-consent-program.

35 Quoted in "Former NHLer Reid Boucher Pleads Guilty to Lesser Charge in Sexual Assault Case," *Sportsnet*, January 17, 2022, https:// www.sportsnet.ca/nhl/article/former-nhler-reid-boucher-pleads -guilty-lesser-charce-sexual-assault-case.

36 Quoted in "Former NHLer Reid Boucher Pleads Guilty."

37 Katie Strang, "Two Women Say Reid Boucher Solicited Photos of Them When They Were Teens," *The Athletic*, January 21, 2022, https:// theathletic.com/3083550/2022/01/21/two-women-say-reid-boucher -solicited-lurid-photos-of-them-when-they-were-teens.

38 Quoted in Mark Malone, "Ex-Star Erased from OHL Club's Record Book after Sexual Assault Conviction," *London Free Press*, January 20, 2022, https://lfpress.com/sports/hockey/ex-star-erased-from-sarnia -sting-record-book-after-sexual-assault-conviction.

39 Harold E. Pepinsky, "Peacemaking in Criminology and Criminal Justice," in *Criminology as Peacemaking*, ed. Harold E. Pepinsky and Richard Quinney (Bloomington: Indiana University Press, 1991), 299–327.

40 Burlington Community Justice Center, "Parallel Justice," accessed February 28, 2022, https://www.burlingtoncjc.org/parallel-justice.

41 Walter S. DeKeseredy, *Understanding the Harms of Pornography: The Contributions of Social Scientific Knowledge* (Sterling, MA: Culture Reframed, 2020), 10, https://www.culturereframed.org/wp-content /uploads/2020/02/CR_Harms_of_Porn_Report_2020.pdf.

42 Michael Kimmel, *Guyland: The Perilous World Where Boys Become Men* (New York: Harper, 2008), 187.

43 Quoted in Jessie Klein, *The Bully Society: School Shootings and the Crisis of Bullying in America's Schools* (New York: New York University Press, 2012), 211.

44 Nick T. Pappas, *The Dark Side of Sports: Exposing the Sexual Culture of Collegiate and Professional Athletes* (Maidenhead, UK: Meyer & Meyer Sport, 2012), 69.
45 This phrase is the title of Spike Lee's 1989 comedy-drama film. The moral of the story told through this film is, according to actress Rosie Perez, "that we have to live together and peacefully coexist." Perez was cast as Spike Lee's girlfriend in the critically acclaimed movie; for more of her thoughts on it, see Juju Chang and Lauren Effron, "How Spike Lee's Film 'Do the Right Thing' Still Resonates, 26 Years Later," *ABC News*, December 10, 2014, https://abcnews.go.com/US/spike-lees-film-thing-resonates-25-years/story?id=27488220.
46 Dale T. Miller and Cathy McFarland, "Pluralistic Ignorance: When Similarity Is Interpreted as Dissimilarity," *Journal of Personality and Social Psychology* 53, no. 2 (1987): 298–305, https://psycnet.apa.org/doi/10.1037/0022-3514.53.2.298.
47 Anderson and White, *Sport, Theory and Social Problems.*
48 Jessica Luther, *Unsportsmanlike Conduct: College Football and the Politics of Rape* (New York: Edge of Sports, 2016), 217.
49 Quoted in Emily Kaplan, "Answer the Big Questions on the NHL's Domestic Violence Policy," *ESPN*, July 2, 2018, https://www.espn.com/nhl/story/_/id/23968215/nhl-slava-voynov-attempts-return-league-questions-league-domestic-violence-policy-lack-thereof.
50 Kaplan, "Answer the Big Questions."
51 Jeff Benedict, *Public Heroes, Private Felons: Athletes and Crimes* (Boston: Northeastern University Press, 1997), 222.
52 See R. Renee Hess, foreword to *Game Misconduct: Hockey's Toxic Culture and How to Fix It*, by Evan F. Moore and Jashvina Shah (Chicago: Triumph Books, 2021), xv–xvii.
53 David Close, "American Hockey League Suspends Player for 30 Games for Racist Gesture toward Black Player," *CNN*, February 8, 2022, https://www.cnn.com/2022/01/22/sport/krystof-hrabik-suspended-racist-gesture-spt/index.html.
54 Alex Prewitt, "The Fight over Hockey's Racial Reckoning," *Sports Illustrated*, January 19, 2021, https://www.si.com/nhl/2021/01/19/akim-aliu-nhl-racial-reckoning-daily-cover.
55 "Hockey Culture Promotes Homophobic Language despite Progressive Attitude: Study," *CBC Sports*, June 20, 2019, https://www.cbc.ca/sports/hockey/nhl/homophobia-in-hockey-study-1.5183136.
56 Kevin Young, *Sport, Violence and Society*, 2nd ed. (London: Routledge, 2019), 272.
57 Kristi A. Allain, "'A Good Canadian Boy': Crisis Masculinity, Canadian National Identity, and Nostalgic Longings in Don Cherry's *Coach's Corner*," *International Journal of Canadian Studies* 52 (Fall 2015): 109–10, https://doi.org/10.3138/ijcs.52.107.
58 John R. Gerdy, *Sports: The All-American Addiction* (Jackson: University Press of Mississippi, 2002), 251.

59 Audre Lorde, *The Master's Tools Will Never Dismantle the Master's House* (New York: Penguin, 1983).

60 Elliott Currie, "Epilogue: Pitfalls and Possibilities," in *Progressive Justice in an Age of Repression: Strategies for Challenging the Rise of the Right*, ed. Walter S. DeKeseredy and Elliott Currie (London: Routledge, 2019), 212–21.

61 Elliott Currie, "The Sustaining Society," in *Crime, Justice and Social Democracy: International Perspectives*, ed. Kerry Carrington, Matthew Ball, Erin O'Brien, and Juan Tauri (New York: Palgrave Macmillan, 2013), 3–15.

62 This is the subtitle of Cheryl A. MacDonald and Jonathon R.J. Edwards's anthology *Overcoming the Neutral Zone Trap: Hockey's Agents of Change* (Edmonton: University of Alberta Press, 2021).

63 Julie Stevens and Andrew C. Holman, "Rinkside: New Scholarly Studies on Ice Hockey and Society," *Sport in Society* 16, no. 3 (2013): 251, https://doi.org/10.1080/17430437.2013.779858.

64 Rus Ervin Funk, *Reaching Men: Strategies for Preventing Sexist Attitudes, Behaviors, and Violence* (Indianapolis: JIST Life, 2006), 207.

65 Ron Thorne-Finch, *Ending the Silence: The Origins and Treatment of Male Violence against Women* (Toronto: University of Toronto Press, 1992), 236.

66 Michael A. Messner, "Women in the Men's Locker Room?," in *Sex, Violence and Power in Sports: Rethinking Masculinity*, ed. Michael A. Messner and Donald F. Sabo (Freedom, CA: Crossing Press, 1994), 50.

67 Jackson Katz kindly provided this information in Box 5.2 in Walter S. DeKeseredy and Marilyn Corsianos, *Violence against Women in Pornography* (London: Routledge, 2016), 100.

68 Donald F. Sabo and Michael A. Messner, "Changing Men through Sports: An 11-Point Strategy," in *Sex Violence and Power in Sports: Rethinking Masculinity*, ed. Michael A. Messner and Donald F. Sabo (Freedom, CA: Crossing Press, 1994), 214–18.

69 Skye Saunders, *Whispers from the Bush: The Workplace Sexual Harassment of Australian Rural Women* (Annandale, AU: Federation Press, 2015).

70 Mary E. Gilfus, Susan Fineran, Deborah J. Cohan, Susan A. Jensen, Lisa Hartwick, and Robin Spath, "Research on Violence against Women: Creating Survivor-Informed Collaboration," *Violence against Women* 5, no. 10 (October 1999): 1194–212, https://doi.org/10.1177/10778019922183327.

71 Quoted in Tony Fahkry, "If You Want to Change the World, Start with Yourself First," *Medium*, January 15, 2018, https://medium.com/the-mission/if-you-want-to-change-the-world-start-with-yourself-first-2e759a460c52.

72 Jackson Katz, *The Macho Paradox: Why Some Men Hurt Women and How All Men Can Help* (Naperville, IL: Sourcebooks), 260.

73 Shawna Lee June Marks, "The Sexual Politics of Australian Football: Social Constructions of Masculinity, Sex, and Sexual Violence" (PhD diss., Flinders University, 2020), 206.

74 Kalle Berggren and Lucas Gottzén, "Rethinking Male Peer Support Theory: Social Network Responses to Young Men's Violence against Women," *Journal of Men's Studies* 30, no. 2 (June 2022): 291–307, https://doi.org/10.1177/10608265211068013.

75 Thorne-Finch, *Ending the Silence*, xviii.

76 Ed Condran, "The Worst Parents in Youth Hockey; True Stories from the Ice," *PhillyVoice*, September 26, 2017, https://www.phillyvoice.com/the-worst-parents-in-youth-hockey-true-stories-from-the-ice.

77 O'Sullivan was the 2002 OHL and CHL Rookie of the Year and the AHL's 2005 Rookie of the Year. He played 334 NHL games over eight seasons with the Los Angeles Kings, the Edmonton Oilers, the Carolina Hurricanes, the Minnesota Wild, and the Phoenix Coyotes. He also played in three World Junior Championships and scored the championship winning goal in 2004.

78 Canadian Press, "Former NHLer Patrick O'Sullivan Opens Up about Abuse," *Sportsnet*, October 19, 2015, https://www.sportsnet.ca/hockey/nhl/former-nhler-patrick-osullivan-opens-up-about-abuse.

79 Michael Caples, "Hockey Parent Horror Story Written by Former Pro a Reminder to Keep Things in Perspective," *MiHockey*, October 20, 2015, http://mihockey.com/2015/10/hockey-parent-horror-story-written-by-former-pro-a-reminder-to-keep-things-in-perspective.

80 Katz, *Macho Paradox*, 234.

81 Ivy N. Defoe, Judith Semon Dubas, and Marcel A.G. van Aken, "The Relative Roles of Peer and Parent Predictors in Minor Adolescent Delinquency: Exploring Gender and Adolescent Phase Differences," *Frontiers in Public Health* 6 (2018), https://doi.org/10.3389/fpubh.2018.00242.

82 Quoted in Berggren and Gottzén, "Rethinking Male Peer Support Theory," 306.

83 For more information on Darlene Murphy's family mediation services, see http://www.darlenemurphymediation.com.

84 See Robin Warshaw, *I Never Called It Rape* (New York: Harper & Row, 1988), 161–4.

85 Colin D. Howell, "Afterword," in *Overcoming the Neutral Zone Trap: Hockey's Agents of Change*, ed. Cheryl A. MacDonald and Jonathon R.J. Edwards (Edmonton: University of Alberta Press, 2021), 271–2.

86 The first three in this list are informed by observations featured in Daniel Dorling's *Injustice: Why Social Inequality Persists* (Bristol: Policy Press, 2010), 1. The fourth is drawn from Colin Howell's afterword to *Overcoming the Neutral Zone Trap*.

87 Sabrina Maddeaux, "Hockey Canada Encouraged a Celebrity Culture That Made Players Feel Untouchable," *National Post*, July 29, 2022, https://nationalpost.com/opinion/sabrina-maddeaux-hockey-canada-encouraged-a-celebrity-culture-that-made-players-feel-untouchable.

88 Renate Klein, *Responding to Intimate Violence against Women: The Role of Informal Networks* (New York: Cambridge University Press, 2012), 127.

Index

Abercrombie, Bill, 226
ableism, 44
abuse, theories of, 68, 77–8, 112–14, 120, 270n30. *See also* sexual violence
academia, 234–5
accountability, 31, 49, 86, 103, 217, 219, 230, 251
action (moment of), 195, 196–7
adjustment, vocabulary of, 120. *See also* male peer support theory
advertising, 167, 175–6, 178, 192, 193–4, 199–201. *See also* capitalism
affairs, extramarital, 82–4, 193
age, 79–81, 270n24
aggression: and alcohol use, 131; and hazing, 141; and hockey culture, 29–30, 38, 39, 229, 242–4; and male peer support, 122, 124–5; and masculinity, 1, 4; and pornography, 180, 189; scholarship on, 234; socialization of, 37, 109–10, 115
aggrieved entitlement, 23–4, 92, 252
Agostinelli, Gianluca, 19
Ak Bars Kazan, 138
alcohol: as coping mechanism, 15, 43; and driving, 147; and hockey culture, 121, 129, 131–3, 172; and male peer support, 51, 117, 129–33; and violence against women, 33, 61, 74, 78, 129–33, 172, 238, 271n42
Aldrich, Brad, 13–14, 17, 251
Aliu, Akim, 18, 144–5
Allain, Kristi, 233
Allen, Bruce, 7, 8
All-Star Games (NHL), 200
alt-right groups, 127–8, 208, 279n50. *See also* anti-feminism; men's rights groups
Amazon, 184–5

American Gaming Association,
194. *See also* betting
American Hockey League (AHL),
102, 151, 231, 295n77
Anaheim Ducks, 18, 99
Anderson, Eric, 205, 212, 217, 226,
230
Anderson, Jacob Walter, 137
Andreff, Wladimir, 197
angry hockey dads, 242–4. *See
also* aggression; childhood
socialization
Angus Reid Institute, 168
anti-feminism, 23–4, 47–51, 60,
190
appeals to higher loyalty, 175, 178
Archer, Christopher, 34
Armour, Nancy, 7–8, 17
Art Ross Trophy, 268n3
Ash, Erin, 50
Asia Pacific, 198
assault. *See* sexual violence;
violence
athletic culture. *See* sports and
sports culture
Atwood, Margaret, 182
Australia, 232, 241
Australian football, 155, 213
authoritarianism, 207
avoidance strategies, x, 27–8,
102–3, 161, 162, 163, 283n8. *See
also* sexual violence

Babcock, Mike, 53
backlash, 47, 53–4, 60
Baldwin, James, 181–2
Ballys, 194. *See also* betting
Baltimore, 149
Baradulya, Alyaksandr, 182
Barton, Bernadette, 177,
285nn47–8
baseball, 37, 82–3, 187
basketball, 29, 69, 198. *See also*
National Basketball Association

Baud, Chris, 27
Baylor University, 135–8, 218
Beach, Kyle, 14–15, 16, 17, 18, 65,
219, 220, 251
Beard, Michael, 76
Beating Wife-Beating (Bowker), 122
Bélanger, France Margaret, 94–5,
220–1, 254
Béliveau, Jean, xiv
Benedict, Jeff, 44–5, 53, 82, 84, 230
Bergevin, Marc: and Chicago
Blackhawks, 13–14; firing and
replacement of, 89, 95, 98, 251;
as former player, 154; and Los
Angeles Kings, 156; and
Mailloux draft, 12, 13, 15, 250–1
Berggren, Kalle, 241, 245
Bertuzzi, Todd, 30
Betfair, 199. *See also* betting
betrayal, institutional, 61, 135,
280n69. *See also* survivors
betting, 51, 193–200
Bettman, Gary, 14, 15–16, 95, 150,
194–5, 234, 249, 252
Betts, Connor, 186
Bible, 167
Biden, Joseph, 127
Biden administration, 86
Biles, Simone, 4
biology, 109–10
Birarda, Bob, 216–17
BK8 (gambling company), 200.
See also betting
Black athletes, 24–5, 31, 209, 231,
260n19
blackface, 5
Black Girl Hockey Club, 231
Black Lives Matter, 9, 207
Black people, 60, 65–6, 69–70, 149,
231, 270n24
Black women, 52, 70, 209. *See also*
women of color
Blake, Rob, 156
Blank, Barbara (Kelly Kelly), 66–7

Michigan Coalition to End
Domestic and Sexual Violence,
225
Middle East, 198
middle school, 36–7, 114, 265n82.
See also high school
Mighty Ducks (Anaheim Ducks),
18, 99
Milano, Alyssa, 52
Milbury, Mike, 123–4
Miller, Pavla, 167
Miller, Ryan, 80
Mills, C. Wright, 78–9
MindGeek, 177. *See also*
pornography
Minnesota Wild, 295n77
minor hockey, 37–9, 142, 168, 222,
243, 265–6n86
misogyny: and anti-feminism, 48;
definition of, 167; and hockey
culture, x, xi, xvi, 168, 170, 251;
and male peer support, 125,
133; and masculinity, 5; and
patriarchy, 167; and
pornography, 171, 173; and
sport, 20
mobile total institutions, 126, 133
Molson (beer company), 132
Molson, Geoff, 89–90, 94, 97
Momentum Hockey, 98
money. *See* capitalism; profit
Monster (2003), 165–6
Montreal Canadiens, ix, xiii–xiv;
and gender integration, 212;
and Mailloux, xiv–xv, xvi,
11–12, 119, 129, 140, 150–1,
250–1; management of, 15,
89–91, 93–8, 220; and mental
illness, 1–4; and Prust, 54;
Respect and Consent Action
Plan, 91–3, 222–4, 227, 254; and
sports betting, 196; and
violence against women, 153,
252–3

Montreal Gazette, xiii, xiv, xv–xvi,
45, 140
Montreal Juniors, 99
Montreal Stars, 97
Moore, Evan F., 22, 43–4, 89, 247
Moore, Melzena, 72–5, 165
Moore, Steve, 30
Moore, Tyria, 165
morality, 31, 107, 136, 152–3, 166,
176, 185–6
mothers, 245. *See also* childhood
socialization
Mulvey, Laura, 200
Murphy, Darlene, 245–6
Murray, Bill, 18
Muzzo, Marco, 148, 149

Nashville Predators, 150, 232
Nassib, Carl, 9
National Basketball Association
(NBA): advertising of, 192; and
Center for the Study of Sport in
Society, 44; drafts, 249; and
marriage, 81–2; media coverage
of, 69; revenue of, 187; and
sexism, 170; and violence, 30–1;
and violence against women,
29
National Collegiate Athletic
Association (NCAA), 44–5, 98,
135–6, 137–8, 157
National Football League (NFL):
Black members of, 260n19;
Center for the Study of Sport in
Society, 44; drafts, 249; and
gender inequality, 214–15; and
racism, 7, 231; revenue of, 187;
and sexism, 170, 201–2; and
STE, 101; toxic culture of, 7–9;
and violence against women, 8,
21, 29, 30, 155–6, 157
National Hockey League (NHL):
and alcohol use, 132; and Black
players, 31; and divorce, 81;

Sportsbet, 199. *See also* gambling
Sportsnet, 233. *See also* journalism
and news media
sports protection hypothesis, 213
Sport, Violence and Society
(Young), 234
stalking, 74, 160–2, 214
Stanko, Elizabeth, 283n8
Stanley Cup, xv, 1, 2, 17, 191, 231,
268n3
status, 51, 119, 196. *See also*
masculinity, hegemonic; power
Steinberg, Jacob, 198
stereotypes, 66–7, 165–6, 186, 239
Steubenville (OH), 10–11, 261n21
Stevens, Julie, 235
Steward, Chris, 24
St. Louis (MO), 149
Strang, Katie, 225, 251
stress and pressure, 1, 3–4, 79,
114–15, 122, 124, 170, 212
Subban, P.K., 24
Subculture of Violence, The
(Wolfgang and Ferracuti), 122
subcultures: and crime shows,
133; hypererotic, 118; and male
peer support, 39–40, 116, 122;
online, 228; and sex
segregation, 125–6; and societal
factors, 128; and violence
against women, 7. *See also*
hockey culture
substance use: and deterrence,
147–8; and femicide, 74, 78; and
hazing, 141; and male peer
support, 51, 129–33, 172; and
professional hockey, 3; and
sexual violence, 43; sports
league guidelines on, 230; and
survivors, 15; and violence
against women, 129–33,
271n42. *See also* alcohol
Suite, Derek H., 115
summer camps, 142

Super Bowls, 201–2, 214
super coaches, 217. *See also*
coaches; prevention strategies
support systems, 64–5
survivors: and hazing, 143–5; and
Hockey Canada, 22; and
image-based sexual abuse,
10–11; and institutional betrayal,
280n69; and male peer support,
120; and NHL, 138, 230; and
parallel justice, 13, 226–7; and
psychological abuse, 161; and
rape culture, 20, 159, 166; reasons
for staying, 72, 75; strength and
resilience of, 66, 67, 68; support
systems of, 64–5; treatment and
silencing of, 60–6, 84–7, 103–5,
108, 135–7, 151, 224–5, 252–3;
and violence, theories of, 77–8;
voices of, xvi, 15, 71, 100–2, 105;
and women's sports, 213–14
suspension. *See* deterrence or
punishment
Sutton, James E., 29
Sweden, 241
Swift Current Broncos, 42

Tallon, Dale, 230
Tampa Bay Lighting, 231
taxes, 192, 194
Taylor, Billy, 199
Taylor, Garrett, 170
Taylor, Maria, 69–70
Team Canada, 30, 97–8
technological advances, 187
television, 133–4, 170–1, 190–2,
193–4. *See also* mass media
tennis, 4, 85–7, 198
Theodore, Sondra, 181
Thériault, Camille, 168
Theron, Charlize, 165
Thorne-Finch, Ron, 241, 246
Thurman, Uma, 52
Timmins, Trevor, 15, 89, 250–1

About the Authors

Walter S. DeKeseredy is the Anna Deane Carlson Endowed Chair of Social Sciences, director of the Research Center on Violence, and a professor of sociology at West Virginia University. He has published 27 books, over 130 scientific journal articles, and close to 100 scholarly book chapters on violence against women and other social problems. He has earned numerous prestigious awards throughout his career, including the American Society of Criminology's 2022 Praxis Award as well as their 2022 Robert Jerin Book of the Year Award. He was named a fellow of the American Society of Criminology in 2022.

Stu Cowan is a sports columnist with the *Montreal Gazette* with over 35 years of experience in the sports department. Before becoming a sports columnist, he worked as a scoreboard-page statistics editor, reporter, and sports editor. He is a regular panelist on the *Hockey Inside/Out Show*.

Martin D. Schwartz is a professorial lecturer at George Washington University and an emeritus professor at Ohio University. He has published 25 editions of 14 books, 80 refereed journal articles, and another 80 chapters and reports. He is a fellow of the Academy of Criminal Justice Sciences and has received a variety of distinguished scholar, teaching, and mentoring awards from international criminology organizations. His work has centered on organizational and peer support for violence against women in school, relationships, sport, and other institutions.